Call Centers

FOR

DUMMIES®

2ND EDITION

by Réal Bergevin, Afshan Kinder,
Winston Siegel, and Bruce Simpson

D1319086

WILEY

John Wiley & Sons Canada, Ltd.

Call Centers For Dummies®, 2nd Edition

Published by
John Wiley & Sons Canada, Ltd.
6045 Freemont Boulevard
Mississauga, Ontario, L5R 4J3

www.wiley.com

For general information on John Wiley & Sons Canada, Ltd., including all books published by Wiley Publishing, Inc., please call our distribution centre at 1-800-567-4797. For reseller information, including discounts and premium sales, please call our sales department at 416-646-7992. For press review copies, author interviews, or other publicity information, please contact our publicity department, Tel. 416-646-4582, Fax 416-236-4448.

For technical support, please visit www.wiley.com/techsupport.

Wiley also publishes its books in a variety of electronic formats. Some content that appears in print may not be available in electronic books.

Library and Archives Canada Cataloguing in Publication Data

Call centers for dummies / Réal Bergevin ... [et al.]. – 2nd ed.

Includes index.

ISBN 978-0-470-67743-8

     1. Call centers–Management. I. Bergevin, Réal

HE8788.C36 2010 658.8'12 C2009-906118-X

Printed in the United States

1 2 3 4 5 RRD 14 13 12 11 10

WILEY

About the Authors

Réal Bergevin is executive vice president of Transcom Worldwide. In 1991, he founded a call center consulting business that he and his wife, Anne, expanded into NuComm International, a global outsourcing call center service provider. NuComm was listed in Deloitte & Touche's *Canada's 50 Best Managed Companies* for five consecutive years and, in 2005, was awarded the National Quality Institute's Canadian Award of Excellence. NuComm was sold to Transcom in 2007.

In 2001, Réal was honored as one of The Caldwell Partners International's *Canada's Top 40 Under 40* business executives. He holds a business degree from Sir Wilfrid Laurier University and is the author of *23 Steps to an Effective Call Centre* (NuComm Solutions, Inc.).

Afshan Kinder (formerly Bye) is a partner in SwitchGear Consulting with more than 20 years' experience running contact centers and more than 8 years' experience as an industry consultant and magazine columnist. She has been a senior vice president of sales and service for companies including Sprint Canada (now Rogers Communications), ING Direct, and Wardair.

She is a past board member of Contact Centre Canada, a current board member of the Greater Toronto Association of Contact Centers, and the author of the "Dear Affy" column that appears in each issue of *Contact Management* magazine.

Winston Siegel is a founding partner in SwitchGear Consulting and a specialist in high-growth service businesses and leadership development. He brings multi-industry expertise to call centers, having run customer service operations in restaurants, musical theater, and retail before seeing the call center light. He was vice president of operations for North America and Australia at Lavalife, growing its call centers from 9 to 20, and became president of the company in 1999.

He is a speaker on call center metrics, leadership, and sales, as well as the author of several white papers, including "The 10 Sacred Cows of Call Center Metrics" (Innovators Roundtable). He has a philosophy degree from York University and an MBA from the Schulich School of Business in Toronto.

Bruce Simpson is a founding partner in SwitchGear Consulting with a sales background in pharmaceuticals, telecommunications, and insurance. He was a founder and chief operating officer of North Direct Response, a call center outsourcer with clients including Royal Bank of Canada, Clearnet (TELUS), and Hewlett-Packard.

He is the author of industry white papers including "The ROI of Coaching" and "How to Control Payroll Leakage," published by Frost & Sullivan.

Dedication

This book is dedicated to the unsung heroes inside every call center. From front-line agents to team leaders and managers, you inspire us — and you inspired this book.

Authors' Acknowledgments

We'd like to acknowledge the work of Réal Bergevin, who — with the support of John Dickhout, Daniel Willis, and other members of the Transcom team — wrote the first edition of this book. It was a privilege to add to your work and wisdom. We hope you approve.

Thank you to Amar Sidhu from Trader Corp., Arleen King and Ian Cruickshank from TELUS, Bernie Herenberg from ServiceOntario, Stephen Gaskin from Scotiabank, Paul Gyarmati from Reliance Home Comfort, Mariflor Di Rienzo from Ceridian Canada Ltd., Mario Perez from Telax Voice Solutions, and Karen Jensen from CI Investments for sharing their insights with us.

To the members of the SwitchGear army, who provided "roadside assistance" whenever we experienced writer's block, thank you for your patience and support. A special "thank you" goes to Suzanne Figueirado, who chased us and prodded us relentlessly for months to make sure that we met the deadlines.

Thank you as well to the team of editors at John Wiley & Sons: Robert Hickey; Kathy Simpson; Pamela Vokey; our copy editor, Laura K. Miller; and our technical editor, Bob Milne. Your feedback and coaching helped us produce a better product and gave us a new appreciation for people who write books for a living.

Publisher's Acknowledgments

We're proud of this book; please send us your comments at http://dummies.custhelp.com. For other comments, please contact our Customer Care Department within the U.S. at 877-762-2974, outside the U.S. at 317-572-3993, or fax 317-572-4002.

Some of the people who helped bring this book to market include the following:

Acquisitions and Editorial

Developmental and Project Editor:
Kathy Simpson

Acquiring Editor: Robert Hickey

Copy Editor: Laura K. Miller

Technical Editor: Bob Milne

Cartoons: Rich Tennant
(www.the5thwave.com)

Composition

Project Coordinator, U.S.: Lynsey Stanford

Project Coordinator, Canada: Pamela Vokey

Layout and Graphics: Wiley Indianapolis Composition Services

Proofreader: Leeann Harney

Indexer: Ty Koonz

John Wiley & Sons Canada, Ltd.

Bill Zerter, Chief Operating Officer

Jennifer Smith, Publisher, Professional & Trade Division

Karen Bryan, Vice President, Publishing Services

Alison Maclean, Managing Editor

Publishing and Editorial for Consumer Dummies

Diane Graves Steele, Vice President and Publisher, Consumer Dummies

Kristin Ferguson-Wagstaffe, Product Development Director, Consumer Dummies

Ensley Eikenburg, Associate Publisher, Travel

Kelly Regan, Editorial Director, Travel

Composition Services

Debbie Stailey, Director of Composition Services

Contents at a Glance

Table of Contents

Introduction

· ·

*W*elcome to *Call Centers For Dummies,* 2nd Edition. If the topic of call centers has piqued your interest, and you're looking for a road map that can help you lead and manage a call center, you've come to the right place. The purpose of this book is to demystify call centers, explaining clearly what they do and how they do it, all in a simple, straightforward manner. We hope that you'll have a little fun along the way, too!

In the first edition, Réal Bergevin clearly laid out his approach to call center management and did an excellent job of covering a wide range of related topics. So why did we write a second edition? Well, call centers have changed significantly because of the advancements in technology and the growing influence of the Internet. A new challenge now exists because customers have many ways to communicate with the call center. In addition to the good ol' phone, customers can use e-mail, online chat, or text messaging to express their feelings or ask questions about products or services.

In addition, many agents can work from home now, so you need to be able to communicate with those home agents effectively. You also have to find innovative ways to lead, motivate, and coach people remotely.

With change coming at a fast and furious pace, how are you going to provide consistently exceptional service to your customers? You can conquer this seemingly difficult task by sticking to the fundamentals, which we cover in this book. This book draws on the experience and insight of four people (us!), but we all lead our businesses by using the same people-first philosophy.

We can't think of a better vehicle for sharing our knowledge, vision, and philosophy for leading and managing call centers than this book. We hope that you enjoy reading it as much as we enjoyed writing it.

About This Book

Many people have developed some pretty strong opinions about call centers. Executives and analysts alike realize more than ever that call centers can have a tremendous impact on a company's revenue, costs, market intelligence, and customer loyalty. Call centers have become a significant part of local and world economies.

A well-run call center doesn't happen by accident or chance. It happens only if the leader of the center has a clear vision of what can be achieved and creates an environment where high-performing teams can flourish. This book can help because it's full of best practices for leading people and managing process and technology.

Because of the complexity of operating a business in today's world, many call center professionals have come to us to deepen their understanding of how changes in business affect call center operations. We hope that you benefit not only from this book's collection of best practices, but also from the depth of knowledge that we've gathered through our combined half century of experience. The difference between this book and the variety of call center publications, seminars, and Web sites out there is that this book doesn't offer a call center "theory of everything." We share with you concepts and practices that have worked for us in our operations. We know that managers benefit from their mistakes as much as they do from their successes, and through these pages, you get the advantage of seeing what to do as well as what not to do.

Foolish Assumptions

If you work in the call center industry, this book gives you an easy-to-use and (we hope) easy-to-read reference guide to the effective operation of a call center. We make some assumptions about who you are and what you may be looking for in this book:

- You're a hotshot MBA tracking through your career, and you find yourself running a call center.
- You're an experienced call center manager, and you're looking for some new ideas and perspectives.
- You supply the call center industry and want to better understand your clients' management perspective.
- You work in marketing, finance, or human resources, so you have some contact with a call center and wonder what goes on in it.
- You're considering a career in call centers.
- You're working in a call center and want to advance your career by unlocking the mysterious, ancient call center secrets.
- You're looking for new material with which you can dazzle members of the opposite sex. (Okay, we don't make any promises about this one.)

How This Book Is Organized

Call Centers For Dummies, 2nd Edition is organized in six parts (plus two appendixes), each covering a different aspect of the call center. Chapters within each part cover specific topics in detail. Each part contains concepts and definitions, interesting facts and anecdotes, and (in most cases) practical how-to suggestions pertaining to the topic. You can take any approach to tackling this book. Unless you're a seasoned call center pro, however, you'll probably get the most out of this book by starting with Part I.

Part I: From the Ground Up: An Overview of the Call Center

This part provides a good overview of many of the topics covered in more detail in later parts. Consider it to be a call center primer, with a little bit extra. If you're just getting started or want a brief indoctrination in all things call center, you may find this part to be especially useful.

In this part, we also discuss planning a new call center and considering outsourcing, and we introduce a business model for building a call center and relate that model to the larger corporate mission and goals.

Part II: The Master Plan: Finance, Analysis, and Resource Management

This part looks at call center analysis, financial planning, and staffing. We provide a simple overview of how (and what) measures come together to drive a call center's operational and financial performance.

Also in this part, we uncover some of the mysteries of how and why call centers perform the way they do, and we explore everything from forecasting to schedule creation and workforce management automation.

Part III: Making Life Better with Technology

Part III reviews call center technologies, including basic requirements, valuable enhancements, and home agent programs. We also cover a simple approach to recommending and justifying new technology, and we show you what this technology can do for your customers, your agents, and your call center.

Part IV: Creating High-Performance Teams

In this part, we cover recruiting; establishing job expectations; offering training, feedback, and support; and creating employee engagement. We also show you how to implement a simple five-step process that can guide the way you manage agents' performance.

Part V: Ensuring Continuous Improvement

In Part V, we explore the call center process and how to manage and improve it. In addition, we examine policies, procedures, and the effects of legislation and employment law on call centers. We also give you the scoop on mastering change, as well as details on various quality programs and certifications for call centers.

Part VI: The Part of Tens

In this part (a *For Dummies* classic), we offer tips and techniques that we've collected from the call center industry. These quick hits can give a boost to your company's revenue and efficiency, employee morale, and customer satisfaction. Even if you don't read the rest of this book, check out this part!

Appendixes

Many industries use a language all their own, and the call center industry is no exception, so Appendix A provides a glossary of key call center concepts. Appendix B gives you access to support services such as call center associations, technology suppliers, and consultants.

Icons Used in This Book

We've placed several icons throughout this book to point out certain information, and these icons have the following meanings.

Material marked with the Tip icon provides a general recommendation about how you can improve your call center or run it more easily.

This icon flags any potential pitfalls that you may want to be careful to avoid.

This content is — you guessed it — the stuff we don't want you to forget.

This icon designates information that you probably don't need to know but may find interesting.

This icon points out real-world stories that we've experienced or that someone told us.

Where to Go from Here

We certainly invite you to curl up on a Saturday night with a nice cup of tea, hot chocolate, or whatever and read this book from cover to cover. We're sure that you hard-core call center types will find it quite gripping — a real page-turner.

We suspect, however, that some of you may not have the desire or need to read this entire book straight through. We encourage you to find the part that interests you most and start there.

Part I

From the Ground Up: An Overview of the Call Center

The 5th Wave   By Rich Tennant

MOUSE PAD HELP CENTER

It sounds like you may still have your pad in the packaging, sir...

No ma'am, the pad goes on the desktop, not the floor.

Try turning the pad over...

Anyone have any experience with a round pad?!

In this part . . .

We answer the question "What is a call center?" and explore what makes a good (or bad) call center. If you just want to know how call centers work, are thinking about working in one, or have ever had any aspirations to start a call center of your own, this is the part for you.

In this part, we introduce a business model for building a call center and relate that model to the larger corporate mission and goals. We examine the organizational structure, exploring the roles you need to fill to ensure that the center performs according to its business model and goals. We also discuss the logistics of building a call center and some key factors to consider if you're thinking about outsourcing your call center.

Chapter 1

A First Look at Call Centers

For years, Réal's mom has been asking him, "What is it you do, again?" Well, here it is, Mom: He works in a call center. In fact, he works in a lot of call centers. Okay, okay — you don't know what a call center is. Well, this chapter explains it all.

Defining Call Centers

Here's a basic definition of a call center: When you call, say, an airline, cable-television company, or bank, the person you deal with at the other end of the phone is a call center *agent* (or perhaps *representative, consultant,* or *associate*), and the office or department that this person works in is a *call center.* Sometimes, a call center consists of just one or two people sitting beside a phone, answering customer calls. Often, it's a very large room that has a lot of people neatly organized in rows, sitting beside their phones, answering customer calls. To the customer, the call center is the voice of the company. If you're angry, you often get mad at the person at the other end of the phone. After all, you're talking to the company, right?

To the company, the call center is many things: cost center, profit center, key source of revenue, key source of frustration, strategic weapon, strategic disadvantage, source of marketing research, and source of marketing paralysis. The role of the call center varies from company to company, depending on how closely the call center works with the parent or client organization to support the company's goals and the ability of the call center itself.

Inbound, outbound, or blended

Call centers communicate with their customers in several ways, depending on the type of call center. Call centers fall into three main categories:

- **Inbound:** In an *inbound* call center, customers initiate the calls. Customers may make these calls to buy airline tickets, to get technical assistance with their personal computers, to get answers to questions about their utility bills, to get emergency assistance when their cars won't start, to get advice from a nurse about minor medical issues, to buy insurance for their cars, or to talk to a company representative about any number of other situations.

- **Outbound:** In an *outbound* call center, agents of the company initiate calls to customers. Your first reaction might be "Telemarketing, right?" Well, yes, a company may call customers in its telemarketing campaign, but companies have a lot of other good reasons to call their customers. Companies may call because the customer hasn't paid a bill or because a product that the customer wanted has become available; they may call to follow up on a problem that the customer was having or to find out what product or service enhancements the customer wants to see.

- **Blended:** Some call centers are *blended* operations, in which agents handle both inbound and outbound calls.

As we outline in Chapter 8, blending, done well, can make call center operations very cost efficient and can improve customer service as well.

Contact or call center: What's in a name?

The explosion in popularity of the Internet and wireless technologies has changed the way people communicate. People still use the phone (although it's frequently a cellphone these days), but they also communicate with friends, Romans, and Walmart by using e-mail, online chats, Web forums, and instant messaging. Call centers have responded to this change. In fact, they're increasingly being called *contact centers* to reflect the fact that they handle more than just phone calls. These facilities are centers for customer contacts in whatever ways customers want to communicate: letters, faxes, Web chats, e-mails, and so on.

Another term that you may have heard is *virtual call center,* in which a group of agents work from their homes instead of being situated at workstations in a building operated by the organization. Some centers are a blend of at-home agents and on-site agents. Working from home is a fantastic arrangement for many employees: The hours are often flexible, and the job has no dress code or commute. Virtual call centers can lower a company's costs because they allow the company to optimize scheduling and spend less on real estate. (We explain scheduling in Chapter 8.)

Bottom line, each customer has to decide how he wants to communicate with the company, and the company has to respond appropriately through its contact center.

As with inbound and outbound call centers (refer to the preceding section), some companies choose to separate the handling of customer contacts by medium — a group for inbound calls, a group for outbound calls, a group for e-mail, and so on. Some call centers, especially those in smaller operations, have opted to create _universal agents_ who handle all contact types. Call centers create universal contact agents for the same reasons that they blend inbound and outbound call-handling agents: efficiency and service.

This book is called _Call Centers For Dummies,_ but we could just as easily have named it _Contact Centers For Dummies._ Throughout the book, we refer to _call handling_ and _call centers,_ partly because we grew up in call centers (well, not literally) and partly because phone calls still represent the bulk of communication between customers and companies. You can apply the concepts in this book to all types of contacts: phone calls, e-mails, online chats, instant messages, and even smoke signals.

Tripping Down Memory Lane: The Evolution of the Call Center

Although we can't really tell you when the first call center opened, we imagine that call centers started around the time that the telephone became a common household device.

The evolution of call centers just makes sense. A consumer can much more easily pick up a phone and call a company than she can start the car (or hitch up the horse), bundle up the kids, and go to town to arrange for the cable company to add extra channels. Likewise, for businesses like the cable company in this example, it's much easier to do business over the phone than to have agents show up on the customer's doorstep.

Consumers and businesses have used the phone as a way to do business for a long time. As a formal business discipline, however, using the phone to communicate with customers is not so old — maybe 30 years or so of development.

Moving from low-tech to high-tech

Before the mid-1970s, airlines and major retailers used *phone rooms* — the precursors of call centers. Phone rooms were located in sites spread across the country or operated in large rooms that had lots of desks, phones with many extensions, and a lot of paper for tracking everything that was going on. We're all too young to have seen these places ourselves, but people say that these rooms were very busy, noisy, and confusing.

One of the most significant advancements in call center technology was the invention of the automatic call distributor (ACD) by Rockwell International. The ACD made large, centralized call centers practical and efficient by providing a way to distribute large numbers of incoming phone calls evenly to a pool of call center staff. With the implementation of the ACD, the call center industry began, and the call center as a business discipline was off and running. We talk more about call center technology and technological advancements in Chapters 9 and 10.

Moving from cost center to profit center

Most important to the call center industry, corporations have changed their view of the call center — from cost center and (in some cases) a necessary evil to profit center and competitive advantage. Today, business owners build entire companies around call center capability. You can buy a computer from a company that doesn't have a retail store, for example, or do your banking with a bank that doesn't have physical branches. These businesses offer the telephone or Internet as customers' only communication options.

Meeting legal and image challenges

Not everyone thinks that call center changes and evolution are positive, however. Partly because of the impact of call centers on everyone's daily lives, and partly because some call centers had bad management and used bad business practices, some call centers have raised the ire of consumers and caught the attention of legislators.

Overly aggressive telemarketing practices, for example, have resulted in laws that regulate how sales are conducted over the telephone, whom telemarketers can and can't contact, and how telemarketers can contact those people. Governments even legislate how quickly some industries must answer incoming calls — a response to the poor service and long delays that consumers experienced in the past.

Call centers are also at the head of the outsourcing debate (see Chapter 5) because many companies are moving their call center operations offshore to countries that have well-qualified but less-expensive labor.

Additionally, privacy legislation has added a level of complexity to the way call centers can collect and use information about their customers, and several countries are considering legislation that restricts how and where call centers can operate.

Poor business practices, as well as the success of the industry, have brought on some of the legislative challenges that call centers face. Explosive demand for call center services, both from business and consumers, has taxed the discipline's ability to grow in size and capability while maintaining excellence. Still, on balance, call centers continue to advance in number, capability, sophistication, and excellence for two reasons: They're effective and efficient business tools, and they satisfy increasing customer demand for convenience.

Today's call centers: Ringing up big numbers

Today, the call center industry is an important part of the global economy. More than 55,000 call centers operate in North America alone, employing more than 6 million people (6 percent of the workforce). Consumers purchase more than $700 billion worth of goods and services through call centers every year, and that number is growing. You can purchase almost anything from the comfort of your home, office, car, or wherever you can get to a phone (or access the Internet).

Call centers continue to evolve at a dizzying pace. In an effort to gain greater efficiencies, provide better customer service, and generate more revenue, call centers are using more sophisticated technology, including customer information databases that give agents a better understanding of customers' preferences, buying patterns, and desired products or services. Based on data collected about each customer, the system suggests options for that customer. This smart technology and its analytical tools give agents the best way to approach each customer as an individual.

Along with improving its use of technology, the call center community is improving its members' knowledge and skills through trade associations, industry publications, trade shows, and specialized training and certification programs. In an effort to better manage people, processes, and technology, the industry has latched onto management approaches and philosophies that can give it an edge, including Customer Operations Performance Center, Inc. (COPC) and Six Sigma. We describe these programs in Chapter 17.

Making Call Centers Work

You can't easily manage a call center well, because call centers are complex places. It's not just the technology; that's the easy part! Call centers are a microcosm of business. To run a good call center, managers need to effectively blend people, processes, and technology to produce a desired result.

Most call centers rely on people — often, a lot of people. Wages and salary typically comprise 60 percent to 70 percent of a call center's budget.

Because customers can ask almost anything of the call center, agents need to have at their fingertips information on just about all the company's policies, procedures, products, and services. With a huge volume and variety of customers, a call center gets a lot of activity. Even if you have the best technology available to smooth things out, when you're dealing with hundreds or thousands of calls each day, the slightest bottleneck can add up to a big problem.

In fact, a 1-second increase in call length in a call center that answers 1 million calls a year creates an additional 280 hours of work requiring approximately 380 additional hours of staffing. (We explain the math in Chapter 6.)

Identifying good call center managers

Good call center managers have the following characteristics:

- ✔ They have a strong sense of purpose.
- ✔ They understand their roles within the organization.
- ✔ They have clear, measurable targets and goals, and understand how to reach those goals.
- ✔ They're part analyst, part accountant, part engineer, part psychologist, part cheerleader, and part coach, effectively blending human resources, process management, and technology without limiting themselves or indulging too much in any one discipline.

For more information on the call center manager's role, see Chapter 3.

Defining the culture

Because call centers rely so much on people, managers need to define and create a supportive culture to make sure that the call center can operate successfully. Think of a supportive culture as being one that clearly defines the values and beliefs that support the call center's mission. (We talk about developing a mission in Chapter 2.)

To make the call center's mission and values come alive, managers are responsible for modeling the right behaviors. As a manager, you should communicate goals and rewards so that they line up with the call center's mission, vision, and values, and thereby help create the desired culture.

Understanding What Makes Call Centers Good or Bad

A good call center has a strong culture in which people work from a common set of values and beliefs, with a common purpose and a strong focus on business goals. Management needs to continually align everything that the call center does with the company's goals and desired culture.

Generally, as Figure 1-1 illustrates, your call center should have four main goals:

- **Efficiency:** Cost-effective operations for the organization. This area includes both operating the call center and completing core tasks for the organization (see Chapters 5–8, 11, 15, and 20).

- **Revenue generation:** Everything that leads to revenue, such as selling, upgrading, collecting, retaining current customers, and regaining lost customers (see Chapter 15).

- **Customer satisfaction:** Really long-term revenue generation, such as building customer loyalty and keeping customers (see Chapters 15, 16, and 17). Call centers should make things easy for customers. Whenever a customer needs it, the call center should be available, and agents should have access to all the information necessary to answer customer questions.

- **Employee satisfaction:** A measure of how happy employees are with their jobs and working environment (see Chapters 13, 14, 16, 18, and 20). In our experience, happy workers are more productive, take fewer days off, and stay loyal to the company.

These four goals are interdependent. Good revenue generation can't happen without some level of efficiency, for example; only satisfied customers continue to buy a product; and motivated employees promote the business effectively. We discuss the four goals in more detail in Chapter 2.

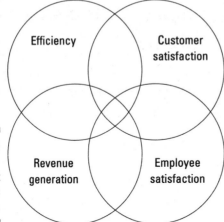

Figure 1-1:
Inter-
dependent
business
goals.

Characteristics of a good call center

When a call center is working properly, it exhibits the following traits:

- ✔ Focuses on its business goals.

- ✔ Answers phone calls and e-mails quickly.

- ✔ Has high employee morale.

- ✔ Resolves a high percentage of customer inquiries on the first contact.

- ✔ Measures customer satisfaction as a service indicator and has high customer satisfaction scores.

- ✔ Provides a significant source of revenue for the organization.

- ✔ Has an effective process for collecting and presenting data on performance. Everyone knows where he or she stands monthly, daily, hourly, and even in real time.

- ✔ Works efficiently. Employees need to do little follow-up on the customer file after the customer has hung up. Calls last for a consistent length of time and require a minimum of customer time to achieve resolution.

- ✔ Keeps everyone engaged and busy with a purpose, with no one being overly taxed.

- ✔ Improves processes continually to make gains in service, efficiency, and revenue generation.

- ✔ Enables the corporation to see the call center as a strategic advantage — an ally to the rest of the organization.

Characteristics of a poor call center

A call center that doesn't function well probably displays the following characteristics:

- ✔ Creates long hold times for customers waiting to get through to the next available agent (and when those customers do reach a call center employee, they're frequently transferred or put on hold).

- ✔ Deals with customer issues that frequently require multiple contacts before they're resolved.

- ✔ Breeds harried staff members running from crisis to crisis, putting out fires but not getting ahead.

- ✔ Lacks understanding of metrics or performance.

- ✔ Scores low on customer satisfaction or has no way to measure customer satisfaction at all.

- ✔ Lacks the appetite to improve working conditions to stay competitive and retain employees.

- ✔ Experiences low employee morale and high turnover.

- ✔ Generates complaints by corporate executives and senior management about costs or sales and service results. Some executives may talk about outsourcing the operation.

A well-run call center doesn't happen by accident. Good people need to do good planning and good execution. This book gives you the strategies, practices, plans, and skills to control what your call center produces.

Chapter 2

Business Basics: Models and Drivers and Goals, Oh My!

A *business model* is a high-level description of how your business is organized and what actions you plan to take to produce results for your
business: profits, happy customers, or whatever you want to achieve in your
business unit. A business model is really no more complicated than a game
plan or playbook ("Our goal is to win the game, so here's what we're going to
do").

The call center business model that we lay out in this chapter attempts to
align the call center's mission, objectives (goals), performance drivers, and
business practices. In our experience, good performance usually results
when call centers are truly aligned with their mission and objectives. Add
to this alignment a strong supportive culture, and you can really increase
results.

Like game plans, business models change and evolve. Over time, your model
becomes outdated, or you find better ways to run your call center, resulting in
a need to modify the plan. But you need to *have* a plan to modify.

Creating a Call Center Business Model

Creating a business model involves understanding cause and effect (do this, and that will happen). The better your understanding of cause and effect, the better you can make your model, and if you have a good model, you probably get good results. This book deals primarily with this pursuit of cause and effect.

Business models vary in the amount of detail that they provide. Some are very general and provide only a low level of detail; others are incredibly sophisticated, including complex economic models that forecast business results. A call center's business model should include

- ✔ A statement of mission and vision for the call center.

- ✔ Identification of the business goals, or *outputs,* that you want the call center to produce in the next year.

- ✔ An economic model made up of the key variables, or *performance drivers,* that affect your call center's business goals. (We explain performance drivers such as occupancy, conversion per contact, and cost per call in Chapter 6.)

- ✔ Identification of the business practices that affect performance drivers (frequently organized in the categories of people, process, and technology).

- ✔ Identification and creation of a supporting culture.

- ✔ A feedback mechanism.

What makes business models so important? History is full of examples of a superior opponent falling to an underdog who had a plan. In 1974, for example, the immensely powerful boxer George Foreman lost the world heavyweight crown to Muhammad Ali, who successfully used his rope-a-dope strategy to win the title.

In business, few companies can find investors if they don't have a sound business plan. Oddly, call centers in successful companies frequently don't have a well-thought-out game plan. As a result, their operations suffer from inconsistent service delivery, high costs, and less-than-optimal revenue generation. Typically, these operations have the necessary tools and talent to achieve their goals; they just need a well-defined business model to help them improve their results.

Figure 2-1 shows a sample of such a model.

Call Center Business Model

MISSION & VISION
(Statement of direction and purpose provided by the corporation)

BUSINESS OBJECTIVES
(Measures of performance supporting the service, efficiency, and revenue objectives of the mission and vision)

PERFORMANCE DRIVERS
(Measures that can be controlled by management and staff that indicate the degree to which the business objectives are being met)

BUSINESS PRACTICES
(The things done in the call center to affect the performance drivers)

People	Process	Technology
Roles and responsibilities	Forecasting and scheduling	Telecom
Skills and accountabilities	Performance management	Network
Motivations	Policies and procedures	Applications
	Recruiting and training	Integration
	Change management	
	Compliance	
	Etc.	

Culture
VALUES   **BELIEFS**

Figure 2-1:
A call center business model.

Lack of model = lack of results

A while ago, Réal and his team had an interesting consulting assignment. The president of a successful retail company, which we'll call PQR Co., approached Réal about PQR's call center. For years, the call center had been producing terrible service and experiencing ever-increasing costs.

The team conducted a fairly quick assessment, interviewing management and staff, analyzing data, surveying customers, and generally reviewing the call center's entire process. It discovered a call center filled with great tools and smart people — frustrated smart people who knew too well that the call center wasn't operating in a cohesive way.

(continued)

(continued)

Interestingly, the employees at PQR had a very high level of sophistication about call center concepts and practices. They tracked all the measures, and then some; they had a lot of training and knew a lot about how call centers worked; and they had a great deal of support, both financial and moral, from senior management.

So why didn't the call center get good results? PQR lacked only a coordinated business model, but it was lacking in a big way. Management and staff had no focus. Most management activities dealt with crises. Management always quickly replaced one important initiative with another.

Priorities changed frequently, based on what senior management was focusing on. Few senior managers seemed to be on the same page. The front-line staff recognized the problems; many sympathized with their managers, who were pulled in every direction. Because of the lack of focus, the call center got inconsistent results at high costs.

Réal's team introduced a simple business model to PQR's call center. Within three months, costs were down, revenue was up, and customer satisfaction had improved. Equally important, the call center staff was more energized and motivated.

Developing your mission

A *mission statement* is an articulation of overall purpose — your call center's *raison d'être*. It's a quick, concise description of your department's purpose, telling the world what the center does and why it does it.

Mission statements vary in length and content, but a one- or two-sentence statement can suffice if the mission statement is part of a bigger overall business model, because the business model adds detail to the mission. Declaring the company's purpose is a leadership responsibility, and the mission should inspire employees to do the right thing.

Some people believe that you create a mission statement as a participative exercise, involving input from senior management, call center management, employees, and even suppliers or customers. Others believe that creating a call center mission statement as a group exercise amounts to management by committee. If the resulting mission doesn't meet senior management's requirements, the mission becomes irrelevant.

We think that senior management — those in the corporation to whom the call center reports — should deliver the mission statement, because the mission statement amounts to the call center's marching orders. Most organizations set goals and expectations at a senior level and filter those responsibilities down.

Mission statements typically include the following elements:

  ✔ **Statement of purpose:** What the organization and its employees are here to do

- ✔ **Statement of values:** What the organization's rules of behavior and corporate beliefs are

- ✔ **Statement of competitive positioning:** What the organization does really well

- ✔ **Vision statement:** What the organization's future looks like

- ✔ **Stakeholder expectations:** What's at stake for everyone involved

You don't need to include all these elements in the mission statement, but you do need to address them somewhere in the business model. At minimum, a mission statement should include the statement of purpose, vision statement, and stakeholder expectations.

Dissecting a typical call center mission

A call center mission might look something like this:

> Our mission is to maximize value to XYZ Corp., our customers, and our employees by providing the highest-value call center services available in our industry. We are a learning organization that constantly improves. As a result, the call center will become a competitive advantage for XYZ Corp., leading the industry in cost control, revenue generation, and customer satisfaction.

This mission statement has a few parts that deserve explanation:

- ✔ **To maximize value to XYZ Corp., our customers, and our employees:** This phrase speaks to stakeholders. Maximizing value suggests that you'll work to achieve what each stakeholder wants out of the relationship with the call center. This phrase suggests that senior management has measured and understand expectations. The word *value* allows the mission statement to define, through the business model, what the stakeholders see as being valuable.

- ✔ **The highest-value call center services available:** This phrase suggests not that the call center will be the cheapest operation, but that it will deliver the most productivity for the money, creating an opportunity to balance cost control, revenue generation, and customer satisfaction.

- ✔ **We are a learning organization:** This phrase identifies the long-term result of consistently following the mission and business model.

Overall, this mission statement provides a neat way to launch into your business model, and you can use it to quickly explain what your call center is trying to do.

The mission describes the message that your senior management, both in the call center and in the corporation, should repeat regularly. If you say it often enough, fairly soon you'll start to achieve your mission without doing a lot of specific micromanagement, because people will gravitate to your overriding purpose.

Mission statements should stand the test of time, so you shouldn't have to change them very often. When you do change them, you should do so as the result of a shift in corporate strategy — changing the call center's focus from a cost center to a profit center, for example.

When Réal and his team first began work with PQR (refer to the sidebar "Lack of model = lack of results"), no one could articulate the call center's mission. How did Réal's team anticipate that this lack of definition might cause a problem? During their initial interview with senior management, the managers said, "We don't have a mission." As the saying goes, if you don't know where you're going, any road can take you there.

Determining Your Business Goals

In the short term, the organization has specific *deliverables* — goals and targets that it wants the call center to achieve. The company needs these deliverables, which generally relate to efficiency, revenue generation, customer satisfaction, and employee satisfaction, and which always support the call center's mission. The call center is a microcosm of the organization. If the call center achieves its goals, this success feeds into the organization's goals and contributes to the success of the organization. Companies frequently set these deliverables once per year, coinciding with the annual corporate budgeting process.

You can make your mission more specific — and achievable — by defining the call center's goals. Business goals measure call center effectiveness and the organization's progress against the four broad areas addressed in the mission statement: efficiency, revenue generation, customer satisfaction, and employee satisfaction (refer to "Understanding What Makes Call Centers Good or Bad" in Chapter 1).

Senior management provides these business goals to the call center, but ideally, the call center has some input, if only to make sure that the goals are realistic.

Don't just pull business goals out of the air; you need to think them through and justify them. When you define goals well, you can use them as gauges that tell you about the performance of your call center, like the gauges in an airplane. On the other hand, the old phrase "Garbage in, garbage out" rings very true of operational goals. Set bad goals, and you'll probably get bad results.

In the case of PQR Co. (refer to the sidebar "Lack of model = lack of results"), when Réal's team asked company agents what their measurable goals were, they produced a lot of measures, including cost per call, average speed of answer, and call length. No one could say which goals were most important, however, and no one seemed to be clear on the right target for each goal. Overall, PQR Co. lacked clear direction from senior management about which goals to focus on.

Specific goals vary by company. Table 2-1 shows a few examples and explains how to measure and interpret them.

Table 2-1	Call Center Goals	
Goal	*Measures*	*What the Measures Tell You*
Customer satisfaction	Postcall satisfaction scores	Whether agents are providing good service.
	Average speed of answer	
	First-call resolution (see "Avoiding misleading measures," later in this chapter)	Whether agents are answering calls quickly enough. (Hanging up is one form of customer feedback!)
		Whether the customer's request was completed on the first call.
Efficiency (cost control)	Cost per contact	Whether agents are handling contacts in an efficient manner.
	Cost per customer	
	Cost per case	Whether customers have to call more than once to get an issue resolved.
	Cost per order	
Revenue generation	(Net) revenue per customer	Whether the call center is making money.
	Revenue generated per call	
	Total customers	Whether the call center is maximizing sales opportunities and upgrading or adding onto the products or services it sells.
		Whether the business is growing.
Employee satisfaction	Employee opinion survey	Whether employees feel valued and respected.
	Retention rates	
	Employee referrals	Whether employees like working in the call center.

Defining a good objective

Here are a couple of important characteristics of good business objectives:

- ✔ They're measurable.
- ✔ They tell a complete story.

Ideally, a measurable goal tells you as much about an area of the business as possible. If you use total call center costs to measure cost control, for example, you can figure out the costs associated with running the call center, but you can't really tell whether the cost is expensive. Understanding this cost in relation to the number of customers, however, provides some context. A call center that costs $1 million per year but has only one customer, for example, is a lot more expensive than a call center that costs $50 million per year but has millions of customers. The most valuable measures tell you about your success without having to refer to other numbers.

You can measure goals as follows:

- ✔ **Cost per customer (efficiency):** Total cost of running the call center divided by total customers.

- ✔ **Revenue generated per customer:** Total revenue generated by the call center divided by the number of customers.

- ✔ **Customer satisfaction:** How satisfied customers are with their call center experience. Customer satisfaction can be measured through post-call surveys, surveys done by a third party, or focus groups. (We discuss customer satisfaction in Chapter 6.)

- ✔ **Employee satisfaction:** How satisfied call center employees are with their jobs. Employee satisfaction is usually measured through surveys and focus groups. (We talk about employee surveys in Chapter 18.)

You can come up with no end of business measures. Just make sure that those measures tell you what you want to know about your operation.

Avoiding misleading measures

When you establish how to measure your business goals, avoid using some common call center measures that don't tell the complete story and, therefore, can be misleading:

- ✔ **Operating budget:** The *operating budget* — how much you spend to run the call center — is a misleading measure. Most companies want to minimize the total cost of running their center, but if the company grows by 50 percent or 100 percent per year, the call center is likely to cost more while the company grows. Looking at the call center budget can be misleading when you're considering cost control, because you need to consider costs in relation to growth of the call center.

✔ **Cost per call:** Another misleading measure is *cost per call,* which is simply the cost of running a call center for a given period divided by the number of calls answered during the same period.

A cost-per-call measure can be misleading because it doesn't consider the effect of poor client interaction and repeat calls. If you overemphasize cost per call, you may tend to focus too strictly on keeping call times low — sometimes at the expense of good customer service. If agents don't do a good job of handling customer calls, rushing customers off the phone before they can satisfactorily resolve the customers' inquiries, customers will probably call back — or switch to the competition. Although your cost per call may appear to be low, a large number of callbacks increases your overall cost per customer.

✔ **First-call resolution:** Although *first-call resolution (FCR)* is a good measure of customer satisfaction, it can be misleading, because different companies have different measures for FCR. If a customer calls back within 48 hours of his first call, for example, some companies would consider this call to be a repeat call; other companies may use a different time frame for a repeat call, such as 72 hours or 1 week.

Also, most companies don't have the technology to link the reason for a call to a callback. If a client calls her bank to make a deposit and then calls back after 24 hours to make a withdrawal, the bank may not have the technology to tell that the two calls were unrelated and is likely to count the second call as a repeat call, thus inaccurately counting the first call as not being resolved.

Similarly, in some situations, a call center has no control over the reason for repeat calls on the same issue. If a customer called to make a purchase but realized that he didn't have his credit card handy, for example, he may decide to call back or to go online to complete this transaction. Such a callback would decrease the call center's FCR rate.

Considering service level

You may be thinking, "What about that grand dame of call center measures, service level?" *Service level* — defined as the percentage of incoming calls answered in a specified amount of time — is probably the most-talked-about standard for inbound call centers (refer to Chapter 1). It actually refers to how fast agents answer the phone, which has implications for customer satisfaction and total call center cost.

Service level directly measures the accessibility of your organization to your customers. It not only provides a good overall indicator of caller treatment, but also provides the foundation for the most fundamental activities in a call center: planning, staffing, and execution. The service-level objective you choose will directly influence the number of people you hire, how many people you need to have on the phone during each hour of the day, and when you need to implement a real-time disaster recovery plan. (See Chapter 4 for details on business continuity and Chapter 8 for information on scheduling.)

Service level balances customer tolerances for time spent waiting to speak with the next available agent; the cost of providing service; and the revenue opportunity that you lose when customers hang up, never to call again. Therefore, service level is a performance driver — that is, it has a direct effect on your call center's performance — but you can't classify it as an actual goal. Rather, it's a variable that will help you achieve your goals.

For more information on performance drivers such as service level, see Chapter 6.

Flowing goals through the accountability funnel

Well-defined goals not only keep the stakeholders happy, but also affect the whole organization, so they shouldn't be created in isolation. Establishing, applying, and communicating appropriate goals to every manager, team leader, department, and employee increases accountability at every level and creates a very focused organization, as illustrated in Figure 2-2.

Figure 2-2:
The accountability funnel.

Your goals must keep everyone accountable to, and focused on, the appropriate performance drivers. If you communicate thoroughly, everyone in the organization will understand how he or she can contribute to meeting those goals. If you don't, you may cause confusion, and your team won't work together to meet the goals.

Make your goals well defined and robust. Ask yourself, "If I achieve these goals or make constant improvements toward reaching these goals, can I achieve my mission? Will my stakeholders in the corporation be happy?" If you can answer yes, you're on the right track.

Measuring Progress with Performance Drivers

You derive your *business objectives* — the goals and targets that you're trying to produce — from your mission. If you want to use your business objectives to manage your call center toward success, you need a good understanding of how to manage and control a business objective. This understanding comes through performance drivers.

Performance drivers are processes and behaviors — expressed as measures — that help you achieve your business goals. Average call length, for example (the amount of time required to fully answer a customer inquiry), is a driver of call center costs and has a direct effect on the business goal of cost per customer, so average call length is a driver of cost.

Performance drivers make up the building blocks of the operation, and by analyzing them, you can mathematically model the business goals, budgets, profit-and-loss goals, and other aspects of operations, thereby creating the economic model for your call center. Performance drivers are like the levers that you push and pull to steer the call center ship toward its objectives.

If you drop by a call center, you're likely to hear discussions of some of these performance drivers:

- ✔ **Service level:** How fast agents answer phone calls, e-mail messages, and so on. You can express this driver in a variety of ways, but it's most commonly measured by the percentage of incoming calls answered in a specified amount of time. If the call center answers 78 percent of all calls taken within 30 seconds of the calls entering the queue, for example, the service level achieved is 78/30. Service level affects cost, revenue, and customer satisfaction.

- ✔ **Average call length:** How long it takes, on average, to process one customer interaction.

✔ **Agent occupancy:** The percentage of time that agents are busy processing customer calls rather than waiting for the next call.

✔ **Agent availability:** How many of your agents are actually available to take a call (meaning that they're not already busy on a call) and, therefore, aren't generating revenue.

✔ **Schedule adherence:** The percentage of time that your agents are actually on the phone during the time when they're scheduled to be on the phone.

✔ **Conversion rate:** The percentage of contacts that the call center converts to sales.

✔ **Retention rate:** The percentage of customers whom the call center persuaded to stay *(retained)* when those customers attempted to cancel their relationship with the company.

✔ **Customer satisfaction:** How satisfied your customers are with the level of service that your call center provides. This driver is often measured by way of a customer survey and is sometimes expressed as a percentage.

✔ **FCR:** The percentage of callers who don't have to call back within a certain time frame (usually, a day) to have their issue resolved.

In Chapter 6, we review other exciting call center–related stuff that you can measure.

By managing performance drivers, you can affect the outcomes of your business goals. Much of the information in this book, in fact, deals with how to manipulate drivers effectively to get desired results, such as the following:

✔ **Make customers happy, and improve customer satisfaction scores.** Answer the phone quickly, be nice to callers, and give them prompt and complete service. We talk about how to make customers happy and improve customer satisfaction scores in Chapter 15.

✔ **Reduce the cost of handling calls.** Reduce average call length, reduce the cost of your service, and make sure that you keep your agents busy while they're available to answer the phones. See Part II for more information on improving efficiency.

In the PQR Co. example (refer to the sidebar "Lack of model = lack of results," earlier in this chapter), the company tracked all the necessary measurable factors relating to its call center. Management didn't see a clear relationship between the performance drivers and the business objectives, however. As a result, managers didn't work in a coordinated and consistent fashion to effect results through manipulation of the drivers; instead, they focused on some performance drivers one day and on others the next day. Because of this scattershot approach, they got mixed results.

Categorizing the drivers

As we discuss in Chapter 1, performance drivers fall into four categories:

- Efficiency
- Revenue generation
- Customer satisfaction
- Employee satisfaction

Which driver is most important to your business depends on your organization's goals and the priorities that you've established for the call center.

Efficiency

Your call center likely comes under the cost-control microscope often, even though call centers tend to offer a very efficient way to communicate with massive volumes of customers. Still, corporations frequently have large call center expenditures, so executives have reason to scrutinize those costs.

Items that affect the efficiency of your call center include

- Call length
- Agent occupancy (defined in "Measuring Progress with Performance Drivers," earlier in this chapter)
- Average cost of making an agent available to answer the phones (wages, benefits, management costs, and so on)
- Repeat calls from customers who don't get an accurate or complete answer on the first call
- Nonproduction time (time that agents spend away from the phone, which is measured through schedule adherence)
- Frequent agent sick leave, absence, and turnover

You should scrutinize these items in great detail because they will help you achieve your call center's goals. Looking at the drivers of cost control is just a start in improving efficiency.

Call center managers who have very good control of their results dig deep into these aspects of operations to better understand why they achieve the results that they do and how to affect those results in the future. Call length, for example, can be broken down into time spent talking with the customer and postcall work (such as time spent processing customer requests after the customer is no longer on the line). You can better understand both aspects of call length when you consider what call lengths result from different types of calls — an information call versus a sales call, for example.

A full-time business analyst can research cost-control drivers to identify opportunities to improve efficiencies, especially in a relatively large call center. (See Chapter 15 for more information on this worthwhile endeavor.)

Revenue generation

It don't mean a thing if you ain't got *cha-ching!* Improvement in your call center's revenue generation can have a greater effect on margins than improvements in cost-control measures. In relatively large call centers, small improvements in *retention rate* (keeping customers who call to cancel service) represent hundreds of thousands or even millions of dollars in saved revenue. Similarly, small improvements in selling and *upselling* (attempting to have the customer purchase an upgrade, an add-on, or a more expensive item) can represent hundreds of thousands of dollars or more.

In addition to your retention rate, consider these key revenue *metrics,* or measures for quantitatively assessing revenue generation:

- ✔ Conversion rate (the number of sales made per contacts handled)
- ✔ Revenue generated per sale
- ✔ Cancellations per call (a variation on retention rate)
- ✔ Revenue lost per cancellation (a measure of the total revenue lost divided by the number of cancellations)

Only when you focus on efficiency and revenue generation with equal dedication and discipline can you experience real improvements in profit.

Customer satisfaction

Some call centers are getting good — very good — at understanding what makes customers happy. Unfortunately, not all of them are good at actually doing what it takes to make customers happy.

Here are some metrics to measure:

- ✔ How fast agents answer the phone, including average speed of answer and service level (refer to "Considering service level," earlier in this chapter).
- ✔ How customers rate their experiences in a postcontact survey. (See Chapter 10 for more about surveys and Chapter 15 for details on developing a customer-experience blueprint.)

Why is employee opinion important?

Your mom probably always said that you should be nice to the people you meet. She meant the people you work with, too.

You have a lot of good business reasons to treat employees well. For one, you spend a lot of time and money to attract and train good people. If those people leave your company to go work for nicer people, you have to attract and train more people (who will probably leave you too). Even if they don't quit, unhappy people don't see the need to work hard to meet company goals. The employee who mentally quits but stays on your payroll can cost your business a lot of money.

Also, in our experience, happy employees create happy customers.

Réal and his team once consulted for two competitors in the same industry. Neither business knew that the team was working with the other business, and neither benefited from the work that the team did with the other business. Still, Réal's team took away some valuable knowledge.

These companies sold virtually the same products for approximately the same prices and had customers in the same location. Customers had to communicate regularly with each company through the call center. In the first company, employees were very happy and rated their job satisfaction as very high. Employee turnover was modest. In the second company, employees weren't so happy, so morale was rather dark, and employee turnover was high.

As far as the team could tell, this difference in employee satisfaction was the most significant difference between the two companies. When they looked at performance data, however, they were shocked. The second company had nearly double the rate of customer cancellations and a significantly lower customer opinion score than the first company. Not surprisingly, the average revenue per customer was much lower in the second company.

This story is far from a scientific study, but it goes to show you that being nice is good for business.

Employee satisfaction

As we discuss in Chapter 6, your employees can tell you in your monthly employee opinion survey what they see as being employee satisfaction drivers. Start by asking general questions about job satisfaction; then ask open-ended questions about the most and least satisfying aspects of the job. In subsequent surveys, include questions about management's performance in relation to the satisfying (and dissatisfying) factors identified in the earlier survey. These points will definitely come up in these surveys as key employee satisfaction drivers:

- **Team-leader support:** Are your employees getting the help that they need?

- **Feedback:** Do they know where they stand in meeting their job expectations and performance standards?

- **Training:** Are they getting the training that they need to do the job well?

Balancing the drivers

To create a good operation, attempt to strike a perfect balance among efficiency, revenue generation, customer satisfaction, and employee satisfaction.

The challenge is that many companies emphasize one of these four areas more than the others, which causes confusion. If you applaud and reward only sales, for example, the other measures will be left by the wayside, causing imbalance. To achieve balance, you have to promote and celebrate behaviors that help employees understand how their actions affect each area.

Table 2-2 summarizes some basic call center business goals and the corresponding performance drivers that affect them.

Table 2-2	Call Center Goals and Performance Drivers	
Goal	*Measure*	*Driver*
Efficiency	Cost per customer	Call length
		Cost per hour of providing the service
		How busy the agents are while on the phone
		Percentage of time agents spend manning the phones
		Percentage of calls resolved on first attempt
Revenue generation	Revenue per customer	Percentage of calls resulting in a sale
		Dollar value of sales made
Customer satisfaction	Postcall customer survey	Accessibility satisfaction survey
		Agent professionalism, courtesy, and ability
		Process (ability to serve the customer and follow company procedures)
Employee satisfaction	Employee opinion score	Behavior and support of managers — especially agents' direct team leaders
	Retention rates	Adequate training
		Consistent feedback
		Other drivers identified by employees

The following sections provide tips on managing each driver.

Don't go overboard on efficiency

You've taken your quest for efficiency too far if you

- Hire people who are unsuited for the job (perhaps because they work for less money than more-qualified people would).
- Skimp on training.
- Don't make time for coaching.
- Don't spend enough on support services.

A business can benefit from greatly reduced labor costs by taking a call center offshore to a far-off country such as India or the Philippines. General Electric, which helped popularize this trend, conducted its move offshore in a well-orchestrated, well-planned fashion. Eager to capture similar benefits, many companies moved their call center operations offshore without the same level of planning and, in some cases, got less-than-ideal results. Delta Airlines, for example, canceled its offshoring in Asia because its customers were very vocal in their disapproval of foreign customer service agents. Some of these companies suffered more in terms of lost customers, lost revenue opportunities, and additional costs of repeat calls than they gained in reduced employment costs. In these cases, an overzealous desire to cut costs resulted in increased overall cost to the organization.

Avoid a surplus of service

You need good customer service, but you need a larger goal than just making customers like you. Customers want call center agents to perform a service, not to be their best pals. Granted, you can find people who want to spend extraordinary amounts of time on the phone with their favorite call centers, but you have to admit that those people are probably not very common.

You'd probably have to spend way too much money to ensure that ten agents are always available, waiting for the next call, so that they can answer every customer call after the first ring. Your average customer is used to waiting at least 20 to 30 seconds before an agent answers. Just try to respond to your customers faster than your competitors do instead of worrying about a number that someone set in-house. This goal will help you keep service level in perspective.

If you overemphasize service, employees can believe that trying to sell the customer something is bad or that keeping transactions quick and efficient can make the customer dislike employees. In our experience, most customers want efficient and professional resolution of their calls, and polite and courteous service.

Killing 'em with kindness

Some time ago, Réal was touring a call center and listening to agents on the phones. One fellow tried so hard to make the customer like him that he virtually held the customer hostage. Despite the customer's best efforts, she couldn't get off the phone with this agent. You could hear the pain in the customer's voice as she feigned interest, not wanting to be rude to this nice fellow who was regaling her with information about everything from the weather in northern Alberta to the dietary habits of his Aunt Martha's cat. Interestingly, but not surprisingly, this agent had very high call times, moderate customer satisfaction scores, and dismal sales results.

Resist revenue-generation mania

If an agent fails to resolve a long-term customer's service concern but makes great attempts to close in for more sales, that customer can get angry, become disengaged from the conversation, and perhaps even decide not to do business with your company.

Although you need an overall focus on revenue generation, overemphasizing short-term revenue gain probably leads to long-term service pain because your call center loses the lifetime value of a loyal customer.

Don't focus on entertaining employees

You can overemphasize making employees happy if your management team attempts to turn the call center into a love-in. In an effort to ensure high employee morale, some companies live with the motto "Try not to upset anyone." If you adopt that motto, you'll probably end up hurting your call center's performance.

People need feedback and coaching on how to do their jobs better. Over time, a fair, honest, and consistent approach wins as much in the morale wars as a soft hand does, if not more, because it keeps the organization on track to meet its goals.

You have to accept the fact that not every employee is going to be happy all the time. Unsurprisingly, the unhappiest employees are often those who don't do a good job.

Carrying Out Call Center Best Practices

If you've read the earlier sections of this chapter, you've developed your mission — the reason why the call center exists — or asked senior management to provide a mission. You've also established your business goals — what the corporation needs from the call center right now. Finally, you've gained understanding of the levers or variables that we call performance drivers, which directly affect your business goals.

At this point, the parts of your business model should begin to align. In a sort of "the leg bone is connected to the knee bone" arrangement, the mission is connected to business goals, business goals are connected to performance drivers, and performance drivers are connected to business practices.

Business practices are the procedures and policies — the specific things that people in the call center do every day — that affect the efficiency, revenue, customer service, and employee morale drivers of the operation, which in turn affect your call center's business goals.

To meet your goals, consider developing business practices as a continuous cycle.

Any call center performs many key practices to ensure success, as we discuss in Chapter 1. You can categorize all these practices and procedures under three headings:

- ✔ **People:** Employ skilled people, and use the best performance-management methods to continue to make those people improve so that they produce better results over time.

- ✔ **Process:** Define, refine, and continuously improve work processes so that you improve your business drivers.

- ✔ **Technology:** Automate efficient, well-defined processes by using appropriate technology to improve driver performance over time.

We discuss all three categories in the following sections.

Focusing on people

Dealing with people is an important aspect of call centers. Folks who want stuff often need to talk to folks who sell (or know about, or provide support for) that stuff. If you have enough people asking, seeking, or buying — as when Madonna concert tickets go on sale, for example — you need a lot of people taking those orders. Sure, customers can order tickets and look for information on the Internet, but a great number of them still want to talk to an actual person about making their purchase.

Generally, the people who are inquiring, ordering, or looking for help want to encounter someone who has a courteous, professional, polite, and friendly manner. You can fulfill that desire almost solely by having great people working in your call center.

You need to establish the appropriate roles, responsibilities, skills, and accountabilities to meet your call center goals. Include clearly defined job descriptions for all roles throughout your call center's organizational chart. Also, hire the best people that you can. In Chapter 3, we discuss organizational design, the key roles, and the importance of work culture in the call center; in Chapter 12, we talk more about hiring the right people; and in Chapter 13, we talk about the importance of developing skills through good leadership and coaching.

No matter how impeccable your processes are or how tantalizing your technology is, without the right people working for your call center, you're headed down the road to mediocrity.

Focusing on process

Any business needs to have the right processes in place to make things happen the way they're supposed to, but you especially need the correct setup if you want to run an effective call center.

Process refers to how work gets done — the organization of tasks for *inputs,* which are anything that you put into a system or that's used in its operation, and *outputs,* which are the results. Call centers are very procedure-driven; in fact, some of the biggest success stories in call center management come from improvements in processes. A more efficient way to schedule staff, a quicker way to service specific types of customer calls, and a better training procedure are all process changes that can have tremendous effects on call center results.

Many call centers seek out quality-control programs, such as International Organization for Standardization (ISO) certification, and call center–specific standards, such as Customer Operations Performance Center, Inc. (COPC) certification. The call center industry also largely accepts Six Sigma, a process-oriented management discipline. We talk more about these programs in Chapter 17.

For virtually every business practice in the operation, you need to ensure that your team develops (and follows) a systematic method to make order from the chaos that a call center can sometimes produce.

Improving process

Process is a call center business practice in which you can always find room for improvement. Fortunately, call centers generally respond well to an environment of continuous improvement, as we discuss in Chapter 15. In fact, because of the dynamic character of the call center industry, you may want to include a process for managing changes — sometimes called, appropriately enough, a *change management process* — in your defined business practices.

Call centers probably grew out of the need for better processes. Imagine, way back in the day, a ticket agency that had just one agent answering a single phone, selling tickets for a Frank Sinatra concert. Eventually, someone likely realized that this setup didn't allow the agency to do business in the most efficient way and hollered, "We need a better process!" The agency rounded up a bunch of people to answer a lot of phones and take a heap of orders, and *voilà* — a call center was born. Call centers have been improving processes ever since.

In Chapter 15, we discuss some process management concepts and methods.

Defining terms clearly

The best-made processes are laid to waste, however, if people don't speak the same language. Therefore, you must establish definitions of terms to prevent frustration. Something as simple as the definition of *call length* — the total amount of time that an agent takes to complete a customer transaction from start to finish, including time spent talking to the customer and any postcall time needed to fill out information in a database — can make the difference between an employee's meeting performance expectations and failing miserably.

To help you avoid costly miscommunication, we provide definitions and concepts throughout this book. Also, for your quick reference, we've included a handy-dandy glossary as Appendix A at the back of this book. Use it to amaze your friends with your astonishing grasp of call center terminology, or consult it when you need a quick refresher.

Talk to your team to find out whether your definitions are clear and specific enough to ensure that everyone understands them.

ANECDOTE

What does "call time" really mean?

One of Réal's team leaders approached him with a challenge that involved coaching one of the team leader's team members. (We discuss the various roles of the call center team in Chapter 3.) It seemed that no matter how hard the team leader tried to explain, this agent simply couldn't get his average call time down to the campaign's requirement, so he wouldn't receive a quarterly raise.

Réal agreed to help and took a look at the agent's stats. He found that the agent's *average talk time* — the average amount of time spent on the phone talking directly to the customer — was shorter than that of many other agents working on the same campaign and that he took almost twice as long as most to complete his after-call work. In other words, his average *after-call work time* — the average amount of time spent doing any postcall wrap-up work associated with the just-completed call — was twice as long.

When Réal spoke to the agent, he found that the agent thought that call time was the same thing as talk time. If the team leader had simply picked up on the fact that the agent didn't fully understand this definition, she could have prevented a few months' worth of frustration for both of them.

Focusing on technology

Technology can be dangerous. Although it can lead to fantastic improvements in efficiency and speed, without a well-thought-out plan, technology can spell disaster. Even if you have good people, when you take a bad process and automate it, you just end up where you don't want to be faster.

In the simplest of terms, *technology* refers to the machines that help make call center processes work quickly and provide the people who are doing the work the resources they need to get the work done. Automation (computers, software, and networks) can supercharge or enable certain processes and increase productivity.

To continue the earlier example about Madonna concert tickets, imagine that when people call to order tickets, all the agents taking all those calls record the pertinent customer information by using only pencil and paper. Those callers probably don't have a very good chance of ever seeing the concert. This setup could work, but the call center would need a lot of paper and a lot more people to process that paper.

You could automate this process, but if you have a poor process, automating it simply adds cost — in some cases, a great deal of cost — without driving performance toward your business goals. Worse, poorly defined and poorly applied technology can take you off track, and if you spend a lot of money on a piece of technology, you have a hard time justifying not using it and may end up entrenching a flawed process.

You can find a lot of great technology that enhances call center processes, however, as we discuss in Chapter 10. Just make sure that you'll be automating sound processes, and research the technology before you invest in it.

Reporting: Providing Feedback

Call centers are data factories. Almost every tool that a call center agent uses collects, stores, and reports on something, and all this data has to be pulled together and analyzed. Used properly, all this information helps call center managers analyze performance, create processes that improve results, and discard processes that don't support the company's goals.

Increasingly, call centers hire analysts who have advanced degrees in statistics and engineering because those analysts make valuable findings about improvements that the call center can make in the business model.

Reporting on performance drivers is an important part of the call center business model. Information reports give managers the feedback that they need to figure out whether their business practices and performance drivers are aligned with the call center's mission and business goals. In Chapter 6, we discuss analysis, and in Chapter 9, we outline many of the types of reports used in a call center.

ANECDOTE

Why you should put people and process first

One call center implemented technology to collect sales data and deliver statistics to each agent's desktop within minutes of that agent's completing a sale. The company used these sales statistics in a very aggressive incentive campaign. The idea was that agents could see their bank accounts grow in actual dollars before their very eyes with every sale they made, which would drive them to make more sales.

This approach was a great idea. Unfortunately, it had a problem: The process for collecting the sales data was flawed, and the technology was double- or even triple-counting some sales. A greater problem, of course, was that the company implemented the technology to deliver the stats *before* it recognized the process issue. That company ended up with a people problem because it had to explain to agents that because of a management error, they wouldn't actually receive the large payouts they expected. Ouch!

Chapter 3

Developing the Cast of Characters

· ·

· ·

*I*n this chapter, we discuss the people you need to run an effective call center — who they are, what roles they have, and how they're organized. Even with the development of self-help technology, call centers are still very much about people helping other people.

Organizational design — how the organization is set up in terms of roles and responsibilities, and who reports to whom — is an important part of the call center business model. You need a coordinated effort among numerous staff members for a call center to achieve its business goals (which we discuss in Chapter 2). It doesn't take too many people working at cross purposes to place a drag on results.

A key part of organizational design is having the right roles in your center, which will allow you to reach your objectives. With the right mix of people and roles, a call center can operate in a highly coordinated fashion. When roles are missing or unnecessary roles creep into the organization, a call center can become overstretched or bureaucratic, and either situation can slow the march toward achieving your goals.

Because you're dealing with people, you need to consider the culture of your call center workplace. A supportive culture can make the call center run smoothly, even if you have a less-than-optimal organizational design. An unsupportive culture can sabotage even the best organization, making it difficult for the call center to improve.

If you put together a good design and a great culture, your organization can produce stellar results even when it faces challenges.

Designing an Organizational Chart

Organizational design — one of the things that the business does to create alignment with the mission — is part of the business model. (See Chapter 2 for more information on developing a mission.) Done well, the design process makes your organization flexible and *scalable* — capable of growing easily without the need for a new design. If you have a good organizational design, people can work together toward the same goals, even though many of those people have unique priorities.

If you create a poor organizational design, while the organization gets larger, it becomes more bureaucratic, inflexible, and bloated.

The most senior person in the call center defines the structure of the organization. This person has some responsibilities of his or her own, of course, in addition to developing the organization structure.

Key considerations

Here are some considerations when you decide how to design your call center organization:

- ✔ **Keep the organizational design stable.** While the call center grows, the number of people supporting a particular function (say, scheduling) might increase, but the structure shouldn't need to change.

- ✔ **Identify the broad critical tasks that need to be done to support the mission.** If the mission statement (refer to Chapter 2) says that the call center should be customercentric, for example, you should have a department that analyzes the customer experience, makes recommendations for improvement, and sponsors the necessary changes through to completion.

- ✔ **Group functions around similar and related processes.** Accounting and payroll, for example, are similar and related processes that can report to the finance department.

- ✔ **Consider how the functions will work together to meet call center goals.** You know that certain functions have different goals, and sometimes, those goals are in conflict. The scheduler may want agents on the phones when the team leader wants agents off the phones for coaching sessions, for example. If you make each function understand the other functions and their relative importance to the organization, people in all functions can work together toward the common mission and business goals.

Key tasks

Several critical tasks must be completed for a call center to function well. Consider these tasks when you design the organization structure and assign roles and responsibilities:

✔ Determine the call center's mission. As we discuss in Chapter 2, you need to craft the mission, communicate it to the employees, and design it into the department's business model.

✔ Work with senior management to determine the call center's business goals.

✔ Identify the key variables — called *performance drivers* (see Chapter 2) — that drive the call center's economic model and that directly affect the business goals.

✔ Assign the roles and responsibilities required to achieve the goals, and determine what roles fall into which function. In your operation, for example, you may have a call center with a director who is responsible for the managers who supervise team leaders who supervise agents. This director may also be responsible for some of the support groups, such as those that forecast calls and schedule agents. Another organizational design may have two directors: one who is responsible for the agents and another who is responsible for the support team.

✔ Recruit, train, and support the management team.

✔ Create and maintain a business culture that supports the mission.

✔ Create a process for documenting policies and procedures, as well as a process for updating policies and procedures when the call center makes any changes that improve the customer experience.

✔ Create an audit process to determine whether employees are following policies and procedures.

✔ Develop a system of corrective action to be followed when someone doesn't follow policies and procedures, or when existing policies and procedures don't optimize results.

✔ Recruit and train agents and support staff.

✔ Manage and support agent performance.

✔ Assess and provide feedback on the quality of agent performance.

✔ Schedule staff and resources to meet demand.

✔ Analyze and report on performance and process, and identify opportunities for improvement.

✔ Implement and manage a telecommunications infrastructure and a computer network.

✔ Identify, build (or purchase), and support applications that support the call center.

✔ Ensure that the call center complies with all legal requirements.

✔ Provide front-line support to customers.

✔ Provide direction and support for the management team.

This list doesn't include everything that you may need to do. You'll identify additional tasks that are important for your particular call center, such as payroll and budgeting or facilities management.

Introducing the Call Center Team: Roles and Responsibilities

The roles and responsibilities that we describe in the following sections are intended only to identify the core work that needs to be done in a call center. Figure 3-1 shows a typical functional organizational chart. Naturally, you may not organize your call center in exactly this fashion; the size of your operation has a significant effect on the structure of your organization.

The precise structure of your organization isn't as important as ensuring that you assign all the major responsibilities and clearly define the accountabilities.

If you have a relatively small operation, one person may handle more than one of the roles and/or responsibilities that we describe. Your team leader might also do recruiting, or the analyst might also do some scheduling. On the other hand, in a large operation, whole departments might handle one role, such as scheduling or reporting functions. Similarly, the team-leader role might be broken into finer areas of responsibility, with one group of team leaders handling coaching and feedback while other groups work on delegated projects that will improve processes.

Senior management

In a corporate call center, you find two groups of customers:

✔ **External:** *External customers* are the people on the phone who are calling for various reasons, perhaps to buy something or (in the case of a TV network) to ask why *Lassie* was taken off the air.

✔ **Internal:** *Internal customers* are members of senior management — the executives who don't work in the call center but tell you what you have to do (such as generate more revenue, cut costs, do both, or make customers happier). If you run an outsourcing call center (see Chapter 5), the internal customer is the client company.

Either way, the internal customer gives you your marching orders, and in your organizational structure, he, she, or it is at the top.

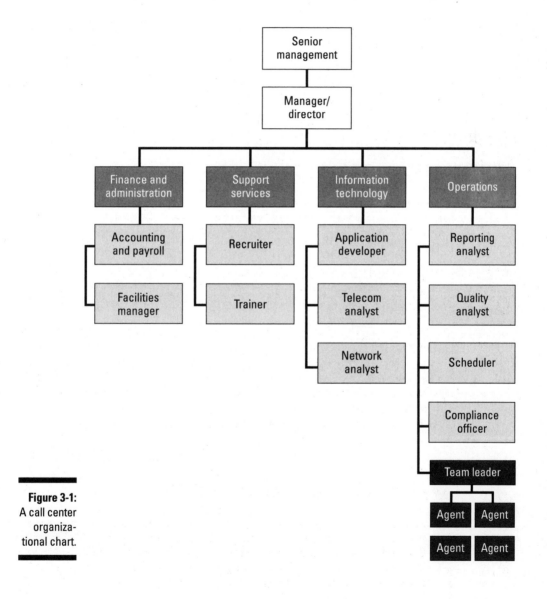

Figure 3-1:
A call center organizational chart.

Senior management has certain responsibilities to the call center, including assigning a general mission (such as "We are here to serve the customer in support of the product. Customers will never leave us for lack of support!"). We talk more about mission in Chapter 2.

Senior management also needs to tell you exactly what your annual business objectives are. A typical objective might look like this: "The company needs the call center to acquire 1 million new customers next year, with average revenue per customer of $100 and a cost per customer of $5. Oh, and customers must rate their satisfaction with the call center experience as excellent 95 percent of the time, with no more than 1 complaint per 1,000 customers." Ideally, some input from the call center went into creating the objectives so that they're based on what's realistically achievable.

Call center manager

Senior management works with the person who has overall responsibility for the call center's goals, processes, and results. If all goes well, it has a give-and-take relationship with this person that results in realistic goals that support the organization.

And who is this wonderful person who has overall responsibility for the call center, this supporter of call center rights and freedoms, this champion of the little agent? It's none other than the wondrous, the celebrated, the awe-inspiring *call center manager!*

Okay, you may not call this person a call center manager. She might be a director, vice president, assistant vice president, senior vice president, super-duper vice president, or "Janet over in the call center." It really doesn't matter what name any organization gives the job. When we say *call center manager,* we're talking about the person who has overall responsibility for the call center's results.

The call center manager takes direction and goals from senior management, communicates them to the call center agents in the form of overall goals and the department mission, and then translates them into internal call center goals and measures. He goes through this process by identifying the performance drivers that affect business and department goals. Cost per customer, for example, may be driven by call length, first-call resolution, cost per hour of agent time on the phones, and agent occupancy. (See Chapter 6 for more information on these measures.)

The call center manager spends much of his time ensuring that performance and all roles, accountabilities, and processes in the department are on track. He has oversight of the following tasks:

✔ Working with senior management to develop realistic annual business goals

✔ Designing the organization structure of the call center, and identifying roles and responsibilities

✔ Reviewing and approving all policies and procedures to ensure that they support the department's mission and business goals

✔ Recruiting, training, supporting, and developing the remaining members of the management team, including people who handle support functions

Agent performance team

Recruiter, trainer, and team leader comprise the *agent performance team.* Together, they perform the core responsibilities that we summarize as the quick method of getting the right agents to be excellent at their job:

1. Hire the right people to do the job.

2. Tell them what to do and why they need to do it.

3. Show them how to do it.

4. Give them feedback on performance.

5. Make supporting them — by ensuring that they have the knowledge, skills, and tools to do their job — your number-one mission.

Recruiter

Here's the ancient secret of call centers: You need people who have the skills (or the potential to develop the skills) to properly support your products and your customers. The recruiter's job is to seek out people who have the motivation and the experience to do the job.

In many small call centers, the job of recruiting is absorbed into the team leader's role. You may not want to create that job combo, however, if your call center does a lot of ongoing recruiting, because your team leader will spend all of her time recruiting, and your existing staff will lack the attention they need. Also, a dedicated professional recruiter can improve the quality of recruits, maximizing the success of your recruits and operations. If you're hiring a lot of people who just end up quitting in six months, you're wasting time. If your call center does more or less ongoing recruitment, look into hiring a professional recruiter.

Being a good recruiter is tough. A good recruiter plays several roles:

- ✔ **Fortune-teller:** The recruiter works with the scheduling department to predict when the call center will need new staff.

- ✔ **Advertising and marketing specialist:** In the process of finding people who are interested in working for the company, the recruiter becomes an advertising and marketing specialist, communicating to potential employees the availability and desirability of jobs in the call center.

- ✔ **Analyst:** After bringing in a sufficient pool of candidates, the recruiter starts the process of comparing the candidates with his own criteria for success.

- ✔ **Researcher/psychologist/tea-leaf reader:** Using the company's selection criteria, as well as interviews, reference checks, and employment tests, the recruiter determines which candidates are most likely to be successful in the job and within the company. This determination, which can be tough, includes two areas of investigation:

  - Does the candidate have the skills or aptitude to do the job well?

  - Will the candidate value the job long enough to be motivated to improve his or her performance?

- ✔ **Lawyer:** When the recruiter finds people who can be successful in the job, he makes offers to those candidates. At this point, the recruiter becomes part lawyer, making sure that the offer of employment is legal and promises only the right things. The recruiter has to make the offer clear. After candidates accept, sign the offer letter, and schedule training time, the recruiter can become a couch potato — for a few hours.

- ✔ **Sleuth:** A very good recruiter is also part sleuth. He reviews the success of employees and looks for patterns that can help with future recruitment. The recruiter interviews employees who quit the company to find out why they're leaving and how he might have predicted their departure during recruitment. (Don't be mistaken here: Some turnover will happen in your call center, as in any business, but you still want to understand why.)

Trainer

You can realize improvements in your call center quickly and easily by establishing good training in sales, call control, anger diffusion, customer service, and similar topics. That training, however, starts with a trainer.

In a call center, trainers offer initial training for new agents; ongoing skill-enhancement training for existing agents; and management and leadership training for team leaders, managers, and other off-phone staff.

In addition to facilitating training sessions, many trainers develop course materials for training. Good trainers are skilled in adult education, management, and motivation. They use a variety of techniques to develop the skills of those they train.

Being a call center trainer is a wonderful job, because things rarely go wrong in training. Unfortunately, things do sometimes go wrong in a day in the life of a call center agent, so the trainer should establish a when-things-go-wrong process and role-play to prepare agents for such events.

Good training and a great trainer have magnified benefits in the call center environment, because call centers are about people — a lot of people working the phones. Call centers are also about numbers. One small positive change can have a big effect on the customer experience or on the improvement of the business, because this change for the better is repeated multiple times across a large number of people.

A call center that has 1 million customers and reduces its contact rate by 1 percent because of effective training reduces call volume by 10,000 calls. Alternatively, imagine taking 10 seconds off call length through call-control training. That translates into about 4,000 hours in reduced staffing.

Often, when an agent comes out of training with a lack of knowledge or understanding about how to apply that knowledge, the team leader points his finger at the trainer, and the trainer points her finger at the team leader. Who has the accountability? Training gives agents knowledge and instruction on how to apply this knowledge. When the trainer hands off a newly trained agent to the team leader, the trainer and team leader need to have a clear discussion about the agent's strengths and areas of development. The team leader must further develop his agent to full proficiency.

Team leader

Probably the most important management job in the call center, in terms of driving operational performance, is the team leader. A good team leader drives agents and a call center to great improvements, but a bad team leader quickly creates poor morale, which leads to agents leaving or not giving their best.

In fairness, bad supervision frequently isn't the team leader's fault. Bad supervision can come from poorly designed team-leader roles. Perhaps the team leader is conflicted about priorities, and as a result, she doesn't focus on the things that motivate employees and drive results. Bad supervision also can result from poor team-leader training (or no training at all). Many team leaders face the "You're a great agent — now get out there and supervise!" dilemma.

Team leaders have several key responsibilities:

- ✔ **Setting expectations:** It's been said that the number-one reason why employees fail is that the employees don't know what's expected of them. Amen to that! We'd go further and suggest that expectations must be very simple, clear, and easy to remember. The team leader needs to communicate expectations clearly and make sure that employees always know where they stand with regard to those expectations.

- ✔ **Coaching:** Coaching includes providing feedback on performance, drilling down to the specific kernel of performance that can result in the biggest improvement for the agent. It also includes providing the agent ad hoc training and guidance on how to make changes for improvement. (For more information on coaching and feedback, turn to Chapter 13.)

- ✔ **Providing support:** The team leader also needs to offer support to the call center agents. Whether he's providing job support or career support, he needs to be there for agents when they need help, clearing away roadblocks and helping them build the skills they need to better their performance. This part of the job is very important, because when roadblocks hamper agent performance, frustration sets in — and if the team leader doesn't remove the roadblocks, the agents will begin to direct their frustration toward him.

Scheduler

Here's a tough job. The scheduler (or, in large call centers, the scheduling group) is responsible for forecasting call-volume demand and planning for sufficient staff, desks, and equipment to meet that demand within call center goals (service level and so on; see Chapter 2).

The job includes multiple phases of forecasting and scheduling, including long-term ("Hey, recruiter, we're gonna need 20 more people next January"), medium-term ("You know, we're going to have to add some people to the evening schedule next month"), short-term ("We're going to be overstaffed Friday afternoon, so we should schedule some training sessions"), and the present ("We're trending over forecast today. Noon to 2 p.m. will be busy; we should reschedule the team meetings for tomorrow"). If you want to know what's going on in the call center, ask the scheduler. We discuss this function in depth in Chapter 8.

A good scheduler can reduce expenses in a call center by 5 percent or more without making any service reductions. In many call centers, 5 percent is worth a lot of bananas.

Analysts

Several analyst roles are critical to the operation of a call center. Each role calls for a person (or people) with specific technical expertise and a high level of skill. The following sections describe the various analysts you'd find in a typical call center.

Telecommunications analyst

A call center isn't a call center without people, but it *really* isn't a call center without calls. Most phone systems are so reliable that people take them for granted. Still, the giant systems at work in today's call centers aren't phone systems as much as they are sophisticated telecommunications servers. Relax — they're still reliable, but they take some TLC to keep them that way. Also, the call center management team always seems to be asking for more sophisticated routing and data from the system.

The telecommunications analyst maintains the phone system and network connection to the outside world's phone network. She changes configurations and assists with sophisticated applications that integrate with the phone system and network. Forecasting capacity within the phone network and phone system frequently falls to the analyst; she works with the help of the department scheduler, who tells the telecommunications analyst how much demand to expect.

Computer and network analyst

The computer and network analyst is responsible for making sure that the call center workstations function optimally as frequently as possible.

Most call centers today rely totally on an agent's workstation to provide that agent the necessary tools and information. When the tools are unavailable, the call center quickly grinds to a halt. Imagine a call center that has 500 agents taking 4,000 customer calls per hour, and the network fails. Aside from the cost of having 500 idle agents, it doesn't take long to frustrate thousands of customers. You can bet that this kind of call center takes downtime seriously.

Another concern for the computer and network analyst is that when workstation response time slows call length, it creates an immediate bottleneck in the call center's work process. This bottleneck results in an increase in call length, which can create long holding times for customers and increase call center costs. A 1-second increase in call length in a call center that answers 1 million calls per year can add more than $10,000 in annual costs — and that's from a *1-second* increase. When computers get slow, they can create much longer delays than that.

As one of these analysts once said, "It's one of those jobs where you know you're doing a good job when you don't hear from anyone, but when you do . . ." Like Mr. Scott on the *U.S.S. Enterprise,* a computer and network analyst can perform miracles, keeping things working and fixing them at warp speed when they don't.

Applications developer

The brother (or sister) of the computer and network analyst is the applications developer. You need this person. A good developer pays for himself many times over in a year . . . but he can be a little scary. How can anyone stare at a computer screen for precisely 1.9 hours, get up, drink a diet cola for 14.5 minutes, and be back in his seat staring at a computer screen for another 1.9 hours? It's not natural.

Still, the application developer creates the tools that make the whole call center world work — and did we mention that you need him? He develops databases, troubleshooting guides, call-management applications, and scripting tools, and also links these tools so that they work together seamlessly. (For details on the use of technology in call centers, see Part III of this book.)

An application developer has superb development, analytical, and problem-solving skills; can work unsupervised for months at a time; and may drink amounts of cola that would make lab rats stand up and sing "Jailhouse Rock."

Reporting analyst

Historically, the person who produced department reports filled the role of reporting analyst. The position of reporting analyst has evolved a great deal. Reporting is still part of her job responsibilities, but now it's a fraction of what she does. Today's analyst isn't just the kid who's really good with spreadsheets. Increasingly, she's someone who has advanced skills in statistics and analysis.

Certainly, this analyst produces reports on how well the call center is meeting its *performance metrics* — business goals and performance drivers (refer to Chapter 2). She produces reports in almost any frequency that management wants — hourly, daily, weekly, or monthly — by using an automated process. The analyst also makes sure that agent performance data is available so that team leaders can provide feedback to their staff. In short, she's sort of the scorekeeper for the call center.

In addition, the reporting analyst can identify numerous opportunities by analyzing the performance of your calls, agents, teams, and the overall department. By studying and researching metrics, she can identify and recommend improvements in processes and tools that can lead to better performance for the call center.

Quality analyst

The quality analyst has to assess agents' work objectively against specific quality standards for information and data-entry accuracy, completeness, and compliance with regulatory requirements. Past industry practice involved a quality analyst assessing customer interaction against a set of quality standards, which included subjective components such as courtesy, tone, and other soft skills. This practice led to a lot of time being spent on internal disagreements about the correctness of the assessment instead of the quality of the customer experience.

Nowadays, in good organizations, the customer assesses the subjective component through postcontact surveys, thus eliminating this subjective component of the quality analyst's job. Combining the analysis with the voice of the customer gives the team leader a full picture of the customer experience.

In many call centers, the team leader often performs this role. If you can, however, separate the responsibilities so that the team leader doesn't have to spend all his time collecting information.

Compliance and procedures officer

This relatively new role for call centers plays an important part in monitoring and documenting your operational process — what you do and how you do it. Call centers are subject to an increasing number of laws that govern their behavior. The compliance and procedures officer is responsible for making sure that the call center knows its legal requirements and that the work processes are adapted to meet those requirements.

Also, as we discuss in Chapter 15, managing call center processes is a powerful and important tool because it allows you to continually improve your operation. This officer is responsible for identifying existing processes, documenting them, and updating the processes when certain parts don't make sense to you or your customer (or the process is too complicated or takes too long). She is responsible for making recommendations for improvements, and she creates an audit process to make sure that employees are following the approved guidelines.

Call center agent

An agent is the person who's on the phone talking to your customers. He's responsible for handling customer contacts in a manner that supports both the call center's goals and his own personal performance goals, which his team leader should outline for him.

The agent is the most vital role in the call center. A call center doesn't work without agents, as they can make or break customers' experience of dealing with your company.

Many call centers have other titles for their agents, including teleservice representative, customer service representative, customer service person, and customer account executive.

Finding the Best People for Your Jobs

If you look at the companies that are most successful, the recipe for success looks pretty much the same at each company. The first ingredient is always having the right talent for the right role. In this section, we give you some tips on finding the best people for the jobs in your center.

Locating a call center manager

A call center manager is a solid business generalist. She needs a well-rounded set of communication, interpersonal, leadership, and analytical skills. Business training, including accounting and organizational behavior, will help her manage people and the costs. Also, understanding call center technology can help her understand how to drive efficiency and make the customer experience better.

You can check many sources for a manager. You might find the manager in your call center working as a team leader, as a trainer, or in another position. You might find the manager somewhere else in the organization, running another business process, or you might even recruit externally.

Don't think that you must hire a manager who has call center experience. Most people can figure out call center skills, tools, and terms fairly easily. Instead, look for a combination of leadership and core business skills, such as statistics, finance, accounting, organizational behavior, and budgeting.

Picking an agent performance team: Recruiter, trainer, and team leader

The recruiter, trainer, and team leader play different roles in the process of bringing and retaining the best agent talent possible. The process starts with the recruiter, who hands off to the trainer, who hands off to the team leader, who is ultimately responsible for the ongoing development of the agent. Here are some tips on hiring your agent performance team:

- ✓ **Finding a recruiter:** It's beneficial to have agents recruit other agents for the call center; likewise, it's beneficial to find a recruiter among your agents. Agents have an intimate knowledge of the job, which they can pass on to candidates, and because they've done the job themselves, they know the type of personality that is best suited for the job. Wherever you find a recruiter, however, you need to train him in human-resources practices and laws as they relate to recruiting.

- ✓ **Finding a trainer:** You can certainly develop a good trainer in your management team or even your agent group. A person with a background in education (child or adult) and human resources can bring training discipline and expertise to the classroom. Even without this background, a bright employee who's an excellent communicator and great problem-solver will do nicely — but make sure that you spend the time to train her in adult education techniques.

- ✓ **Finding a team leader:** The team-leader job is a great advancement opportunity for call center agents, but not everyone can be a great team leader. The ideal candidate has communication, interpersonal, and analytical skills. A background in leadership and possibly some business education can help the team leader understand human behavior and both motivate and lead agents. At a minimum, a new team leader needs training in leadership, coaching, and human-resources practices.

Hiring a scheduler

A scheduler needs to be analytical and should have a solid mathematical and problem-solving background. Without computer skills, too, a scheduler might have a hard time.

You might find a good scheduler in the accounting or finance department, on the reporting team, or maybe even in the agent group — especially if he has an educational background in accounting, business, or engineering. An external candidate might also work, especially if he has the necessary skills (which we talk about in the section "Scheduler," earlier in this chapter). Having worked in a call center in the past can really be an asset, particularly if that experience comes with good references.

Expect to pay well for someone who's been a success in the scheduling role at another call center.

Acquiring analysts

Not all analysts are created equal! Each one of the following roles requires very specific technical expertise and skills that are unique to that role. You may have to look in different places to find the analysts you want. A telecommunications analyst may be sourced externally from a technology vendor, for example, whereas you may find a quality analyst internally in your pool of call center agents.

Here are some tips on finding good analysts:

✔ **Finding a telecommunications analyst:** Telecommunications analysts are special. Certainly, you can find a person who has a lot of analytical skills and some computer background, and then train her. You can also find a good candidate externally or working in other areas of the company.

✔ **Finding a computer and network analyst:** You can find a computer and network analyst inside your call center. Look for young people who have strong computer and network backgrounds and who are eager for an opportunity to use their skills. Those people may work in other departments, and you can even find them outside the company. A good computer and network analyst has the required computer skills, is analytical, and is great at solving problems.

✔ **Finding an application developer:** This position is another one that you may be able to fill from inside your call center.

Frequently, you may be able to hire an application developer right out of school. The smarter a candidate is, the better.

✔ **Finding a reporting analyst:** Consider people who have advanced degrees in engineering, business, math, or statistics because of the complexity of the data analysis that is required. A candidate who has experience in root-cause analysis, a discipline such as Six Sigma (see Chapter 17), research, or another analytical discipline would be the best fit.

✔ **Finding a quality analyst:** The role of quality analyst is a good training ground for agents who want to move up in the call center world as trainers and team leaders. You can probably find a lot of potential quality analysts among your call center agents.

Rounding up a compliance and procedures officer

The compliance and procedures officer role requires someone who's well organized, detail-oriented, and a good communicator. If this person has experience with documenting quality standards, such as ISO 9001/2000 (see Chapter 17), he will be better equipped to get the job done.

Recruiting agents

Agents come from a variety of backgrounds. When selecting agents, develop a profile of ideal candidates. We discuss agent recruiting in Chapter 12.

Creating and Managing Call Center Culture

A lot of people recognize that a company's *culture* — how people in the company think, act, and view the world around them — is important and fundamental to operating any business. You may hear a lot of talk about understanding culture, but not a lot of people understand how to *create* culture.

Leadership is a topic that would require a whole different book, so we can't go into it in too much detail, but we *can* show you how to have a positive influence on the culture of your call center. Here are some approaches that can change your workplace culture for the better:

- **Make creating culture a team exercise.** Designing a culture is a great team exercise. Even if you can't involve everyone associated with the call center in the exercise, everyone needs to be involved in the communication and training that come out of it.

- **Review the mission and vision.** In Chapter 2, we talk about creating a mission, which is a quick, concise description of your department's purpose that tells the world what you do and why you do it. The *vision* is a very specific statement about what you want the organization to look like in the future. The mission and the vision are assignments that the people in your call center have to complete as a team.

- **Define what a culture is.** We define *culture* as being the behavior that results from a team's shared beliefs and values. The behavior, values, and beliefs should support your mission and vision; they certainly can't contradict the mission or vision. If you want to define certain codes of behavior, you have to define some values and beliefs that you want to incorporate into your team members' work lives. Following are our definitions of *values* and *beliefs:*

  - **Values:** *Values* are the organization's stated rules of engagement. Values describe how the people who are involved with your call center — management, staff, customers, clients, vendors, and so on — should treat one another and expect to be treated. Examples of values include honesty, dignity, and respect.

  - **Beliefs:** *Beliefs* are definitive, bold statements of how a company or department will achieve its mission by using the power of its values. If your call center's mission is to be a world-class provider of customer service, for example, a belief would be "Together, we will achieve our goals through teamwork and integrity" or "We will work with our customers as partners to achieve their goals."

✔ **Decide what you need to do to turn the values and beliefs into a culture.** Ask yourself how you're going to incorporate values and beliefs into your management practices, policies, and rules of conduct. The company reinforces beliefs through actions, decisions, and initiatives such as competitive learning (say, promoting teamwork), continuing education, and research. If you tie enough threads between values and beliefs and the operation of your business, and the members of your management team demonstrate these values in their daily interactions, the fabric of the culture that you want will emerge in time.

Sizing the Organization

The basic design of a call center organization shouldn't change depending on its size, because the roles that you need in a 20-seat call center are the same ones that you need in a 500-seat center. The key difference is that in small organizations, you might group tasks so that fewer people can handle them.

In a large call center, you might subdivide tasks because you need several people to complete a task. In a small call center, the team leader might handle recruiting, training, and feedback, whereas in a large center, an entire department may do recruiting, another department may do training, and so on.

You can determine the number of people required to complete any task based on the complexity of the task and the volume of work to be done. In Chapters 7 and 8, we discuss how to determine the number of agents that you need. In most call centers, agents make up the bulk of your workforce.

Your ratio of team leaders to agents (see the following section) determines how many team leaders you need. If your call center has another layer of reporting — team leaders who report to managers, for example — you need to determine the optimal ratio of managers to team leaders so that you can calculate the size of the management team.

Other groups that should be sized in relation to the call center are the various roles that support the agents and the center, such as trainers, schedulers, and quality analysts. The ratio of these roles varies with the type of work that is required. Scheduling one center of 100 agents requires only one scheduler, for example, and if you grow your center by another 100 agents, you still require only one scheduler. For those same 100 agents, however, you may have 2 trainers who impart specific sales and service skills as well as technical knowledge, and if you grow your center by another 100 agents, you might need to add 2 more trainers.

Ensuring the best management span

Call center managers spend much time discussing *management span* — how many agents any one team leader can supervise, or how many team leaders any one manager can manage. Make management span for your organization directly proportional to the amount of support your agents require. The span of control really depends on the complexity of the work done in the center, the experience and capability of the staff, and the amount of job support that agents can get through technology and tools.

Some call centers prefer a relatively low span of management control because it provides more time for the team leader to spend with each call center agent, improving the quality of call handling, reducing the employee learning curve, and improving employee morale. The obvious downside is that it costs the company more money, because when you have fewer agents on each team, you need more team leaders.

A span of 15 to 1 seems to be the de facto standard, but spans vary with the type of work that is being completed by agents. Often, call centers that require lower skill on the phones, such as taking orders for pizza, can work with a 30-to-1 span. Other types of call centers, such as those that handle insurance underwriting, may work with ratios as low as 5 to 1; in these organizations, the team leader is responsible not only for coaching, but also for approving the work completed by agents.

Most call centers fall in the area of 10 or 20 to 1, with an average of about 15 to 1. We encourage you to use some of the criteria in the following sections to determine the right span of management for your organization.

Increasing span

These factors can allow you to increase the span of management control:

- ✔ Technology that supports call center agents, such as performance feedback that goes directly to their computers or knowledge bases that contain answers to even very difficult questions

- ✔ E-learning, which allows agents to take training right on their computers

- ✔ E-mail, which allows team leaders to communicate more effectively with staff members

- ✔ Automated call recording, which increases team-leader productivity, making it possible for team leaders to provide feedback to more staff in the same amount of time

- ✔ The creation of a dedicated call-evaluation team that listens to agent calls and assesses them for the team leader, essentially offloading some of the team leader's tasks

- ✔ A strong team of agents who know the job well and can work on their own

Employing support tools

Imagine that one of your team leaders comes into the office to do her job of supporting and coaching her staff. To start her day, she prints a variety of reports from various systems that tell her about the team's performance. She summarizes these reports in a spreadsheet so that she can better understand each agent's strengths and weaknesses. Next, she spends a few hours listening to agents' calls. (This process takes a while, because not many customers are calling today.) After she hears some complete calls by a few agents, she reviews and evaluates those calls. Now, with reports and work samples prepared, she's ready to provide coaching. Unfortunately, the day's almost over, and she needs to wrap some things up before heading home. Oh, well, coaching can wait until tomorrow.

Now imagine the same team leader with better support tools, such as electronic reports. When she comes into the office, she starts her computer, and waiting there for her is a statistical performance analysis for each agent. The analyses are very detailed, containing more history than she could ever collect on her own, and identifying the strengths and weaknesses of each agent. Also, her agents have already seen these reports, which include a list of coaching points for improvement.

Also available to the team leader is a large sample of calls for all agents. The calls have been scored, and the scores have been sent to the respective agents. With all this work done, your team leader can start her day by approaching agents and offering help in working on their already-defined coaching areas.

You can use these tools in your own call center; we discuss them in greater detail in Chapter 10. By using these tools, team leaders can spend more of their time supporting their agents through coaching and feedback, which allows for a higher span of management control.

Recognizing overly high span

Having too low a span of management is rarely a problem. Concerns about cost control, growth in the call center, and movement of management to new assignments place constant upward pressure on management span. You need to be able to recognize the signs of a span of management control that's too high:

- Call center agents complain that they don't get enough time with their team leaders.
- Quality of call handling decreases or needs improvement.
- Team leaders can't do everything that they need to do.

If your call center's span of management is too high, you either need to change the way that team leaders' work gets done (through the addition of new tools or processes) or increase the number of team leaders.

Planning for growth

While your call center grows in size and complexity, you may find that some processes and tools don't work the way they used to. In fact, you may find that some tasks fail altogether. In some small call centers, one person who uses some fairly basic tools — perhaps homegrown spreadsheets — can do the center's scheduling. When the call center grows in size and complexity, however, that person may find that he can no longer get his job done in a day.

You can handle the increased workload that results from a growing organization by adding more people or changing the work process. In many cases, while a company grows, its old work processes no longer meet the needs of the business, so that company needs to change a process or get some new technology — not necessarily more manpower. In the case of the scheduler, a new, fully automated scheduling package might change the work process enough so that he could again do the entire job of scheduling for the call center.

It's best to add more people *after* you've looked at your processes and found opportunities to create efficiency.

Chapter 4

Building a Call Center of Your Own

. . . .

. . . .

*T*he implementation of a call center starts with a need — sometimes, an urgent need. Okay, *frequently* an urgent need! An organization finds itself receiving a lot of calls from customers — perhaps because business is booming — but the organization doesn't have anywhere for the calls to go. So someone declares, "We need a call center!" Often, and particularly in urgent cases, the organization builds the call center quickly to expand the company's existing customer contact capability.

Other organizations plan their call centers well in advance. If your company is rolling out a new product or business, for example, and you expect to have a lot of calls coming in, you can plan to meet the need for more call handling.

In this chapter, we provide some of the questions and answers on the why, what, where, when, and how of building a call center.

First Things First: Asking Questions

You need answers to some basic questions to determine your call center's logistics:

✔ What are the call center's business goals?

✔ What functions will the call center perform?

✔ What support services will the call center require?

✔ What skills do you need on your planning team?

     ✔ How big will the call center be?

     ✔ Will the call center stand alone, or do you plan to network it?

Answering these questions helps planners create the list of requirements that ultimately becomes a project plan for building the call center. We discuss all these questions in the following sections.

You also need to consider what sort of technology the call center requires and whether to outsource the call center's work. These topics are so large that we cover them in separate chapters — outsourcing in Chapter 5 and technology in Chapter 9.

What are the call center's business goals?

As we discuss in Chapters 2 and 3, senior management in the corporation sets the call center's strategic direction by defining its mission. Getting an early understanding of what's expected from the call center can help you begin to define future capabilities and requirements.

In Chapter 2, we provide more information about service level and other call center goals, along with a model that can help you ensure that you're meeting those goals.

What functions will the call center perform?

The types of services provided by your call center dictate the skills that you need, and those services may also influence the call center's location. If you're taking highly technical calls, for example, you may want to locate in an area that has a technical school. If a lot of your callers speak Spanish, you need agents who do too, so you may want to locate in an area that has a highly concentrated Spanish-speaking population.

Here are some typical tasks that agents might perform in your call center:

     ✔ **Inbound customer service:** Providing general product information, service help, or advice to customers

     ✔ **Inbound technical support:** Helping customers use their product or service, and offering troubleshooting advice for technical problems

     ✔ **Inbound sales:** Helping customers make purchase decisions

✔ **Inbound billing:** Helping customers understand their invoices and providing them general account information

✔ **Outbound telemarketing:** Selling new offerings to customers

✔ **Outbound service:** Following up with existing customers on inquiries and problems, as well as providing information about relevant product offerings, gathering opinions, or conducting surveys

✔ **Outbound collections:** Attempting to pry payment from people whom you may no longer choose to call customers

✔ **Inbound collections:** Receiving payment from people whom you probably do still call customers

✔ **Back office:** Processing customer requests and orders for new products or services

What support services will the call center require?

Call center planners need to ask what services, other than call handling, the call center will perform. (In addition to providing call handling, a customer support center may want to provide e-mail support for customers who prefer to use that method of communication, for example.) Some of these services may be obvious, such as management support functions, which are performed by team leaders, schedulers, trainers, and the other roles that we discuss in Chapter 3. Other services may not be so obvious, and you must identify them before you start the call center design.

Consider the product and service support functions that your call center may require, such as the following:

✔ Communicating with customers via fax, e-mail, or online chat

✔ Processing mail

✔ Entering customer orders into company systems

✔ Ensuring that customers receive products and/or services within the promised time

✔ Reviewing and approving (or denying) customer requests for claims, credit, and so on

✔ Distributing the product

✔ Processing warranty claims

What skills do you need on your planning team?

Because a call center's requirements cross several disciplines, you want people on the planning team who have a variety of skills. People with necessary expertise include specialists in project management; human resources; and facilities, technology, and staff planning. You also need someone who has experience running the type of call center that you're building — perhaps the future call center manager.

A project team made up of people who have these skills is less likely to miss important requirements.

How big will the call center be?

The size of your call center depends primarily on the number of agents that you need to manage all your customer contacts, so you must predict the workload that the new call center will handle. Conduct a long-range forecast — say, five years out — so that you can plan some room for growth. In Chapters 7 and 8, we discuss forecasting and staffing, and explain how to determine how big a call center you need.

Determining your future call center's size tells you a lot, including the type of community in which you need to locate it (one with a sufficient labor pool that has the skills you need) and the type of building you need (one that has sufficient space, utilities, telecommunications infrastructure, convenient access, and parking).

Will the call center stand alone, or do you plan to network it?

As part of your sizing discussion, you want to know whether you're making the call center a separate entity — a stand-alone facility that does all the work itself — or part of a network of call centers that perform similar functions. A new operation requires more planning and research because a blueprint on which you can base decisions may not exist. Many companies start with one call center. To ensure that they can continue operations during a disaster (see "Planning for Problems," later in this chapter), companies often launch another site or hire an outsourcer, or they implement a home agent program. We cover outsourced centers in Chapter 5 and home agents in Chapter 11.

You may want to create a network of centers if your customers feel that a regional presence is important or you can get attractive financial benefits (government subsidies or lower agent turnover, for example). You may find adding to a network of call centers to be fairly easy because the new operation can rely on the model developed by the existing operation.

X Marks the Spot: Situating Your Call Center

The major factors that influence your call center's location are

- ✓ Access to a readily available pool of talent, such as that provided by universities or military bases
- ✓ Level of competition for the agent skills you need
- ✓ Labor and regulatory laws that affect your ability to operate
- ✓ Access to public transportation
- ✓ Reliability of local providers of telecommunications and utilities, such as power and water
- ✓ Local government interest in your success (including incentives such as business tax breaks and subsidies)
- ✓ Cost of real estate or rental facilities
- ✓ Cost of operating the call center

Some companies also want to locate their call centers close to other corporate locations or to their customers. Simply add whatever criteria are important to your company to the core location factors in the preceding list to give yourself a great basis for comparing operations.

Consider each criterion when you decide on the best location for your new center. You have a lot of options. With the worldwide availability of the Internet and telecommunications services, new labor markets all over the world have opened to call center operators. Every market has its benefits, and everything else being equal, you can locate a call center anywhere in the world and still achieve the operation's mission and business goals.

You don't even have to limit your call center to a physical location: You can create virtual call centers that have agents working in different locations around the world while serving the same group of customers. See Chapter 11 to find out more about setting up a virtual call center.

Considering infrastructure

Naturally, the area that you select must be equipped with the latest and greatest telecommunications infrastructure, not to mention other utilities, such as power.

Because of technological advancements, it doesn't matter whether you're locating your call center in a different city, county, region, state, or province from the company's other operations; telecommunications can link everything seamlessly. Call centers have been locating away from the home office or customer base — a practice called *geographic outsourcing* — for a long time. If a company that was based in New York moved all or part of its operations from New York to Iowa, for example, that move would represent geographic outsourcing.

Considering the available workforce

Whether or not you decide to build close to home, you always have to consider the availability of sufficient employees who have the skills that your call center needs. Here are a few factors to consider:

- **Labor costs:** You must find out the average wage rate in the target area. To justify locating your call center away from home, it makes sense to gain an advantage — preferably, a significant advantage — in labor costs. Generally, you can staff a call center more cheaply in a small town than in a booming metropolis. When you consider that labor accounts for more than 60 percent of your costs, you need to take this consideration seriously.

- **Population base:** Factor in the percentage of staff turnover in a year, as well as call center growth. The population base of your target area has to be able to sustain more than just your immediate needs.

To test whether a market has sufficient qualified labor, call center managers place newspaper recruitment ads and then review the volume and quantity of candidates who come forward. A good response makes the market a candidate for the new call center.

Réal's company has developed a recruiting application by using interactive voice response (IVR). (We talk more about IVR in Chapter 9.) When looking for new sites, the company advertises in several communities, giving each community a unique number to call. Candidates call the IVR system, which prescreens applicants. Then the IVR system gives the company the volume of interest and an initial indication of the quality of applicants.

- **Educational institutions:** Does your target area include educational institutions? If so, do those institutions offer programs that support your business's needs, providing training in the skill requirements that you'll be hiring for? Additional training is a significant call center cost, so it pays dividends to locate your center in an area that has an abundant supply of educated employees. Also, communities that include university or college campuses are a great source of part-time and summer-replacement employees.

✔ **Availability of qualified managers:** Make sure that you can get a qualified management team in your new location. Many planners have built a call center in a remote location only to have a tough time placing a qualified management team there. Sure, you may be able to train some of the call center agents to be managers, but that training takes time.

Locating near other facilities in the corporation

Is your call center integrated with your organization's other functions? Does corporate management need to have an ongoing presence in the call center? If the answer to both of these questions is yes, you want to locate close to the corporate head office.

Also, can you consider a call center job to be an entry-level position that leads to other roles within the company? If so, staying close to home makes sense, because the call center can become a labor pool for the organization.

Building the call center near existing corporate facilities and capabilities — data processing, human resources, recruiting, and training — can provide cost advantages. You can save on personnel costs because you don't necessarily have to fill certain roles that duplicate those in place at your head office, and the availability of facilities such as training and meeting rooms can help avert the cost of extra buildings for the call center.

On a more warm and fuzzy level, your organization may want to promote a strong sense of corporate community and teamwork, and keeping the call center close to the home office can certainly contribute to that feeling.

Getting close to your customers

You may find advantages in locating close to your customers, especially when your product or service requires a significant degree of local knowledge.

You can ensure cultural familiarity by keeping the call center in the market that serves your customers. By locating within your own country but in a different state or province, however, you may not lose much in the way of customer service while gaining the advantage of lower costs and increased capacity — particularly if your market is one with relatively high labor costs, such as Los Angeles, New York, Toronto, or London.

In Chapter 10, we talk about customer relationship management (CRM) software, which gives agents information about customers' interests and preferences. If you want to create a trusting relationship with customers, your agents should know a bit about where those customers reside. Therefore, include in agent training geographical information about the countries and cities that your call center serves.

Being far, far away from your customers

If your company wants to reduce operating costs and feels that cost-saving options won't significantly affect customer service, you have three options for locating a call center:

- ✔ Offshore (far from your company's country)
- ✔ Near shore (in a neighboring country)
- ✔ A combination of offshore and near shore

We discuss all three options in the following sections.

Locating offshore

By far the least costly alternative on a purely operational basis is moving your call center operations offshore. Locating in places such as Central America, the Caribbean, South Africa, India, the Philippines, or China can greatly decrease labor costs. It can also provide a large pool of highly educated and skilled people who are looking for work. (In India, for example, millions of people graduate from university every year.) In many of these countries, the availability of jobs falls well behind the country's ability to produce a skilled workforce.

Also, contrary to the stigma sometimes attached to working in a call center in North America, call center jobs are coveted in many other countries. Although an MBA grad in Montreal might not give much thought to a call center job, an MBA grad in Manila would jump at the chance. As we discuss in Chapter 14, motivation is at least half of what makes up agent performance, so finding a location where qualified people truly value the work may be the single most important site criterion.

Moving your call center offshore comes with significant risk, because cultural differences can create communication and operational challenges. You also need to do a lot of research and project planning, and possibly create a permanent home-office management presence on-site to alleviate potential control and communication issues.

Locating near shore

Near-shore locations are call centers placed in a neighboring country. U.S. corporations often locate call centers in Canada or Mexico, for example, and many firms in England locate call centers in Ireland.

Locating your call center near shore is an easy and often viable alternative to offshoring; the center is close to the company's home country, so you probably don't have to deal with significant language, education, and cultural issues.

A near-shore location is essentially just an extension of the geographic diversification within your company's own country, and you can gain some significant advantages in available labor pools, cost of labor, education, and skill level of interested labor.

Implementing a combined option

If you're seriously thinking about pursuing an offshore location, you may want to consider moving your call center operations in two steps:

1. **Move a portion of your operations to a nearby location in a less-expensive labor market.**

   After your organization gains experience running a remote location, you can begin the offshore project.

2. **Run the two operations simultaneously, or begin the process of moving all operations offshore.**

The company benefits from multiple labor pools, redundancy in case any call center needs to be shut down (say, during a snowstorm), and a blended wage rate that's lower than what the company has onshore but higher than the lowest rate possible if all the calls went offshore. For some businesses, this approach provides a nice mix of cost control and capability.

If you're not sure about taking your call center to a far-off land, consider testing the waters by sending some of your simpler calls or other work offshore. By creating a blend of your local call center (doing the more complex and valuable work) and the offshore call center (doing the simpler and less valuable work), your company can test the offshore option and lower its overall cost. Sending only your simple calls offshore may be all you need to do.

Going big-city versus rural

Although locating your call center in a big city can increase the availability of labor, the competition for labor at higher wages also increases. A call center in the middle of a large residential community has its employee base close by — a prime consideration for people who may come to work for you. An inaccessible call center throws up a roadblock to attracting the greatest number of highly qualified employees.

Small communities, on the other hand, often have a strong culture of support for customer service operations. Often, a new call center becomes a significant employer in a small community, reducing unemployment and building immediate company loyalty within the entire community.

You can staff call centers more easily if you locate them in or near the communities where people live — meaning near the skilled target labor that you require. Attract employees to your center by making the commute easy for them.

Setting Up Shop

Regardless of where you decide to locate your call center, you need to think about what that call center will look like and any special needs that you may have. Creating facilities for disabled agents, for example, can broaden the number of candidates you can attract.

Beyond bricks and mortar: Planning the facilities

After you settle on a location for your call center, what will you actually put there? The term *call center* describes the operation quite well, actually. Agents answer *calls,* and you *centralize* the operations by handling them in one place, either real or virtual.

Most call centers have one or more large rooms that have a lot of grouped workstations, which include desks for the agents, electronic terminals, phones, headsets, chairs, and so on. Workstations come in many designs, including the everyone-wedged-in-together "I can hear your heart beating" style and the everything-exposed-to-the-all-powerful-corner-office "I've got an eye on you" style. Somewhere in the middle exists a nice place to work, which is spacious, quiet, and pleasant.

Design the call center for one major purpose: to answer calls. Focus on the actual call center — the big room that holds all the people. Set up everything else that you add to the facility so that it supports the call center. Make washrooms easily accessible, for example, so that agents aren't required to make long walks. Similarly, make the washrooms large enough to prevent lineups that could cause agents to miss parts of their shifts. Design all other rooms in the facility in a way that ensures convenience.

Usually, a call center includes specialized rooms set up in different areas of the building:

- ✔ **Data center:** A secure and separate room that holds the computer servers and telephone equipment.

- ✔ **Training rooms:** Rooms in which your business conducts training sessions. Many training rooms include whiteboards and audiovisual equipment, and some have workstation setups for simulations and role-playing scenarios.

  Make your training rooms large enough and plentiful enough to accommodate more than one training class at the same time.

- ✔ **Meeting rooms:** Rooms for conducting meetings. A meeting room can be anything from a small room with a desk and a couple of chairs (which you could use for conducting interviews or one-on-one meetings) to a lavish boardroom with leather chairs and a mahogany table that could seat the population of a small country.

- ✔ **Lunchroom:** Yep, a room in which employees can eat lunch. Generally, call center lunchrooms include cafeteria-style tables and chairs, as well as a kitchen for agents who bring their lunch and vending machines for agents who work in the middle of the night. Make sure that the lunchroom really accommodates your employees and their shifts. Providing too few seats frustrates employees, and not providing enough amenities (such as microwaves) leads to lineups that can delay agents' return to work after lunch. Some call centers have on-site hot/cold food services, which you may want to consider, especially if your call center isn't near a lot of outside facilities.

- ✔ **Offices for various managers:** Most centers have offices for executives, directors, and any managers who require more privacy than the typical cubicle world affords.

You may want to go further, as some operations do, and add some nice amenities for the staff. You don't need the following amenities, but they make the call center environment a little more fun and a nicer place to work:

- ✔ **Game room:** The job of a call center agent can be stressful, so some companies provide their employees a room in which to unwind and enjoy their break time. Some game rooms include videogame consoles, television sets, table-tennis and air-hockey equipment, and the like.

- ✔ **Quiet rooms:** Quiet rooms offer a place to unwind after or in the middle of a hectic day. These rooms often include reclining chairs or sofas and books or magazines for agents to read.

Designing the ideal space

Your call center needs a good design because you want to build it for maximum efficiency — from a cost-reduction standpoint, of course, but also for efficiency in operations. You don't want to have team leaders hunting for agents, agents hunting for team leaders, or *anyone* hunting for the tools that he needs to do his job.

Average workspace depends largely on the type of culture you want to create. Make sure that your agents have ample room to do their work, with their team leaders in their row working alongside them. When you use this setup, agents can get the support they need, and the team leader has access to the pulse of the business.

When designing the layout for your center, make sure that all your employees have ample room to work. The workspace-per-call-center-desktop area can vary substantially, from less than 50 square feet per desk to upward of 150 square feet per desk. To encourage open communication, many centers use low partitions between workstations to enable line of sight across the call center without increasing noise levels.

One possible call center layout is what we call the zigzag configuration. Often touted as being employee-friendly and efficient, this configuration places the team leader's workstation at the end of the row. Other possibilities include linear and pod configurations. Base your choice on the amount of real estate available and the type of culture you want to create.

Don't scrimp on office furniture, getting some tattered hand-me-downs to save a few dollars. Agents may feel that the company doesn't value them if you give them chairs that provide poor back support or that have stains, or if you offer a dingy, poorly ventilated work environment. Also, you may have to spend a lot of money later to bring your facilities up to par, because a poor work environment could lead to agent turnover or absenteeism.

Naturally, for cost control, you want to maximize the use of your space, but if you try to cram too many desks into one operation, you have to worry about noise control. No bunk-bed-type stations, please!

Understanding environmental issues

The environment that your management team creates — how management treats agents and whether those agents feel valued — has greater impact on employee morale than creature comforts and paintings on the walls do.

Still, some environmental factors can go a long way toward making your call center a great place to work:

- ✔ Availability and control of natural light and temperature
- ✔ Noise control
- ✔ Comfortable desks and chairs
- ✔ Cleanliness/neatness
- ✔ Ample eating and resting areas
- ✔ Conveniences such as a hot-food cafeteria, relaxation rooms, and lockers
- ✔ Convenient access via public transportation and affordable parking

In today's multicultural society, religious needs may arise, such as a place where people can pray during their shifts. Good call centers make accommodations to meet those kinds of needs without disrupting the business.

Taking special needs into account

Your call center can open doors to people who have a variety of special needs because technology makes it possible to overcome many disabilities in the workplace. Some special-needs concerns include

- ✔ **Wheelchair access:** The call center should have wide aisles and wheelchair-accessible desks, offices, elevators, washrooms, and parking.

- ✔ **Amenities for visually impaired employees:** The call center can provide reader software, which reads text information from computer systems to the employee, or special monitors that expand the size of text on a computer screen. You may also want to consider in your design how you can help visually impaired employees navigate the call center, perhaps by providing Braille signage, railings, and the like.

Creating accommodations for employees who have special needs isn't only a socially responsible thing to do, but also good business, because people who have disabilities are a large, often-overlooked source of highly skilled labor.

Building a Call Center One Step at a Time

Table 4-1 summarizes some of the tasks that Réal's company performs in building call centers. Your call center probably has to take other considerations into account, but you can use this table as a good start.

Table 4-1	Tasks Involved in Building a Call Center
Task	**Steps**
1. Establish site goals and reasons for building.	Create a mission statement for the call center.
	Develop your business goals.
	Determine whether the call center will be stand-alone or part of a network.
2. Determine the capability requirements of the call center.	Identify the types of services that the call center will provide to customers: inbound and outbound calls, support, sales, e-mail, and so on.
	Identify the support functions needed in the call center: team leaders, trainers, schedulers, and so on.
	Determine specific skills that agents need to perform the work.
	Determine the technology requirements.
3. Determine the size of the call center.	Size the facility based on seat requirement and planned space per seat.
4. Select a location for the call center.	Identify hours of operation. Do you need to have the call center open to provide service to customers who are in different time zones, for example?
5. Set criteria for cost, available labor, telecommunications, and facilities.	Assess the availability of physical locations in each region.
	Assess the government and business environment for that region.
	Select a region.
	Identify potential markets in the region that meet size and skilled-labor requirements.
	Advertise for applicants in each market.
	Measure the response rate in each market.
	Develop a short list of markets that have sufficient response.
	Assess the caliber of candidates in each market.
	Determine each market's ability to support the center's capacity and growth.
	Assess telecommunications and utility availability in each market.

Task	Steps
6. Decide on renting, buying, or building.	Contact the local economic development office in your area to see whether you can get any subsidies or information about facilities that are suitable for a call center.
	Contact local commercial real estate agents.
	Consider zoning within municipalities, because a call center qualifies as commercial real estate. Check whether you can locate in a residential area or have to stay in a commercial-zoned area.
	Investigate government subsidy or support programs: skills training, facilities-related subsidies, tax reductions or deferrals, and so on.
	Create a short list of suitable properties for lease or purchase.
	Conduct a comparative analysis of leasing, buying, or building.
	Contact an architect to design the call center to your specific needs.
7. Create a project plan.	Create a budget for construction or renovation, as well as for running the center.
	List all tasks (such as installing the technical infrastructure and ordering equipment), timelines, and the people who are responsible for those tasks.
	Get approval from senior management.
8. Implement the plan.	Assign a project manager to orchestrate the implementation of the plan, and get going!

Creating the plan

After the project team determines the building and budget details, it can create an implementation plan. This plan identifies all the steps necessary to launch the new call center, including creating budgets for how much the center will cost to build and to run; defining and documenting initial work processes; hiring and training staff; installing furniture, equipment, and technology; and answering the first calls. The implementation plan should include time frames and deadlines for launching the call center.

When you complete the implementation plan, you can present it to someone in senior management for approval. If you have a sponsor in senior management who created the mission for the call center and will work with the call center to establish annual business objectives, she provides the mandate to build the call center; makes the final decision about where to locate; and approves the budget, including commitment of capital.

Managing the project

First, you want to assign a project manager — the person responsible for keeping the call center project on track. The project manager tracks tasks and accountabilities, and hounds anyone who falls behind. Be sure to select someone who has experience with project management.

Also pull together a team of people who have expertise in human resources, facilities management, technology, staff planning, and general call center management.

After senior management blesses the project, the project manager assembles the project team, and the team members begin to go through the planning process, during which they cover the tasks listed in Table 4-1 (refer to "Building a Call Center One Step at a Time," earlier in this chapter).

Planning for Problems

Business continuity is all about ensuring that you can continue to do business if something disastrous happens to your call center's location, people, or tools. *Disaster recovery* involves getting your call center back to the way it was before that disaster befell it.

Every call center needs some form of plan for business continuity and disaster recovery. The sophistication of your plan and the protection it offers depend largely on the effect on the organization if it loses the call center for even a short time.

Some companies can't function without their call centers; therefore, they consider the call centers to be critical. An airline's ticket and reservations center, for example, serves a critical purpose for that organization. It deals with customers purchasing tickets and offers customer service for travelers when they want to change their travel dates. If the call center shuts down for any extended period, the airline loses money because customers will go to other airlines to purchase their tickets. Having a business continuity and disaster recovery plan in place ensures that customers can always reach the ticket and reservations center.

A disaster recovery plan may involve ensuring that you back up all call center data daily so that you can access that data if something happens to the primary facility. To ensure business continuity, you might reduce your risk of a loss of service by having multiple centers or employing home agents (see Chapter 11), as well as having a complete mirror backup of the call center and its tools on standby, just waiting to be used.

You can plan for almost anything — at a cost — and when you're planning for business continuity and disaster recovery, you have to balance the cost with the risk of loss. For more information on this critical topic, see *IT Disaster Recovery Planning For Dummies,* by Peter Gregory (Wiley Publishing, Inc.).

Many call centers conduct simulated crisis situations on a regular basis to assess the effectiveness of their business continuity and disaster recovery plans. Recording and reporting the results from these exercises provides the opportunity to fine-tune your plans and make them more effective.

Multiple locations

Business continuity and disaster recovery provide good reason to have multiple sites in separate cities, if possible. This way, you can duplicate your system requirements, building in some *redundancy* — meaning that you can route calls in several ways so that if one route goes down, you still have the other routes available and open. Having multiple sites also provides some security against temporary localized issues, such as severe weather, power interruptions, workforce fluctuations . . . or a plague of locusts.

Stand-alone call centers

If you're in a stand-alone operation, consider the following:

- ✓ **Remember your ABCDs (Always Back up Critical Data).** Your operations should include a backup of critical data at least daily.

- ✓ **Have redundant services.** You may want to make your entire data center redundant (meaning that you have a copy of the data center) and locate it off-site. You also need some sort of redundancy to power your center. As a short-term option, you can have an uninterruptible power supply (UPS) for your computer system. A UPS may work for about

20 minutes to an hour and will keep you going while the longer-term solution — a diesel generator — kicks in.

✔ **Use a business continuity service.** Business continuity services offer sites that sit empty, with the capabilities that your call center needs (telephone systems, computers, and operating systems) just waiting to be used. They can also include data backup capabilities, which can help you with disaster recovery.

✔ **Engage an outsourcer.** Splitting work with an outsourcer (which we discuss in Chapter 5) can help you balance workload, act as a frame of reference for the quality of your service, and provide a level of business continuity.

You can work with an outsourcer in many ways:

- Send the outsourcer a consistent percentage of your overall volume. In this case, the outsourcer gets the same call types that you do.

- Use your outsourcer's call handling to see how well your internal organization handles calls.

- If your call center ever has a weather-related power failure, route all your volume to the outsourcer. Sure, the outsourcer may become overwhelmed by the additional volume, but at least you're not out of business.

- If you outsource work that you can stop at a moment's notice, such as outbound collections or telemarketing, the outsourcer may be able to temporarily increase the number of calls it can take in the event of a disaster at your primary site.

Networked call centers

If your call center is part of a network of call centers, you already have a degree of business continuity and disaster recovery built in. In this case, you need to consider the following:

✔ **Whether your network has a single point of failure:** Can one thing bring down the entire network if that thing fails?

✔ **Whether the remaining center(s) can handle the additional volume:** If so, for how long? If you have two centers working at full capacity, and if one center goes down, the other center can't take the first center's calls. You'd need to find an outsourcer that could take these additional calls or build another center that would go to work only if a disaster occurred.

Preparing for a possible disaster

Disaster preparation might include provisions for quickly accessing the following:

✓ **Backup batteries and generators:** As we mention in "Stand-alone call centers," earlier in this chapter, you need to install a UPS and a diesel generator.

✓ **Your manual (paper-based) processes:** You need to be able to access customer information and call tracking in the event that the data network fails.

✓ **Your telephone network:** For a fee, you can gain control of your phone network so that you can route customer calls to another center quickly.

✓ **The services of a business continuity center:** This type of center is ready to go when you need it, using your own staff.

✓ **The services of a third-party outsourcer:** Keep an overflow agreement in place so that the outsourcer becomes familiar with your business and customers.

Chapter 5

Choosing the Outsourcing Option

A Google search for *call center outsourcer* generates results for more than 15,000 companies that do call center outsourcing. Some of these companies claim to do everything from inbound and outbound sales, customer service, and help lines to technical and product support. Which type would you choose, and why? How would you go about making that decision?

Mix into that decision the opportunity to choose an outsourcer that operates in some faraway place, where you can supposedly save so much money that it sounds too good to be true. With the ever-present pressure to reduce operational costs, examining all options (which includes moving your calls to an outsourcer) can give you a competitive edge.

In this chapter, we introduce you to the possibility of getting someone else to run your call center and what it means to you and your company on both the upside and the downside. We help you compare the costs, benefits, and risks of outsourcing your operation versus keeping it in-house.

If you decide to move forward, the rest of the chapter is devoted to getting you started, providing tips on choosing an outsourcing partner and creating a contract that allows you to meet your goals. To keep your new relationship productive and strong, we also share with you best practices that can set you and your outsourcer on the road to success.

Understanding the Benefits and Risks of Outsourcing

Throughout the industry, you can find passionate discussions about the pros and cons of outsourcing. The following sections present the well-known benefits and risks of outsourcing.

Potential benefits

Here are some good reasons to outsource. Outsourcing allows you to

- ✔ **Reduce your costs:** The most compelling reason to outsource is that it can potentially save you 30 percent to 50 percent of your call center costs. An outsourcer typically pays lower wage rates for comparable jobs (such as agent wages and management salaries), provides centralized support functions such as human resources, and offers technology and technology-support personnel that can help increase productivity. An additional cost advantage comes from sharing technology, processes, and support functions within the entire client base (meaning other companies just like yours).

- ✔ **Control your costs:** Customers' calling patterns aren't always predictable, and during unpredictable periods, call volume can move up or down by as much as 50 percent. Also, during these periods, you may have little control of your customers' experience and may have to deal with extra unknown costs. Outsourcing your operation to cover business peaks or off-hour operations converts these unknown costs to known costs. If you use an outsourcer, you can increase your flexibility, provide a better customer experience, and change these unpredictable fluctuating costs (*variable costs*) to ones that you can predict (*fixed costs*).

- ✔ **Speed time to market:** Companies that are just starting up or perhaps launching a new business unit, product, or marketing campaign often outsource some or all of their call center operations. Giving this part of their business to an outsourcer allows these companies to focus on other areas and gives them the advantage of getting to market faster.

A startup bank gave back-office operations to an outsourcer that had the regulatory knowledge and operational competency to process its transactions. Even though the bank was in a different location from the outsourcer, the service was transparent to customers, and the bank was able to provide good service at a lower cost because it outsourced — a win–win situation for both the bank and the outsourcer.

- ✔ **Increase your capability and expertise:** As technology and business processes become increasingly specialized, you might consider outsourcing for capability, not cost. Some companies use an outsourcer to broaden their service offering to customers by combining a process with an outsourcer's technology. Some outsourcers have multimedia capability and the expertise to handle Web chat, e-mail, and text messaging; others specialize in areas such as outbound calling to prospect for customers.

One financial-services company that we know outsources its outbound calling for two reasons: It doesn't have highly proficient and skilled agents who can make this type of call, and it doesn't want to disrupt its agent pool because many outbound calling programs can run for a short time. Outsourcing makes sense in this case, because the company doesn't have to deal with reallocating or terminating agents when the program is over.

Potential risks

Calculating risk isn't a perfect science, so you may have to make a best guess to estimate the costs of these risks. When you add these estimated costs to your cost comparison, you can get a balanced view of the true cost of outsourcing, which includes the costs of risks like the following:

✔ **Decision made on cost alone:** Based on the many juicy stories about significant cost savings from outsourcing, some companies make this decision without doing any analysis. You can take the potential risk out of the decision by taking time to do a comparison, using the age-old pros-and-cons method for choosing an outsourced center versus running your operation yourself. Cost is just one of many factors to consider.

Uh-oh . . . we didn't guess that would happen!

A telecommunications company with declining revenue and profit decided that outsourcing was the key to reducing costs both significantly and quickly. It moved forward without doing too much planning and without understanding the length of time it would take to integrate its systems and processes.

During the outsourcer's first implementation of the call center, technology installation took three months longer to install than planned, and it took the new agents more than six months to perform at the level proclaimed by the business plan. As a result, the company lost revenue and added expense because of the number of

customer complaints that were streaming in. Because those complaints took time to handle, and because it's difficult to sell to a customer who is unhappy and wants a resolution of his or her problem, costs went up, and sales went down.

By working with the outsourcer, this company rectified its challenges. Still, the call center took 12 months longer than planned to achieve the results that senior management was promised, so first-year savings were actually first-year losses. The lesson: Plan for and understand the level of effort it will take to move calls to an outsourcer.

✔ **Failure to fix internal service problems first:** Some companies think that starting outsourced call centers with brand-new agents will solve their customer service problems. What really happens is that the service goes from bad to worse, because the outsourcer's agents have less experience than the company agents who were handling these service issues. The right thing to do is figure out what is causing your service problems and fix them before you hand your calls over to an outsourcer.

✔ **Selection of the wrong partner:** Choosing the wrong partner can cost even a small company more than $500,000 U.S. per year in lost revenue, customers, and productivity. You can minimize this risk by defining what you're trying to solve, obtaining tangible evidence that the outsourcer can deliver, and completing an objective assessment. (For tips on selecting a partner, see "Picking the Right Outsourcing Partner," later in this chapter.)

✔ **Loss of flexibility:** Your ability to change direction may be hindered by an outsourcing relationship or contract. You may not be able to make changes as quickly as you want because you have to go through many channels of communication first. In addition, you need to think out all changes carefully, because those changes may result in additional fees charged by the outsourcer.

Deciding Whether to Outsource

On first thought, you may be very excited about the prospect of saving money and having someone else deal with the trials and tribulations of running a complex operation. In the following sections, however, we give you a framework to help you figure out the best option for your company based on facts, not on opinion.

Going through this process gives you not only greater clarity about the decision, but also confidence about the decision. By presenting these facts, you can bring others in your company on board, therefore making the final decision easier for those who may be affected by the decision.

Clarifying your internal costs

If you understand how much it costs you today to serve your customers, you can use that information to determine whether you can indeed save any money if you move your calls to an outsourcer.

In the majority of cases, companies can run their call centers more cheaply through outsourcers than through an in-house call center while getting the same quality of work. Many in-house call center people argue that outsourcing isn't actually cheaper. They say, "I pay my staff $12.50 per hour, but the outsourcer wants $29 per hour."

That statement, however, is like comparing apples and gorilla feet. The out-sourcer's $29 per hour includes everything from agents' pay to the team leader's pay, the trainer's pay, the cost of the desks and phone system, the cost of having the carpet cleaned when a visitor drops a cup of coffee on it, and so on.

Building your own call center can cost more than $10,000 on a per-seat basis. By using an outsourcer, you can turn this capital cost into a variable cost. Réal's research and experience suggest that outsourcing typically reduces a company's call center operating costs by more than 30 percent.

Most in-house corporate call centers should look at their true hourly costs. To do a comparison, you have to create a point of reference. We call that reference point, which consists of your true hourly costs, your *baseline*. Measure all other options or possibilities against this baseline.

We suggest that you use cost per hour as the measure for this comparison because many outsourcers use this measure or a variation of this measure (such as cost per minute). To calculate your true cost per hour, you need to define what's included in your costs and in the time measurement.

Some outsourcers charge by cost per call or some other measure. Just ask them to convert that charge to cost per production hour so that you can make an apples-to-apples comparison.

Determining overall costs

We've seen many faulty comparisons of the cost of running an in-house call center versus outsourcing — comparisons that include certain expenses that shouldn't be included. Take the time to identify the expenses that will remain in your budget regardless of who answers the phone.

A good example is the credit or money back that you may give customers to compensate for errors made or inconvenience caused. This type of expense will continue regardless of who handles your calls: you or the outsourcer. If you tally up your costs and don't include the line item called Credits or Refunds in your list of expenses, your overall costs will appear to be higher than the outsourcer's costs. By removing these kinds of expenses from your calculations, you level the playing field, allowing you to complete a valid comparison of costs.

The budget categories shown in Table 5-1 can help you group your costs. From this table, you can easily determine which costs will continue to be your responsibility and which ones the outsourcer's fee includes. We've boldfaced the costs that many companies should leave out when they calculate their internal cost per hour to run the function or operation that they're considering outsourcing. In Chapter 6, we describe these costs in detail.

Table 5-1	Budget Categories	
Category	*Description*	*Examples*
Direct variable costs	These costs fluctuate with volume of contacts.	Wages and benefits of all employees who interact directly with customers Telephony costs
Indirect variable costs	These costs cover the salaries for team leaders. The number of team leaders will fluctuate with the total number of agents that you have working in your call center.	Wages and benefits for team leaders, the managers who supervise team leaders, quality assurance, training, workforce or resource management, and any administrative staff **Incentives, credits, or refunds to your customers,** and cost of recruiters
Support and management	These typically fixed costs relate to supporting the department and don't vary significantly with changes in customer contacts.	Wages and benefits associated with employees in **senior management, planning and forecasting, the project team, reporting,** and **analysis** Other support costs, such as **external training, conferences, travel,** and **entertainment**
Corporate overhead	These costs are associated with the infrastructure required to run your center. Areas within your company share some costs and allocate those costs based on use.	Workstations, rent, business taxes, and heating and air conditioning costs Other facilities costs, such as coffee, office supplies, repairs, and maintenance PCs, telephones (hardware), and **technology hardware and software costs** **Cost for services performed by other departments for the call center** (such as services rendered by human resources, finance, and information technology support) **Software licensing and maintenance fees**

Determining your measuring stick

The industry-standard efficiency measure is *cost per production hour,* which references the time devoted to serving customers directly. You calculate production hours by adding talk time, after-call time, and time waiting for the next call.

Be sure to know which time measurement you're paying for. Does the outsourcer charge you for paid hours or production hours? *Paid hours* include all the hours that the outsourcer uses to run your operation: breaks, lunches, vacation hiring, training of new agents to replace those who left the company, and so on. In the outsourcing industry, the outsourcer typically bears these costs, which are included in the hourly rate. *Production hours,* on the other hand, are hours devoted to serving the customer: talk time, after-call time, and time waiting for the next call. Before you go any further with a potential outsourcer, make sure that it charges only for production hours, not for paid hours.

Calculating baseline costs

Because we recommend using cost per production hour, you can easily tally all the costs in Table 5-1 and divide them by your production hours (talk time plus after-call time plus time waiting for a call) to get your cost per production hour. With this figure, you can accurately compare in-house costs with an outsourcer's cost per production hour.

Adding hidden costs to your outsourcer's cost

In determining the overall cost of moving to an outsourcer, many companies don't factor in ongoing costs, which include the labor cost of managing the outsourcer relationship. Also, they often forget the one-time costs associated with the transition to an outsourcer and ongoing costs for future events, such as training for a new marketing promotion. Include these costs in your comparison, and add them to the overall cost associated with the outsourcer. The following sections discuss costs that you should include in costs associated with moving to an outsourcer.

Cost to launch

Determine who else you need to involve in your company to select, negotiate, and set up the operation at the outsourcer's site, as well as the person whose full-time or part-time job involves being the main point of contact for your outsourcer (the *vendor manager*). One person may take on all these tasks, or a team of people could be responsible for recruitment, training, finance, and setting up computer or telephone networks. You may need to create a job profile for agents (recruitment); document core knowledge and soft skills required to deliver your service (training); create design and project plans of your computer systems for the outsourcer's operation (IT); and set up financial tracking, controls, and reporting (finance).

Factor in the labor costs for these additional resources when you determine the costs associated with your outsourcer. After you launch your program with the outsourcer and move into production, you may not need these resources to the same extent.

Following are some additional costs that you will incur and should factor into your cost comparison:

- ✔ Integrating your technology at the outsourcer's site
- ✔ Procuring new telephone numbers and lines
- ✔ Designing and printing training and marketing materials
- ✔ Recruiting, orienting, and training new employees and managers
- ✔ Paying various fees (such as licensing fees for technology, insurance, and government fees)
- ✔ Hiring consultants to help you with the whole process (from selecting the outsourcer to transitioning your calls)
- ✔ Upgrading your Internet and intranet to accommodate the new location and people

These costs can grow significantly, depending on the complexity of the work that you're outsourcing.

Cost of travel

Before and after you move your calls to an outsourcer, you and others involved in this project occasionally need to go to the outsourcer's site. The outsourcer needs your expertise to solve problems, train its staff and managers in your systems and processes, and further understand your expectations. You have to add costs for time and travel based on the distance of travel, frequency of travel, and length of stay. If you pick an outsourcer that's overseas or on another continent, for example, you may have significant direct travel costs and lost productivity for the travelers, and those costs carry on for the length of the relationship.

It's a best practice to have your team on site for a minimum of one month — maybe more, depending on the complexity of your products, services, and processes. One of our clients sent a team of four to its outsourcer, and that team stayed two months to train, roll out new processes, and put the client's quality-assurance program in place.

Your first-year savings may be less than you expect because of these one-time costs — especially if your call center doesn't get many calls in the first place. If you outsource 30 people to a faraway country, the cost of sending over your technology, human resources, and training teams could equal what you'd pay for 130 in-house agents.

Cost of severance

If you have to lay off staff from your current operation, you have to distribute severance pay, maintain benefits for a given period, and possibly provide outplacement support. These costs may reduce or even eliminate your first-year outsourcing savings.

If you're *really* going to realize savings, you must reduce employee head count. You just don't have an option. Many companies shed the required number of agents but miss the fact that other groups that support the agents also need to be downsized. If you need 10 support-staff members to assist 100 agents, you probably can assume that 60 agents need 6 members of support staff, not 10.

Cost of setting up technology

When you move your calls to an outsourcer, you have to pay to divert existing phone lines or perhaps set up new phones lines, provide remote access, or integrate your computer systems with the outsourcer's systems. Sometimes, you have to pay extra software licensing costs for a different site, even if you use the same number of agents. Check with your software provider to find out whether outsourcing would lead to software-related additional costs.

Cost of lost revenue from lost productivity

You create a flawed comparison if you don't include assumptions of lost revenue due to lost productivity during employee training.

If you lay off 100 agents who have high collective competence and replace them with 100 rookies, you should absolutely expect a period of time in which the new agents are building their knowledge and honing their skill. (Think about it: When you started your first job, were you performing at the same level as others? Most likely, you were learning from your mistakes instead.)

During this time, you will incur expenses such as the cost of errors, the need for *rework* (doing the same thing many times before getting it right), and the frequency of customer complaints. (Because we visit three to four centers every month, we can tell you that most complaints involve an average of four to seven calls from the customer before resolution.) All these errors and complaints drive additional calls into your center, thereby increasing cost.

Many outsourcers keep their prices low by paying agents and team leaders less than the wages offered by your company (which is probably why you're considering this option). But an outsourcer often has significantly more *attrition* (staff turnover) than you do, and its team can never be at the same level of competence as your current team because it always has a higher percentage of agents in training. Some well-run outsourcers mitigate the wage difference quite well, but we've seen others that have 100 percent turnover each year!

Putting your comparison together

Creating a formal and well-defined recommendation document that captures all the elements we discuss in the preceding sections has its benefits. It can help you organize your thinking and force you to consider all the elements of your comparison, not just a few. Also, many large companies require an executive or board decision to make this strategic move, and the higher-ups will want to know that you have done your homework.

The following sections lay out a framework for a recommendation document.

Problem statement

Make your recommendation clear, and support it with a few well-thought-out reasons for your position on whether to outsource your call center. These reasons, when you put them together, can make a persuasive argument.

Qualitative benefits

You can't quantify certain benefits, but they're just as important as the cost benefits. Typically, these qualitative benefits increase customer satisfaction and loyalty, but you may have trouble putting a number on the cost of customer dissatisfaction. Companies often cite the benefits to your customers of having access to the outsourcer's state-of-the-art technology or the outsourcer's ability to implement a process that your company doesn't (or can't) implement.

Quantitative benefits and return on investment

Include your cost comparison, which benchmarks your cost per hour against the outsourcer's. You can best show the comparison by doing a *return on investment (ROI)* calculation — the money that you plan to spend to transition to the outsourcer minus the money you save after you pay off the money that you spent.

You may spend $500,000 to transition to an outsourcer, for example. If, by the end of the first year, you save $100,000, you have a return of 20 percent ($100,000 ÷ $500,000). It'll take you five years to pay back your initial investment of $500,000.

Although calculating ROI may not be a perfect science (you have to make many assumptions, some of which won't be accurate), you want to know when you can see your investment paid off. After that point, you get to keep the savings.

Use this equation to calculate an expected ROI on outsourcing:

Annual difference between outsourcing costs and your current costs ÷ Investment to ramp up × 100 = ROI percentage

Risks

Be realistic about the possible risks and the ones that have the greatest likelihood of occurring. Any company that's thinking about moving part of its existing call center to an outsourcer needs to consider the morale of the employees who remain. Because outsourcing tends to generate lower morale among employees, your business could experience higher attrition and/or lower productivity. Get feedback from others in the company, and incorporate possible risks from their points of view.

Another risk is possible negative publicity for the company if it moves work outside its home country — a significant risk if the business is well known nationally.

Implementation plan

Should you recommend moving to an outsourcer, you want to present a clear picture of the transition plan and the effects on the current business. After all, timing is everything! Including this section in your document helps senior management look at all the other projects going on in the business and determine whether outsourcing is the right place to invest the company's time and money. For more information on creating an implementation plan, see "Planning the Transition," later in this chapter.

Picking the Right Outsourcing Partner

After you do your homework, if you decide to proceed, you need to find the right partner. We say *partner* — not *vendor* — for a reason. This relationship is like a marriage. Take the time to do the research, and find out all you can about your "dates" before you pop the question. When you meet a potential partner and experience a spark of interest, you'll have a lot of questions about what that company is and what it can do. That company will be happy to present to you all the things you want to know — but it will present that information in the best possible light because you'll be interacting with salespeople, not necessarily the folks you'll be working with day in and day out.

Following are some good questions to ask to help you determine whether an outsourcer is the right fit for you, regardless of cost:

- ✔ How has this company shown that it can fulfill all your primary needs?
- ✔ Does your company have a true connection with this outsourcer in terms of values and philosophy?
- ✔ Did the outsourcer even think of having you meet the team members who would be responsible for the day-to-day operations of your business?
- ✔ What was your first impression of the leadership team (not sales team)?
- ✔ Did the company pay attention to the details, respond promptly, and follow through on its promises during the due-diligence process?
- ✔ How confident are you that this company has the expertise to deliver what you need?
- ✔ Do you trust this company?

The profit motive causes some outsourcers to do things that they shouldn't, such as cutting corners on technology, recruiting, and training costs, or taking on more clients or campaigns than they can effectively handle. Using a bad outsourcer can cost your business money, as well as damage your corporate image and customer relations.

Looking for outsourcers in all the right places

To find a list of reputable outsourcers, contact your regional call center association, ask others in the industry for referrals, or consider saving some time by hiring a call center consultant who knows the top-quality outsourcers in your area.

Requesting information and proposals

The typical evaluation process starts with putting together a *request for information (RFI)*, which is like dipping your toe into water to test the temperature. This request gives you a sense of what's out there and whether those companies' capabilities can satisfy your needs.

You create a *request for proposal (RFP)* when you're sure that you want to move forward and invite a good selection of top-quality outsourcers to respond. Send your RFP to each of the candidates, and attach a nondisclosure agreement that both parties can sign.

Table 5-2 lists some do's and don'ts to consider when you request proposals from outsourcers.

Table 5-2	Do's and Don'ts of Requesting Proposals
Do	**Don't**
Be clear about what you want the outsourcer to do.	Ask for the world — and be surprised when it comes with a high price tag.
Stick to your timetable and promises that you make to outsourcers about decisions.	Underestimate the time it takes to evaluate and make decisions, especially when many people are involved in the decision-making process.
Set expectations, internally and externally, about the process and the time it takes to find the right partner. The timeline from RFP to decision-making can range from 6 to 12 weeks. Most of the delay involves internal decision-making rather than waiting for the outsourcer to respond.	Make an outsourcer spend time responding if you don't see it as being a serious contender. It's better to have a few high-quality candidates than to have many.
Ask your contenders to respond by using the same unit pricing so that you don't have the extra work of converting cost-to-call figures to cost-to-productive-hour numbers.	Make the RFP long, and give the contenders a short time to respond. You may lose quality candidates that may not have time to respond.
Demonstrate your willingness to partner, and assume some of the burden of preparing the response yourself. A good rule is to ask for one signed hard copy and one electronic copy.	Overburden your contenders with labor- or resource-intensive tasks. Asking for things like multiple hard copies, fancy bindings, and secure drives takes time away from the content of the response.

Evaluating responses

You can save time during the evaluation process by creating a list of your five most important needs. We've used this system with great success over the past few decades (goodness, are we dating ourselves?) by assigning a weight to each need that appears in the top five. This distinction helps a business prioritize its needs and determine whether the outsourcer can really support them. If your business needs specialized skills, such as Spanish or French service, to have successful customer interactions, you might place that skill in your top-five list.

Examples of other typical criteria are

- A track record of top-quality service to customers
- If you have a multilingual requirement, the ability of the outsourcer to attract agents who have your specific language requirements
- A track record of meeting and exceeding given targets
- Expertise and experience in your industry
- Cost

After you evaluate the responses, create a short list of outsourcers that meet all or most of your requirements. Then make your final choice from this list, as outlined in the following section.

Choosing an outsourcer

To choose the best outsourcer on your short list, follow these steps:

1. **Invite each outsourcer on the list to a private meeting.**

   At this meeting, have the outsourcer's representatives expand on the company's responses through a question-and-answer session.

2. **Narrow the list of candidates again to two or three finalists.**

   Based on your weighted point system (see the preceding section) and interviews, a few outsourcers will bubble to the top.

   If you have enough call volume to divide the work between two outsourcers, consider that strategy. Healthy competition drives the desire for higher performance and allows you to raise the bar over time.

3. **Visit (don't tour!) the finalists' sites.**

   A *visit* means that you meet and interview the leadership team and, if possible, some or all of the support staff (such as trainers, quality analysts, and perhaps agents) who handle customer complaints to find out the outsourcer's level of expertise and its fit with your company's culture.

   We recommend that you sit with some of the outsourcers' agents and listen to their calls. This may not be possible, due to customer privacy issues, but it doesn't hurt to ask. We also recommend that you make your visits on short notice so that the outsourcer doesn't have much time to prepare. Short notice allows you to get a glimpse of what the call center typically looks like.

4. **Complete your comparison, and make your decision.**

5. **Put together a recommendation document for senior management (as outlined in "Putting your comparison together," earlier in this chapter).**

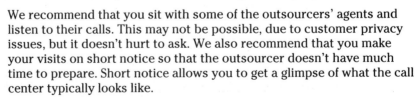

Designing the contract documents

After you choose your partner, you need to create a contractual agreement. This agreement consists of two main parts:

- **Master service-level agreement (MSA):** Contains all the legal language and requirements that typically never change during the term of the agreement.

- **Statement of work (SOW):** A series of numbered schedules outlining your specific requirements. The SOW is more operational than the MSA, and you can adjust the requirements according to changes in circumstances during the course of the contract.

We describe both types of documents in the following sections.

 Although you can have an unlimited number of SOWs, don't get so specific that you can't make a change when your business needs change. Spending countless hours documenting and mandating everything that you want your outsourcing partner to do isn't a good use of time and money. Keep the document simple and focused on the key issues. Your goals should be to create a good working relationship with your outsourcer partner and to establish a set of operating guidelines that reflect the intention of the MSA and associated SOWs.

Elements of the master service-level agreement (MSA)

Here are the contents of a typical MSA:

- **Definitions (in alphabetical order):** You should provide definitions so that both parties understand all the terms used. You might include a definition of what constitutes a business day or specifically explain the term *intellectual property,* for example.

- **Nonoperational expectations associated with program management and key personnel:** These expectations may include the exclusivity of your business — whether you allow your outsourcer to work with your competitors and, if so, how you keep the programs separate.

- **Contract information:** This information may include the term of the contract, the notice period for nonrenewal, how and when both parties can call it quits, the dispute procedure, and a reference to the schedule that contains payment terms and fees.

- **Notice requirements:** These requirements may include notice of changes in work or site location. You may also specify that certain conditions of the contract can't change — an increase or reduction in the amount of work or a change in the type of work performed, for example.

✔ **Guarantee of quality of work performed:** This guarantee may include a requirement to comply with standard operating procedures and the right for you to audit the outsourcer's work on-site or remotely, as well as have access to the outsourcer's site.

✔ **Guarantee of the outsourcer's ability to keep data secure, confidential, and private:** This part of the agreement may specify which party owns new customer data and any inventions created during the course of the contract. Other stipulations may require the outsourcer to ensure compliance with privacy legislation, as well as confidentiality of data and information related to your business (such as status of your business and inside knowledge of your sales volume and revenue).

✔ **Legal issues:** These issues could include *indemnity,* which means that the company or the outsourcer will not be liable to pay damages to customers for information that was given inaccurately *(error)*, left out *(omission)*, or provided on behalf of the other party without authority to do so *(misrepresentation)*. A large call center has many interactions with customers and, therefore, many opportunities for any of these situations to happen. As a result, many companies and outsourcers buy insurance to protect themselves against customer complaints in the event that customers hold one or both companies liable and potentially sue for damages.

Other legal points to put into the contract involve what happens when either party doesn't meet its contractual agreement. To resolve the dispute, follow the arbitration process spelled out in the laws of your state or province.

Elements of the statement of work (SOW)

A SOW usually contains these elements:

✔ **Scope:** This element outlines the scope of work that your business outsources and specific service requirements, such as key roles required for your program and service-level agreements (refer to Chapter 2).

✔ **Fees:** These fees are associated with the services provided to you by your outsourcer. Certain services are included in your hourly rate, such as new-hire training, standard reporting, and management salaries. Extra fees include services defined in the scope of work, ad hoc training, custom reporting, and any technical work associated with changes or upgrades to computer systems.

Many outsourcers are familiar with gain share/risk share programs, and a program of this type typically appears in the fee schedule. *Gain share* means that you give your outsourcer a bonus if it overachieves on your targets, and *risk share* means that you get some of the fee back if the outsourcer continually misses your targets.

✔ **Specific procedures:** These procedures are what you require your outsourcer to follow, such as quality testing, disaster recovery planning (what if the outsourcer's site is no longer functional?), customer complaint handling, and so on.

Negotiating the contract

Before you start a dialogue with your potential outsourcer, figure out what you need versus what you want to have. Make items such as privacy, confidentiality, customer data, and some of your service standards non-negotiable. You can discuss and negotiate other items, such as specific performance targets, your gain share/risk share program (see the preceding section), the term of the contract, and the fee associated with services.

Reacting negatively to a request without finding out the motivation or need behind the request can only lead to further misunderstanding. You're possibly starting a long relationship, so try to start out on the right foot.

After you negotiate all the terms in the MSA and the SOW that would include a service-level agreement, you're ready to sign the contract. You need to work with your new outsourcing partner to devise the transition plan for moving the calls to the outsourcer, as we discuss in the following section.

Planning the Transition

Set up your transition as you would any other project plan, ensuring that all activities are delegated to the right people. Integrate your outsourcer's project plan into the overall plan. Hold regular meetings with the outsourcer, and when you're about two weeks away from moving your calls to the outsourcer, meet daily to keep the project moving along.

When you're planning the transition, consider the events taking place in your organization before you decide when to move calls over. If your company is launching a new initiative (such as a new bill design), absorbing an acquisition, or installing new technology, all these events will affect the transition because they increase call volume and customer interaction. You want to set your outsourcer up for success, so schedule the transition for a time during which you don't expect to be unusually busy.

Elements of a typical transition plan

A typical transition plan addresses the following elements:

- ✔ Physical location of the call center and facilities, including the number of workstations
- ✔ All the technical components: computer systems (including knowledge base), telephone system, and so on
- ✔ Design of call routing and number of phone lines

- ✔ The number of unique groups of agents needed, as well as the number of agents needed in each unique group
- ✔ Recruitment and hiring plans for both agents and the leadership team based on the skills required
- ✔ Training strategy, design, and materials
- ✔ Mapping of key processes to ensure exceptional customer experience
- ✔ Performance metrics for agents, teams, and the overall program, including a gain share/risk share program with respective reporting
- ✔ Customer feedback mechanisms

You want your outsourcer to seem like an extension of your own business — one that has particular call center expertise. Set goals and work closely with the outsourcer to ensure that it can (and does) achieve these goals. Clarity is vital — clarity of purpose, expectations, and communications . . . the works!

Roles and resources required

Identify the roles and skills that you need to lead this transition. If you don't have these skills within your company, consider this option: Pick a function in your center, such as e-mail response to customers. Starting with a smaller volume allows you to cut your teeth on the first transition and apply what you find out to the next transition.

Consider taking a phased approach to outsourcing, starting with a just a few agents doing simple work. If this phase is a success, you can increase the volume or complexity of the work. By doing things this way, you reduce your risk by testing the outsourcer with a smaller part of your business.

Developing a Strong Relationship with Your Outsourcer

After you move the calls to the outsourcer, your job isn't over. You need to assign a vendor manager who's accountable for building a strong relationship with the outsourcer to ensure that your business achieves its goals. In the following sections, we share some best practices about creating and growing a good relationship with your outsourcer.

If you don't have trust within the relationship, you can't sustain these practices; both parties must take part in them.

Setting expectations and creating operating guidelines

Setting expectations between two parties helps determine how to mesh personal working styles with what both parties need to accomplish. You have to be honest about what you want and what you commit to do for the other party. Establish how you want to work together and what's important to you in a relationship.

Verifying the outsourcer's understanding

In the words of business guru Stephen Covey, who has written several books about leadership and management, "Seek first to understand, then to be understood." This guideline applies to both parties. It's the basis of good communication, as it minimizes misunderstandings. Often, outsourcers complete a requested task without understanding the business reason for that task and its effect on the business. Take the time to give your outsourcer the background and context for a request, making sure that the outsourcer understands what you want it to do (and how).

A great example of getting clarity involves a typical requirement for outsourcers to complete quality evaluations. From a business point of view, you want assurance that the outsourcer's agents are providing great service and taking care of your customers. It's important that both you and your outsourcer clearly understand what a good customer experience sounds like, which you can do only by listening to taped or live calls and discussing them both from the customer's perspective and from the business perspective. You should ask two questions during this activity:

- ✔ Did your customer leave with a positive feeling and confidence that his or her issue was resolved?
- ✔ Did you give the customer the required information accurately and ensure that all transactions were completed without error?

You can communicate clearly what your business expects from an outsourcer by listening to calls and having a good conversation about how the service that the outsourcer delivered matches the service you want to provide your customers.

Take the time to talk

When Afshan was in telecommunications, she contracted an outsourcer that provided Internet technical support for her company's customers. The contract required the outsourcer to provide a specific level of service, with a penalty to be levied if that service level wasn't achieved. The contract didn't specifically mention, however, how long low service would be allowed to continue before the penalty was levied.

After the contract was signed, Afshan and the outsourcer sat down and created a set of operating guidelines that made specific parts of the SOW clearer. Her first step was explaining the effect of prolonged low service levels on the customer and her company, with the understanding that low service might occur on occasion for one or two days at most. She and the outsourcer agreed that if low service levels continued for five days in a row, the outsourcer would provide an analysis of why low service was occurring and a plan to rectify the problem.

Lo and behold, three months into the contract, the outsourcer struggled with low service levels for five days in a row. As it had agreed to do, the outsourcer came forward with a reasonable plan of action that left both parties confident that the situation was being rectified. Because Afshan had this conversation with the outsourcer at the beginning of the relationship, the outsourcer was able to meet her expectations — no mess and no fuss!

Staying involved

Some companies feel that providing direction and stating expectations at the beginning of the relationship are all that they need to do. But when you work with an outsourcer, you need to stay connected through short daily meetings or weekly status updates so that you can understand the outsourcer's challenges and help by removing roadblocks. This relationship is a true partnership when you face the challenges together, and holding regular meetings helps you get to satisfactory solutions faster.

Another best practice is having regular quarterly performance reviews for your outsourcer. Just as employees do, the outsourcer needs to know what it has done well and what needs to improve or change.

We had a client who asked us for help with an outsourcer that wasn't meeting the client's revenue-per-call targets and that had high turnover. When we visited the outsourcer to see what was going on, we found out that no one from the client company had come to visit the call center, let alone provide direction about what products it should offer first or how to sell those products better. The outsourcer was doing the best it could with the little knowledge and understanding that it had. After we started a conversation between our client and its outsourcer, eyes started popping all over the place, and light bulbs went off. The agents changed their approach, and the client immediately realized the benefits. Revenue per call was no longer a challenge, and the client was happy with its outsourcer.

Knowing when to jump in

When things are going awry at your outsourcer, it's difficult to stand back. You just want to take the reins and start fixing the problem. But you've given these reins to someone else who has the expertise to solve this issue. How long should you wait for things to improve, and what should you do if they don't?

Don't add more stress and pressure to the situation. Be part of the solution, not part of the problem. Your role could include being part of a brainstorming team that looks for solutions. Through collaboration and open discussion, suggest options that work for you and your outsourcer. After all, you want to set all parties up for success.

Part II

The Master Plan: Finance, Analysis, and Resource Management

The 5th Wave   By Rich Tennant

"I tried calling in sick yesterday, but I was put on hold and disconnected."

In this part . . .

This part brings the call center business model — analysis, financial planning, and staffing — to life. We provide a simple overview of how *metrics* (things you can measure) come together to drive call center operational and financial performance to achieve forecasted results.

Staffing is probably the biggest mystery and frustration to most call center professionals. In this part of the book, we also explore everything from forecasting to schedule creation and workforce management automation. We uncover why call centers perform the way they do.

Chapter 6

Analyze This!

*Y*ou may find the thought of call center analysis a little boring, and you might even feel a little pain at the idea, but trust us — it really isn't that difficult, and it can make your call center more successful.

Call centers can be complex beasts, and they run very much by the numbers, so analysis plays a significant role in operating them effectively. Call centers can get very big, and although they offer a cost-effective way of doing business, they can require a lot of dollars from the parent organization to make them go.

In this chapter, we discuss a simple approach to analyzing your business goals and setting targets to help you achieve them. Our approach aligns performance drivers (and the ways you measure them) with your business goals. We also talk about call center operating budgets and costs, methods of tracking satisfaction at both customer and employee level, and various ways to increase efficiency.

Adding It Up: Call Center Math

Most of the math that you use in call centers every day is simple. Sure, you can get really fancy, using sophisticated techniques such as multiple regression, but your super-keen business analyst will be only too happy to do the work and translate the results into English for you. (For a discussion of the roles of analysts in a call center, see Chapter 3.)

Understanding the fundamental concepts

Most call center analysis involves basic concepts, such as the following:

- Percentages and cumulative percentages
- Averages and weighted averages
- Standard deviation
- Simple charts, such as bar charts and pie charts
- Charts that illustrate variation, such as control charts and run charts

We discuss these tools in greater detail wherever they come up throughout the book.

A detailed discussion of statistical analysis is beyond the scope of this book, but you can find more information and a definition of standard deviation in *Statistics For Dummies,* by Deborah Rumsey (Wiley Publishing, Inc.).

After you establish your business goals (as we describe in Chapter 2) and know what you need to do to achieve them, you can use mathematical models to figure out what levels to aim for, or create and analyze what-if scenarios for costs per contact, cost per customer, call center budget, and other measures.

If you can model call center results by using the business and operating drivers to create an economic model of your operation, you gain valuable insight into how your call center works.

Using models in calculations

You can calculate contacts per hour based on *occupancy* (how busy call center agents are while they're logged into the company phone system) and average call length. Just use the following formula:

Contacts per hour = Occupancy × 3,600 ÷ Call length (in seconds)

In this formula, 3,600 represents the number of seconds in an hour. So if your call center's occupancy is 75 percent (0.75), and the call length is 360 seconds, your equation looks like this:

$$0.75 \times 3,600 \div 360 = 7.5$$

The result is 7.5 contacts per hour.

You can see from this model that to increase contacts per hour, you simply have to reduce call length or increase occupancy.

We discuss call length and occupancy calculations in "Performance Drivers: Managing the Results," later in this chapter.

Analyzing Business Goals

You generally group your call center's business goals into four areas: customer satisfaction, efficiency, revenue generation, and employee satisfaction. (Chapter 2 covers these areas in detail.)

You can target and measure the call center's mission and business goals in various ways, as well as measure the performance drivers (see Chapter 2) that have a direct effect on your call center's performance. Table 6-1 summarizes the relationships among the four business goals and the performance drivers that affect results.

Table 6-1	Business Goals, Measures, and Performance Drivers	
Goals	*Measures*	*Drivers*
Efficiency	Department budget	Occupancy
	Cost per contact	Cost per agent hour
	Cost per customer	Call length
	Cost per resolution	Contacts per customer
		Agent utilization
Revenue generation	Total revenue generation	Sales-conversion percentage per contact
	Revenue per contact	
	Revenue per customer	Dollar value per conversion
Customer satisfaction	High customer-satisfaction survey scores	Ease of access to agents
		Agent call quality
		First-call resolution
Employee satisfaction	High employee-satisfaction survey scores	Value placed on the work
		Team-leader support
		Recognition
		Working environment

Measuring Business Goals

As we discuss in Chapter 2, business goals are the desired results of the call center — what the corporation needs from the call center by way of customer satisfaction, efficiency, revenue generation, and employee satisfaction.

In the following sections, we outline some common ways to measure whether you're meeting your call center business goals.

A note about employee satisfaction as a business goal: Some companies believe that it's the obligation of a socially responsible employer to provide a quality work environment; others believe that maintaining high employee satisfaction is good business practice. Few dispute the strong link between happy employees and the satisfaction level of customers with whom those employees interact.

Breaking down the operating budget

As with most departments or divisions of a business, you need to know your operating budget to complete your call center business planning effectively. The *operating budget* is the sum of the costs associated with running a call center for a given period — usually, a year. The message is fairly simple when it comes to budgets: Don't exceed a budget, and if you can keep your expenses lower than the budget, that's great.

You may not have an accounting degree, but you need to understand the financial aspects of managing customer contact. Some people inside your company might see the call center as a big cost pit, so you need to show them the value of the call center and explain your costs. If you're talking to senior executives about your call center's financial results or considering outsourcing (which we discuss in Chapter 5), you need to answer the question "How much does it really cost to run our call center operations?"

When you have that figure, you can calculate your fully loaded cost per call, cost per minute, and cost to service an existing account or customer. *Fully loaded* means that you total your costs (labor, telephony, overhead, and so on) and divide it by the number of calls you take over one year.

You can calculate these costs over a few months, but things like depreciation, amortization, and rent usually are calculated annually. Alternatively, you can divide your total costs by the number of labor minutes or hours that your operation uses in the course of a year.

Budgets have their limits, however. Meeting or beating an operating budget doesn't tell you whether your call center operated efficiently or your general business activity was lighter than planned. In a growing company, operating budgets for call centers generally go up, and an increasing budget doesn't tell you much about whether you're running the call center less efficiently than you did the year before.

Also, sticking strictly to an operating budget without using comparative data — such as percentage of revenue or comparison with last year's results — can lead to the wrong business decisions. Most people probably would agree that if demand for your product greatly exceeds the demand that your call center budget planned for, and as a result, your call center is swamped with calls from people who want your product, you probably want to exceed your budget so that you can accommodate these purchasers.

Categorizing operating costs

We present a few categories that can help you organize your thinking and costs. (In Chapter 5, we talk about these costs in more detail.) These operating-cost categories are

- **Direct payroll costs:** Labor costs directly associated with handling customer calls, e-mails, online chat, and so on. This category includes not only your agents' hourly or salary wages, but also the additional costs of health benefits, taxes, vacations, and other payroll-related costs (which can add 10 percent to 20 percent to wages, depending on jurisdiction and company policies).

- **Indirect payroll costs:** Costs such as payroll for team leaders, managers, trainers, and people who fix computers, as well as at least part of the cost for groups such as human resources. You also need to add benefits, payroll taxes, vacations, and so on to these costs.

- **Support and management costs:** Costs related to supporting the department, such as wages and benefits associated with senior management, reporting and analysis, meals, entertainment, food (what call center agent doesn't like a free meal?), travel, and agent incentives. The person who manages the service center has direct control of all these costs.

- **Corporate overhead costs:** Costs that typically are beyond your day-to-day control, including facilities (rent, utilities, maintenance, and property taxes), insurance, security, software licenses, telecom maintenance, phone lines, and Internet access.

- **Capital expenses:** Costs of acquiring long-term physical assets such as land, buildings, or technology, which appear in this year's operating budget as amortization and/or depreciation. Amortization or depreciation reflects the portion of the asset that was "used up" this year. How much you apply is regulated by accounting and tax rules.

Many one-time purchases (such as technology) include ongoing costs. You group these costs as new operating costs (such as licenses and maintenance).

Your company might also look at costs as being fixed versus variable. A *fixed cost* doesn't change when call or work volume decreases. Fixed costs typically include rent, insurance, and payroll costs such as managers and the information-technology staff. A *variable cost* does change with call volume. Typically, a call center's variable costs include agent hourly wages (plus taxes, benefits, and vacations associated with these hourly wages).

If your call volumes fluctuate, but the number of paid agent hours doesn't, your cost per call, cost per minute, or cost per customer measurement increases. You can solve this problem in several ways, including moving or reducing agent hours (moving some agents to part-time or casual hourly employment), or giving agents some other type of work to do instead of waiting for calls to arrive.

The largest cost in the call center budget typically is labor. You base budgets on assumptions about the number of calls that the call center will receive, how long those calls will be, and how quickly agents need to answer the phone. You use these assumptions to determine how many agents, managers, and support people your call center needs. In Chapters 7 and 8, we discuss how to calculate the number of people you need to answer the phone.

Companies need operating budgets, and managing with the budget in mind can help a company achieve its goals. Very effective call center managers have a great deal of control of their costs and generally know how much they need to spend in any month long before the finance department produces a cost report.

Modeling the operating budget

Modeling the call center budget gives you the opportunity, through what-if scenarios, to see the real effect on the bottom line of changes in various drivers. The following formula, which is a simplified version of the call center budget model, is an easy way to do a simple cost–benefit analysis:

Call center budget = Customer base × Forecasted calls per customer × Average call length ÷ Planned occupancy at service level × Cost per hour

Assume the following:

- **Number of customers (customer base):** 1 million
- **Forecasted calls per customer (annual):** 1
- **Average call length:** 360 seconds
- **Planned occupancy at service level:** 75 percent (0.75)
- **Cost per hour:** $45

In this scenario, your equation would look like this:

Call center budget = $1,000,000 \times 1 \times 360 \div 3,600 \div 0.75 \times \$45 = \$6,000,000$

If you could reduce call length by 30 seconds, your new calculation for the department budget would be

Call center budget = $1,000,000 \times 1 \times 330 \div 3,600 \div 0.75 \times \$45 = \$5,500,000$

In this example, reducing call length by 30 seconds translates into a $500,000 savings. To reduce call length, management might make some significant changes in the call-handling process, introduce call-control training, or perhaps introduce some new software that streamlines the way that agents retrieve information. Doing a quick calculation of the effect of changing the call center's drivers may motivate management to find ways to make improvements.

To figure out what occupancy levels you'll have when you hit service-level targets, look at your results over time, and determine what occupancy level you typically hit when you're at the service-level target. (For more information on service level, see Chapter 2.) You can use this information as a benchmark, which you can improve on.

We talk more about occupancy later in this chapter, and we discuss forecasting in Chapter 7. Also, knowing your optimal occupancy (see Chapter 8) can help maximize productivity without burning out your agents.

Measuring cost per contact

Measuring cost per contact tells you something about your call center's cost control. If cost per contact is getting lower, your boss is probably happy.

This measure doesn't tell the whole story, however. If your call center's cost per contact is low because your agents are rushing off calls to keep their call length low, or if you have a very high percentage of repeat calls, cost per contact can simply mask a problem.

Calculating contact costs

You calculate cost per contact by dividing the total cost of running the call center for a given period by the total contacts to which agents responded in the same period. Even with the concern about short calls and repeat calls, you want this measure to decrease over time.

Figure 6-1 illustrates a run chart of cost per contact. A *run chart* is a line graph that shows data points plotted in the order in which they occur. Run charts illustrate trends, so you can identify possible causes if you see spikes or dips.

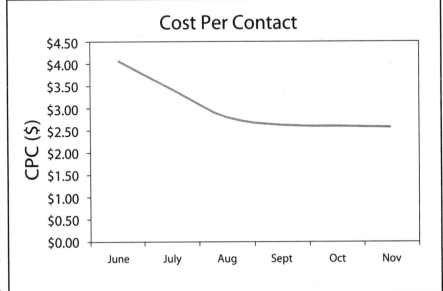

Figure 6-1:
A run chart
illustrating
cost per
contact.

Running with run charts

To create a run chart, simply chart any data point, such as how long each agent's calls last over a given period, and *voilà* — instant analysis.

You can even illustrate control limits on a run chart when you track an agent's performance, even though doing so isn't common practice. *Control limits* are horizontal lines drawn on charts usually at a distance of plus or minus three standard deviations of the plotted statistic from the mean. When you include the control limits, you can much more easily compare an agent's performance with the trend of the group and see exactly how much variation has occurred over time.

Although we don't go into statistics in detail in this book, *Statistics For Dummies*, by Deborah Rumsey (Wiley), provides more information on common statistics terms and concepts.

Determining cost per contact

By using the formula for contacts per hour (which you can find in "Using models in calculations," earlier in this chapter), you can easily calculate cost per contact if you know your cost per hour:

Cost per contact = Cost per hour ÷ Contacts per hour

If your cost per hour is $45, for example, and your contacts per hour are 7.5, your cost per contact is $6 ($45 ÷ 7.5). To reduce this cost per contact, you have to reduce your cost per hour (maybe by improving agent utilization, which we discuss in "Performance Drivers: Managing the Results," later in this chapter) or increase calls per hour (perhaps by improving occupancy, which you can read about in "Occupancy," later in this chapter).

Models provide a simple but effective way to create and experiment with what-if scenarios. You can use models to do very accurate cost–benefit analyses.

Measuring cost per customer

Cost per customer addresses the problems with cost per contact by eliminating the variable of call length as long as you have a finite customer base. Cost per customer tells you more than cost per contact does, because it takes repeat calls into account and doesn't penalize an operation that smartly took simple shorter calls and moved them to a self-service interactive voice response system (IVR; see Chapter 9) or Web site. You calculate cost per customer by using this formula:

Cost per customer = Cost of running the call center for a certain period ÷ Average number of customers for the same period

If your cost per customer reduces continually, your overall call center costs keep going down — and you can bet that you'll be talked about favorably in the executive lunchroom.

Measuring cost per resolution

Cost per resolution is a great way to measure progress toward your business goals. Cost per resolution recognizes that sometimes, agents can't satisfy customer issues in a single contact. It also recognizes that customers sometimes call back because of new issues.

You may find cost per resolution difficult to calculate because you can't always track unique issues accurately, but if you use customer relationship management (CRM) software, which tracks customer contacts and unique issues, you can at least get a close approximation. If you have that data, plug it into this formula:

Cost per resolution = Total costs for the period ÷ Cases resolved

You want to see your cost-per-resolution number decrease, showing improvement over time.

Ringing up revenue

Revenue refers to the money that your business makes before it pays expenses and taxes. *Profit* (or *earnings*), on the other hand, refers to the money that you have left after you subtract from your revenue the expenses of producing, selling, and delivering a product or service.

Determining total revenue generation

Total revenue generation and the call center operating budget (which we talk about in "Breaking down the operating budget," earlier in this chapter) coexist in the annual planning process.

Your finance or marketing department calculates total revenue generated. It probably estimates the number of sales-inquiry calls that you're going to get for the period, the percentage of these inquiries that your agents will convert to sales, and the average value of these sales.

You can always look at beating the revenue-generation target as being a good thing, but you don't know how good it is until you put it into the context of how many customers contacted the call center. If customer calls exceeded your plan by 100 percent, and revenue generation exceeded the plan by only 50 percent, your agents didn't generate as much revenue per customer as you had planned.

Calculating revenue per contact

Revenue per contact gives you a fairly good measure of how much revenue your call center agents are bringing in per contact — and the higher, the better.

You can calculate this value easily:

> Revenue per contact = Total revenue generated by the call center for a given period ÷ Number of contacts for the same period

Revenue per contact offsets cost per contact. You can also include the effect of customer cancellations in the revenue-per-contact measure to arrive at net revenue per contact. When you measure revenue per contact at the agent level, you see which agents best maximize all revenue opportunities, including sales and retention opportunities. Here's the formula for these relationships:

> Net revenue per contact = Total revenue generated by the call center for a given period ÷ Number of contacts for the same period – Revenue lost from cancellations

Include all calls when you're calculating revenue per contact. Don't make an attempt to qualify which calls to count ("Well, if you take out calls made to wrong numbers, my conversion rate goes way up!"). In the world of call centers, everyone gets the same percentage of misdirected or non-revenue-opportunity calls. Qualifying which calls count and which ones don't introduces subjectivity, interpretation, and error into the measure. Use all calls — for absolutely everyone.

Calculating revenue per customer

Revenue per customer provides a nice comparison with cost per customer, giving your call center a good visible contribution to the organization on a per-customer basis. Here's how you calculate this measure:

> Revenue per customer = Total revenue generated for a given period ÷ Average number of customers over the same period

If you continually reduce cost per customer and increase revenue per customer, you'll have a key component of a successful performance evaluation.

Scoring satisfaction

We all want to be part of an organization that people not only enjoy working for, but also enjoy working with. To find out whether your customers and employees (whom you can consider to be internal customers) are satisfied, simply ask them by conducting satisfaction surveys. When you conduct these surveys, make sure that you have a clear idea of when and how you gather this information and what you ask your customers. To get true value out of the survey results, consider that the actions you take after you analyze this data can help you improve both employee and customer satisfaction.

Measuring customer satisfaction

Your call center needs to provide exceptional customer service, of course — and not just because your mother, the president of the United States, or the queen of England plans to call. Customer satisfaction drives future business.

At the very least, lack of customer satisfaction is a primary cause of loss of future business. You certainly don't want the call center to be the reason why customers stop doing business with your company, so you need to deliver good customer service.

In some cases, call centers provide such great service that callers say, "Wow, thanks!" If you can impress customers in this way often enough that the call center actually increases the number of customers your company has, you and your team will have the satisfaction of a job really well done.

How often should you survey employees?

You may hear that an annual or semiannual survey is more appropriate than a monthly or quarterly one. We can't agree with this assessment, however. You certainly wouldn't measure cost-per-call performance semiannually, so why measure employee satisfaction any less often than you do your other business goals? Frequent measurement of employee satisfaction allows a call center to track not only progress, but also the effect of initiatives designed to improve employee satisfaction.

If you do surveys monthly, however, don't promise that you'll resolve every new issue quickly. Gauge employees' attitudes frequently, but also manage their expectations about resolutions so that you don't create employee cynicism.

Measuring employee satisfaction

Employee motivation is a complex topic, which we don't dive into too deeply here. (For a full discussion, see *Motivating Employees For Dummies,* by Max Messmer [Wiley].) In Chapter 14, we talk about employee engagement. But just know that you need to give it a lot of attention, make it one of your business goals, and try to improve it so that you have happier employees.

You can start measuring employee satisfaction by conducting regular employee surveys, maybe once per month and certainly no less than quarterly (see the sidebar "How often should you survey employees?" in this chapter). These surveys give you a continuous view of how employees view their jobs and the company.

Include a few consistent questions in the monthly survey, such as "Do you like working here?" and "Do you find your team leader to be helpful?" In addition to these standard questions, you can list a few questions-of-the-month to take a closer look at particular issues, such as new initiatives and program rollouts.

You may want to ask open-ended questions to determine what your employees think you could improve in your operation. After you have a good idea of what is and isn't working, you can make changes.

In our call centers, we use a Web-based survey that we can edit and launch on a moment's notice. The survey includes room for employees to write their recommendations and concerns. Participation is confidential, which helps foster open discussion. The application automatically tabulates results and produces trend data on overall satisfaction, as well as satisfaction relative to the individual questions.

As you do for other measures, you want a high level of employee satisfaction. You want to see improvement — graphs that go up. A bad score can, and should, be cause for concern and quick action.

Keep your employees by keeping them happy

Here are some characteristics of happy employees:

✔ **They value the work.** Hire people who like the work and want to continue doing it. No job is for everyone, and if you hire someone because she needs some quick cash, you run the risk of having an employee whom you can't motivate. We discuss recruiting in Chapter 12.

✔ **They get the team-leader support that they need.** One of the biggest turnoffs for employees of call centers (or any other business) is not being able to get help when they need it. A competent staff of team leaders contributes to employee satisfaction.

✔ **They get recognition for doing a good job.** If they do something truly good, employees want someone to notice it.

✔ **They feel that the environment is positive.** A positive environment can include a positive corporate culture, friendly coworkers, clean carpets, adequate lighting, and so on.

You can measure all these aspects of employee satisfaction in your opinion survey by asking employees to rate each element on a scale — say, from 1 to 5, with 1 being lowest and 5 highest.

Performance Drivers: Managing the Results

As we discuss in Chapter 2, *performance drivers* are variables that affect your call center's business goals. They're called performance drivers because, like the software programs that make computers work, they make other things go. In the case of call center employees, performance drivers are the behaviors and actions that improve business goals.

The models that we discuss in this chapter show that the measures you identify really do drive results, especially in the very measurable goals of cost and revenue. Understanding this relationship is just the beginning, however; you want to use that information to plan new business activities to improve the way you work.

A key component of controlling and manipulating outcomes is designating responsibility throughout the organization — especially to the call center's agents, because each agent is a microcosm of the operation.

Formula for success

Statisticians might think of the relationship between business-goal measurements and performance drivers in these terms:

- ✔ y = business-goal measurements

- ✔ x = performance drivers

- ✔ $y = f(x)$ (which means that y is a function of x)

Budgets are a function of call length, among other things.

Table 6-2 shows how to track and improve results at agent level. Individual agent improvement creates improvement in overall average agent performance, which in turn drives overall improvement in the call center.

Table 6-2	Tracking Results at Agent Level
Call Center Drivers	*Agent-Level Drivers*
Cost per hour of agent time	Wage rate
Agent utilization (logged hours/paid hours)	Schedule adherence
Call length	Call length
Contacts per customer	First-call resolution
Occupancy	N/A
Conversion per contact	Conversion per contact
Dollar value per conversion	Dollar value per conversion
Accessibility	Average handle time (see "Calculating call length," later in this chapter)
Agent professionalism and ability	Agent professionalism and ability
Policies and procedures	Application of knowledge

Some measures in Table 6-2 — the ones that agents can't influence or control through their own actions — don't correlate with agent-level measures because they're not considered to be agents' responsibilities. Occupancy and service level, for example, are group measures that individual agents can't control. Also, agents can't directly control company policies and procedures.

In Table 6-2, cost per hour becomes wage rate at the agent level because apart from their wages (which correlate directly to them), agents generally can't control any other costs.

You measure the call center driver called agent utilization as schedule adherence at the agent level. *Schedule adherence* is the percentage of expected phone time that an agent is actually on the phone.

Use these driver calculations to help agents achieve continuous improvement in the areas for which they're responsible.

Wherever possible, break the drivers into the smallest unit of measure that you can. Break call length into talk time and after-call work, for example, and then try to break those measures down further, perhaps by contact type. Tracking these drivers at agent level is just another way of breaking down the data so that you can understand the driver better.

Hundreds of performance drivers probably affect a call center's results. The business analyst (see Chapter 3) needs to identify these relationships to gain a better understanding of how performance drivers make business objectives work. In the following sections, we look at the variables that have the greatest effect on call center results. Master these variables, and you can develop a great deal of control of performance and profitability.

Cost per agent hour

A call center manager needs to know the center's cost per agent hour, which amounts to the total cost of operating the center for one hour during which an agent is logged into the telephone system. To calculate this value, use this equation:

> Cost per agent hour = Total call center cost for a given period ÷ Total hours logged into the phone system for the same period

Track cost per agent hour over time because it fluctuates with call volume.

You can control this measure, and if you do, you gain a great deal of control of the cost-management goals in your call center.

After you calculate your cost per agent hour, you can analyze the result. Break the total cost per hour into agent labor, benefits, management, rent, and so on.

Next, you may want to compare your cost-per-agent-hour figures with those of other organizations — a process called *benchmarking.* Benchmarking can give you a feel for whether your results are high or low (keeping in mind that the company you're benchmarking against may be in a different industry or may not provide comparable services). Through benchmarking, you may find that you're doing well, or you may find that you can improve. If you find other companies that run good operations and have a lower cost per agent hour, at least you know what's possible.

You may want to benchmark with outsourcers, too; they know their cost per agent hour only too well and typically remove all inefficiencies. We discuss outsourcing in Chapter 5.

Cost per agent hour is influenced by variables such as average wage rate, benefits, and logged hours over paid hours (L/P). Here's the equation for L/P:

> L/P = Total logged hours by all call center agents ÷ Total payroll hours for the same period

Some operators use the term *agent utilization* for L/P. Whatever you call it, this ratio illustrates the overall productivity of your call center. We've seen it range from less than 50 percent to more than 80 percent.

In a large operation that Réal helped, a 1 percent increase in L/P reduced total call center expenditures by approximately $1 million, or about 2 percent of the total budget, so you may want to consider paying close attention to this measure.

To manage L/P, account for all the time that agents don't spend on the phones — the difference between your L/P number and 100 percent. After you account for this time, you can probably find savings by reducing *nonproduction time* in your operation — any time that agents aren't talking to customers or doing after-call work.

The cost associated with agent time represents 60 percent to 70 percent of the call center's costs and can be broken into these categories:

✔ **Total paid time:** This category is subject to a markup percentage for health benefits and payroll costs that human resources or finance may not always share with managers of the call center.

✔ **Nonproduction time:** Some of this time may be paid (such as training and meetings), and some of it may be unpaid (such as breaks or lunches). Check with the payroll person to determine the time your company pays agents for and the time it doesn't pay agents for. Even if the company doesn't pay for a certain period of time, that nonproduction time still affects your operation; if an agent isn't there to take a call, you have to pay someone else to replace her.

Between total agents-paid time and agents-working time, a typical call center can lose anywhere from 7 percent to 12 percent, depending on its absence policy (paid versus unpaid) and on whether it has any new hires in training. (The call center has to pay for these new hires but doesn't yet have them in the operation talking to customers.)

✔ **Production time:** This category represents the time when an agent is waiting for a call *(idle time)*, performing after-call work (finishing a customer's file after hanging up with the customer), or talking to the customer.

✔ **Talk time:** Talk time is the most important part of production time. During this time, the agent is helping customers and producing revenue.

Payroll efficiency represents how well you turn total paid time into talk time, and this number gives you a good overall view of organizational efficiency. Unlike measures of quality, generation of revenue, or first-contact resolution (see "Contacts per customer," later in this chapter), however, payroll efficiency doesn't tell you how effectively your call center delivers great service or generates revenue.

Call length

Call length is a major building block of a call center. Together with call volume and *service level* (how quickly an agent answers the phone), call length tells you how big to build your operation — how many people, how many desks, how large a phone system, how many phone lines, and so on.

Managing call length

Call centers often put too much focus on call length without paying appropriate attention to other measures. Focusing too heavily on call length can make agents feel pressured to reduce call times, which can result in a reduction in the quality of customer service. Still, this measure can tell you much about your operation, as follows:

✔ **Long calls:** Our research has shown that customers want quick, accurate, and complete resolution of their problems or inquiries. Long call times suggest that customers may not be getting what they want. Frequently, long calls are the result of complex problems.

✔ **Short calls:** Short call length may suggest that the agents don't fully serve the customers. Usually, calls are short because they deal with simple problems, but sometimes, the call-handling process doesn't allow agents to fully support customers. In these cases, you actually want call length to increase — along with customer satisfaction and call resolution.

Your efforts to improve call-handling processes and reduce call length not only save the call center money, but also satisfy customers by providing faster access to an agent. You can achieve high satisfaction with low call lengths only if you can equal or improve service and call resolution.

Calculating call length

Most companies use this standard equation to calculate call length (see Chapter 7):

Talk time + After-call work = Call length

These companies, however, may be missing other times that have been recorded by the phone system, such as holds or transfers. Therefore, this call calculation may be understated.

The following formula, which Réal has used for years, produces a consistent measure of call length, or *call service time (CST)*. You can use this measure for analysis and scheduling:

Call service time = (Total time agents are logged into the phones – Time agents spend waiting for calls) ÷ Number of calls answered

You may find that your CST is slightly different from *average handle time* (AHT) — the total time (measured in minutes or seconds) that agents spend on the phone over a given period — that your phone system reports because of the different ways that phone systems calculate AHT.

Charting call length

Bar charts (or *histograms*) can help you see how one thing compares with another or how frequently something occurs. In your call center, you can chart calls received by day of the week or types of calls received by day.

Figure 6-2 shows the average call length for different types of calls plotted on a bar chart.

To use this type of chart, follow these steps:

1. **Track your call times by the different types of calls you take, and create a bar chart of that data.**

2. **Determine the longest call type.**

3. **Map out the step-by-step process for a typical call of that type.**

4. **Try to determine a different way to handle this type of call that doesn't take as long.**

5. **Continue to track the length of this call type for 30 days.**

   Ideally, you'll see some improvements.

6. **Repeat Steps 1–5 for each call type.**

   Over time, you should increase cost control and customer satisfaction.

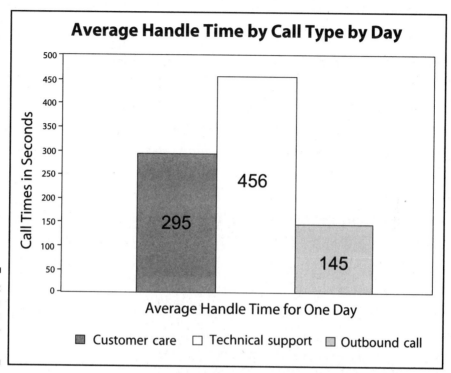

Average Handle Time by Call Type by Day

Call Times in Seconds

500 —
450 —
400 —
350 —
300 —
250 —
200 —
150 —
100 —
50 —
0 —

295

456

145

Average Handle Time for One Day

■ Customer care   ☐ Technical support   ◻ Outbound call

Figure 6-2: Tracking average call length by call type.

Contacts per customer

Contacts per customer is a measure that can help you forecast and track cost control. Tracking the number of contacts per customer on a monthly or daily basis and then multiplying that figure by the current number of customers gives you a forecast of call volume demand (specifically, the demand for agents' time).

Reducing contacts per customer can help you gain efficiency and create high customer satisfaction. The more times a customer calls, the more total calls you have to take and the more agents you need to schedule to handle the calls. If customers call back because they're irate about errors or problems with their transactions or orders, you have to take a double whammy: Handling a second call costs you money, and so does correcting the error. Reducing or eliminating errors and unnecessary callbacks plays a major role when you're striving for improvements in customer satisfaction and efficiency.

For this reason, you need to measure *first-call resolution* (FCR), which refers to the percentage of customer inquiries that your agents can complete on the first attempt. If customers have to call back once — or many more times — because the call center didn't resolve their inquiries or concerns the first time, your FCR percentage declines.

You may have difficulty tracking this driver because the call center must keep track of all callers, as well as their reasons for calling. Customer tracking software can make tracking FCR easier, however. (For more information on this software, see Chapter 10.)

You can get big benefits from tracking FCR. Improving this measure affects customer satisfaction because customers want quick, accurate resolutions of their problems and needs. It also improves efficiency because it reduces calls per customer and repeat calls.

Occupancy

Occupancy refers to how busy call center agents are while they're logged into the company phone system. Occupancy has a great effect on efficiency.

You calculate occupancy as the percentage of call center agents' logged hours — the time agents are logged into the telephone system, busy, and unavailable to accept customer calls — against the total hours that the agents spend at work (being paid). The formula looks like this:

Occupancy = Logged hours ÷ Total time spent at work

Occupancy is the opposite of *idle time* — time that agents spend waiting for customer calls.

What are logged hours?

Everyone in the call center must fully understand and agree with what it means to be logged into the phone system. Agents are logged in whenever they're handling customer calls, including all work associated with handling calls: talking to the customer, placing the customer on hold while the agent looks up the solution, doing after-call work, or waiting for the next call.

When agents are at work but not handling customer calls, they shouldn't be logged into the phone system. Agents should log out for breaks, meetings, training, and so on.

Reserving telephone logged hours exclusively for time spent handling customer calls makes it much easier to keep the data associated with call handling clean. Some call center managers might disagree, arguing that the phone system can track many uses of agent time. We've invariably found, however, that when agents stay logged into the phones for non-call-handling reasons, it becomes unclear what time they used for call handling and what time they used for breaks. You can find other ways to track total agent time. Keep logged hours pure.

It's worth noting that if agents are going to remain logged in, auxiliary (AUX) codes in the phone system and/or shift segments in the workforce planning software should identify production versus nonproduction time, providing a more complete picture of the day.

You can consider agents who are doing certain activities to be occupied. These activities include talking to customers, researching customer issues while the customer is on hold, and working on customer files after the customer has hung up. This final occupied state is referred to as *after-call work,* and a button pushed at the agent's phone tells the system that the agent is temporarily unavailable to accept calls.

Here are a couple of notes regarding occupancy:

- **How fast agents answer the phone:** When occupancy decreases, agents can answer customers' calls more quickly (because a lot of agents are waiting for those calls). But if occupancy increases, agents answer the phones more slowly, and customers have to wait for "the next available agent."

- **The size of your call center:** You want consistent occupancy throughout the day, meaning that your agents receive a steady but comfortable pace of calls during the whole day. In this ideal situation, you optimize the use of your agents, and your agents aren't stressed because they don't receive a ton of calls at the same time.

Because of economies of scale, the larger the call center, the higher the occupancy at any service level should be. So if you have agents waiting in different queues to take different calls, by consolidating *call queues* (in which customers wait until their turn to speak to an agent) or entire centers, you create a steady level of work and a more sustainable occupancy level.

The effect of random call arrival

Unless your call center gets swamped with calls, you'll never have 100 percent occupancy. Call centers often experience occupancy of 65 percent to 75 percent because of the random nature of call arrivals. To put it simply, customer calls come in bunches.

As we discuss in great detail in Chapter 8, the call-arrival pattern in a typical call center is random (and looks spiky if you graph the calls over time). Imagine that you work in a chocolate factory: The spikes represent chocolates coming off a conveyor belt, and you have to wrap each chocolate individually. If you're working alone, you probably miss many of the chocolates, especially during the spikes in chocolate arrival. If you absolutely can't miss any chocolates, you ask a few friends to help you catch and wrap all the chocolates. Now you and your friends don't miss any chocolates, but for the most part, you're not very busy. In fact, it's very slow on the chocolate-wrapping line during the valleys in chocolate arrival.

Call centers experience the same kind of situation. If you have too few agents answering phones, you miss calls, but if you add people so that you don't miss calls, your agents spend time waiting.

Because of the variation in call-arrival patterns, you can't just staff the phones for any given period based on the average number of calls; the peaks will kill you, just like in the chocolate-factory example. To answer all calls reasonably quickly during the peaks in caller demand, you must staff higher than the average number of calls.

The difference between the workload represented in the calls you receive and the actual amount of staff used to answer those calls represents time that your call center agents spend waiting (idle).

If you want to answer customer calls quickly, you need some agent idle time. Conversely, if you want to make your call center agents more productive (increasing occupancy), you need to staff fewer agents, reducing idle time and making your customers wait for an agent.

As we discuss in Chapter 8, *optimal occupancy* (what you can achieve with perfect scheduling) and *expected occupancy* (what you get from the imperfect schedules that you have to work with) differ. Getting as close as possible to optimal occupancy is a goal of every scheduler. You can achieve that goal by creating more flexible schedules with shorter shifts and by using part-timers and home agents (see Chapter 11). In large call centers, even a 1 percent improvement can add up to significant savings.

Occupancy as a driver of cost

How does occupancy affect your cost objectives? For any given caller demand, you can easily determine how much work the demand represents. If you're going to get 10 calls in a half hour, and each call takes an average of 3 minutes to handle, some quick math tells you that you have 30 minutes of work to do. In half an hour, you need one agent to answer those calls, but that agent becomes 100 percent occupied for the half hour. If calls arrive randomly — and you know that they will — some callers won't get an immediate answer. If you need to answer calls quickly, you have to add another agent. The second agent can help you make sure that calls get answered quickly, but because these two agents have only 30 minutes of work, your occupancy falls from 100 percent to 50 percent, and the cost of answering these calls has doubled.

You have to consider optimizing occupancy when you plan a call center, and you need to manage it hourly to help manage costs and productivity.

Conversion per contact

A *contact* is any occasion when you communicate with a customer (via the phone, e-mail, chat, or whatever). A *conversion* is any occasion when you generate or save revenue during a contact.

When it comes to conversion, higher is better. Period. Full stop. Even if the customer just called to ask you what time the store in Upper Rubber Boot is open, if you manage to sell him something when he calls, you help build revenue for the company.

In most call centers, the revenue opportunity associated with improving conversion per contact is big. Managers and sales coaches spend a lot of time in call centers finding ways to improve this variable. Conversion per contact affects total revenue generated and other revenue goals.

Dollar value per conversion

Sure, you can make a lot of sales, given the universe of opportunities, but you want to make a lot of *big* sales. The terms *upsell* (which means selling the customer more than she initially planned to buy) and *cross-sell* (which means moving the customer to a new product line that he didn't think about before) are the skills that agents need to achieve this goal. If you can make big sales or create cross-sells, this variable increases, which adds to total revenue generated, revenue per customer, revenue per call, and so on.

Accessibility

We use the term *accessibility* to describe how easily callers can get through to an agent — how fast someone answers the phone. Accessibility affects both customer satisfaction and efficiency.

A well-selected accessibility target can balance customer satisfaction with the cost of providing that level of accessibility. Accessibility affects cost by influencing how many agents the call center needs for any particular level of demand. As a result, accessibility influences cost through occupancy.

Here are three common measures (among many) that you can use to calculate accessibility:

- ✔ **Service level:** Service level is probably the most common term used to define accessibility. It refers to the percentage of callers whose calls are answered or who hang up within a defined time. If your time threshold is 20 seconds, you may have a service-level objective of answering 85 percent of calls arriving in the call center in 20 seconds or less.

  Just to keep you on your toes, service level is also sometimes referred to as *telephone service factor*. Also, the target number of seconds — 20, in the preceding example — is referred to as the *telephone service factor threshold*. Oh, boy.

Service level gives you a very specific measure, which you can use to make decisions about the cost and benefit of service-level objectives. We discuss this topic in more detail in Chapter 2.

✔ **Average speed of answer:** This term refers to the average amount of time that your customers wait before they can speak to an agent. Generally speaking, a lower figure is better.

✔ **Abandonment rate:** This measure is the percentage of callers who hang up before an agent answers their calls. This percentage, rather than a service-level measure, is more a measure of customer satisfaction. If your customers are hanging up a lot, guess what? They don't like the speed of your service. If they don't hang up very often, you likely offer them an acceptable average speed of answer (see the preceding paragraph).

Be careful with this guideline, however. If customers don't hang up simply because they absolutely *must* speak with someone, making them hold through a long delay can result in some nasty exchanges between frustrated customers and overworked agents.

Agent professionalism and ability

Whether they're phoning a call center or shopping for shoes, most customers expect the same things of the customer service people whom they deal with: They should know what they're talking about, and they should be nice.

The customer-satisfaction measures that we discuss in this section can help you find out how capable your agents are. Customers will tell you about agents who aren't nice or can't do the job. When you ask the right questions, customers can also tell you specifically what your company needs to do to improve. This information can make for excellent training material.

Many call centers have people listen to agent calls to determine whether their agents are professional and capable; this process is frequently referred to as *call assessment* or *call monitoring*. Quality analysts or team leaders often perform this role. When listening to agent calls, they score those calls against a template of key call behaviors. We discuss this role in Chapter 3.

In measuring customer satisfaction, many call centers rely on two methods:

✔ Team-leader or quality-assurance-team assessments of agent calls

✔ Customer-satisfaction surveys

We discuss both methods in the following sections.

Assessments of agent calls

You've probably heard the recorded message "This call may be monitored for quality purposes." That recording refers to this process.

This type of assessment (or *call monitoring*) involves a couple of challenges:

- ✔ **Volume:** Team leaders can't possibly assess enough calls to get an accurate view of call quality. In most operations, team leaders may listen to only three to five calls for each agent every month.

- ✔ **Subjectivity:** Even if team leaders could listen to enough calls, their assessments of the quality of these calls usually are based on subjective ideas of what makes a good call. You can't easily get two managers to agree on these criteria. Only the customers know whether they were happy with their call experiences.

  Many large companies have a team dedicated to quality-assurance monitoring to ensure that the calls are heard and that the scoring process is followed uniformly.

Customer-satisfaction surveys

Many companies conduct these surveys annually, but more sophisticated companies conduct them quarterly or even monthly (using different customers each month). Standard questions include evaluating speed of answer, agent knowledge, agent style and attitude, and possibly loyalty measures such as these:

- ✔ Will you continue to buy from us?
- ✔ Will you buy additional products or services?
- ✔ Will you recommend us to others?

Call monitoring and scoring can help agents meet and correct basic service standards (such as using the proper greeting or delivering the company's privacy statement), but you really need to survey customers first to determine what's important to them. Saying the customer's name three times, as some quality-assurance score sheets require, may not be as important as giving the customer a quick, courteous answer and allowing her to get off the phone and get on with her life. The customer rules. Long live the customer!

Company and call center policies and procedures

The drivers discussed in this chapter aren't the only ones that influence your operation. A large part of your business analyst's job involves figuring out how to identify and manipulate all the drivers of call center performance.

Your management team can control and improve performance drivers throughout the operation and improve agents' ability to apply their skills and knowledge. Create detailed documentation of company policies and procedures — right down to how processes work. If you have well-documented processes, when you want to review a process, you don't have to spend a lot of time researching it. In fact, the act of documenting a work process can help improve everyone's understanding of how to do it. While you lay out a work process on paper (or in a word processor file), you or others may look at it and say, "Wow, that doesn't make any sense!" Then you can change the process for the better. You can find a lot more about process management in Chapter 15.

Also, have a strong coaching culture (see Chapter 13) to help both new hires and existing agents achieve the skills they need to create a memorable customer experience. Your agents must be able to coordinate all the tasks they have to perform and what they need to say, making the interaction feel like a natural conversation with the customer. The customer should feel that the experience both met his needs and provided other options that he hadn't even thought about. Coaching has been shown to be the best strategy for achieving this goal.

Setting Performance Targets

People work better when they have specific performance targets. Unfortunately, many call center operations generally set unrealistic performance targets (or none at all), probably because it's not easy to set them effectively. You can easily say, "Tomorrow, I want you to answer 25 calls and make all the customers happy," but knowing whether those targets can be achieved effectively is another matter.

First, you have to figure out the right thing to target; then you have to determine what level of performance to expect for that target.

If you set a target that's too low, your operation underachieves. If you set a target that's too high, you frustrate the people in your operation.

Targets for accessibility/service level

Sorting out this mess and selecting the perfect performance targets can be difficult. The following sections give you methods that you can use to set performance targets specifically for service level.

Do what everyone else does

The default level of service for answering phone calls tends to be 80/20 — which means that 80 percent of calls are answered or hung up in 20 seconds or less. In most operations, this service level results in a relatively short average wait time for customers (8 to 18 seconds), and most customers hang in there for that long.

Although 80/20 is good enough for many operations, the wait time on the other side of the 80 in 80/20 (meaning the 20 percent of people who wait more than 20 seconds) can be a long time — one or two minutes, or even longer. A person who's calling to claim her lottery winnings probably wouldn't mind, but the guy who calls because his television set stopped working three minutes before the big game probably wouldn't be satisfied.

Go with your industry's direction

Several industries are self-regulated, or even government-regulated, in terms of how fast call centers must answer the phone. Utilities such as electricity providers come to mind; many have penalties for long answer times. The government regulates these companies' service levels so that consumers can get access to these essential services.

Develop a business case

Do a cost–benefit analysis to determine your service-level goal. Work out the cost of providing faster service through a broad range of service levels: 50/20, 60/20, 70/20, 80/20, 85/20, 90/20 . . . you get the idea.

Next, work out the benefits of providing faster service:

- More customers get through to your call center (meaning that they don't hang up and call the competition).

- When customers do get through, they aren't grumpy from long waits.

- Your agents aren't fraying at the edges from taking one call after another for eight hours (so they don't call in sick or take extra breathers between calls).

- You aren't paying additional toll-free (800-line) costs for your customers to listen to a repeating loop of elevator music.

Beyond an optimal point, providing faster service doesn't lead to higher customer satisfaction or more revenue. Work with your business analyst to determine what your optimal point is, and don't spend more than you need to.

In Table 6-3, we illustrate a simple analysis that you can use to determine your ideal service level.

Table 6-3			Analysis of Service-Level Targets			
Service Level	Staffing Cost	Abandonment Rate	Lost Revenue	800-Line-Delay Cost	Incremental Benefit	Incremental Cost
50/20	$200,000	18%	$180,000	$2,100	N/A	N/A
60/20	$220,000	12%	$120,000	$1,733	$60,367	$20,000
70/20	$244,000	8%	$80,000	$1,281	$40,452	$24,000
80/20	$270,000	5%	$50,000	$851	$30,430	$26,000
85/20	$290,000	3%	$30,000	$508	$20,343	$20,000
90/20	$320,000	2%	$20,000	$336	$10,172	$30,000

Here's an explanation of the information in the table, column by column:

✔ **Staffing cost:** To increase service level, you need more agents on the phone, so staffing costs rise.

✔ **Abandonment rate:** This measure decreases when you have increased service level because customers don't hang up due to a long delay.

✔ **Lost revenue:** Fewer lost customers mean less lost revenue.

✔ **800-line-delay cost:** Because agents are answering calls more quickly, customer wait time decreases, so your toll-free telephone costs decrease.

✔ **Incremental benefit:** This measure combines the incremental lost revenue and incremental 800-line-delay costs that you avoid.

✔ **Incremental cost:** This measure represents the staffing cost associated with raising your service-level objective.

The first two rows of figures in Table 6-3, for example, represent a change of your service-level objective from 50/20 to 60/20:

✔ Staffing costs go from $200,000 to $220,000, for an incremental cost of $20,000.

✔ Lost revenue (because customers abandoned calls) goes from $180,000 to $120,000, for an incremental benefit of $60,000, and the 800-line-delay costs decrease from $2,100 to $1,733, for an incremental benefit of $367. Totaling these benefits gives you a total incremental benefit of $60,367.

Analysis, then, involves finding that sweet spot where the incremental benefit starts to exceed the incremental cost.

Targets for call length

Call center mystics, gurus, and shamans have posed this question for eons: "What's the correct benchmark for average call length?"

Honestly, we don't know. You can't know! *Way* too many variables, all of which are changing all the time, go into determining call length. Here are a few to consider:

- ✔ Product complexity
- ✔ System capabilities
- ✔ Responsiveness
- ✔ Availability
- ✔ Working environment
- ✔ Temperature
- ✔ Noise level
- ✔ Training
- ✔ Competitive environment
- ✔ Policies and procedures
- ✔ Work distractions

All these variables, and many more, affect call length. Add the individual difference that each of your call center agents brings to the situation, and you have a very complicated process. Identifying the one *right* call length is nearly impossible.

What you can — and should — do is try to understand as much as possible about your own call center's call lengths (or, more accurately, the call lengths for each of the call center's campaigns). You should also attempt to make call length as consistent as possible.

Tracking variations

Consider what would happen if your call center produced exactly the same call length day after day, and every agent produced the same call length as the others day after day. Then you could be fairly certain that the call length produced was the product of your defined work processes. You'd be certain that all agents were following the same processes day in and day out. Then you could experiment with making changes in the work processes and measure the effect of those changes on the resulting call length. This experimentation could give you a great deal of control of call length, which would greatly simplify the task of making improvements.

Unfortunately, your call center and its employees can't behave that consistently. Most call centers see a great deal of variation in call length from one agent to another. Day after day — often, even hour after hour — your call center produces very different call lengths, making planning and process improvements difficult.

Using variation analysis

To find the outliers (or underperforming agents), follow these steps:

1. **Plot whatever you want to analyze (usually, one of the drivers) on a control chart.**

   A *control chart* is a specific kind of run chart that allows you to differentiate significant change from the natural variability of the process.

   Figure 6-3 shows a control chart of average handle time.

2. **Identify those agents who are *out of band* — the ones who are above the top acceptable limit or below the bottom acceptable limit.**

   Make this determination by choosing a percentage of variance above and below your group average.

3. **Target those agents for coaching and follow-up.**

To perform your actual analysis of what behaviors or skill gaps are causing the variances, follow these steps:

1. **Look for differences.**

   What causes these agents to be statistical anomalies for this driver (metric)?

2. **Act on the differences.**

   You have the following options:

   - If the differences are better than the average, use them to inspire other members of the team to perform the same way.
   - If the differences are worse than the average, work with the individual agents to correct skill or behavior gaps.

   The overall goals of this analysis are to reduce variation and increase your understanding of what creates performance variance.

Note: Use this approach with all agent metrics, including FCR and conversion rate — not just call length.

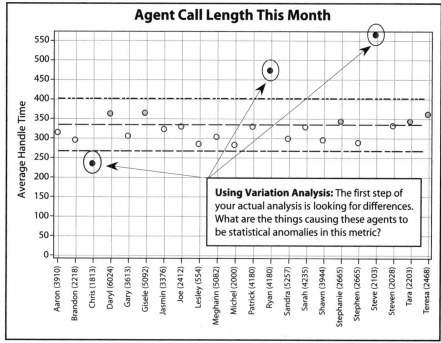

Agent Call Length This Month

Using Variation Analysis: The first step of your actual analysis is looking for differences. What are the things causing these agents to be statistical anomalies in this metric?

Figure 6-3:
The con-
trol chart
illustrates
variation in
agent per-
formance.

For planning purposes, such as scheduling resources or creating your budget, simply use your call center's historical average call length. In Chapter 7, we provide details on how to do long-range workforce planning.

To increase consistency and to help your call center reach its performance targets, use a process of variation analysis, performance diagnostics, and corrective measures to identify exceptions in overall operation performance and individual agent performance.

If you feel that your call center needs a specific target for call length, try using the top or bottom acceptable level. If your target for call length is 300 seconds, for example, and you choose a margin of 10 seconds because most agents (say, for example, 84 percent) achieve this target, your acceptable top limit for call length will be 310 seconds. For some metrics, you may use a lower accept-able limit. An example is *sales conversion* — the number of calls on which an agent make a sales attempt and closes the sale. If your agents close sales on three out of ten calls, your conversion rate is 30 percent. If you allow a margin of 5 percent for conversion, you have a bottom control limit of 25 percent for conversion. Make sure that you've established these limits over a reasonably long period — say, 90 days. Incremental improvements in performance can help you reach your targets.

If something of consequence changes in your call center and affects call length, the control limits change, and so should the targets — the top and bottom acceptable levels of performance that most people achieve. Many people who don't achieve the bottom limit fall just below it. Because the top or bottom limit is based on performance that the staff actually achieves, it gives you a reasonable minimum target. Through coaching (see Chapter 13), you can motivate agents who are just shy of the bottom limit to improve their performance to at least the minimum standard.

Operationally, track the daily average call length on a run chart (see the sidebar "Running with run charts," earlier in this chapter), along with the top and bottom limits at plus and minus one standard deviation, as Figure 6-4 illustrates. You want to control the metric, so dive into the exceptions — where the metric is exceptionally high or low, or where variation is greatest — to see what happened and why.

For more information about this type of calculation, see *Statistics For Dummies*, by Deborah Rumsey (Wiley).

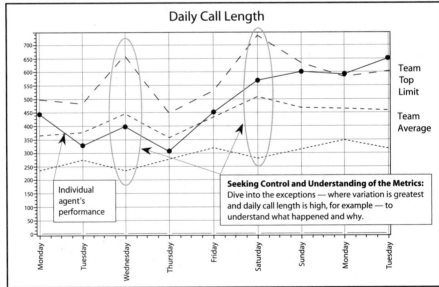

Figure 6-4: The run chart illustrates trends in variation.

If you notice that during a particular week, call lengths increased significantly compared with previous weeks, you can look for the reason behind that increase. Maybe you had a bunch of new hires on the phones that week, the computer systems were slow, or you had a complicated billing problem that affected a lot of customers.

Whatever the case, this analysis can help you understand and quantify the effects of events, and you may be able to use the analysis to justify changing the way your company works.

Targets for occupancy

Occupancy can be a tough performance measure to get a handle on, but you need to consider it because it's a key contributor to your productivity and costs. Much debate exists among call center professionals about how to target and manage occupancy. Some people incorrectly believe that you simply need a good service-level target and that by achieving your service-level target, you maximize opportunity. If you have a well-thought-out service-level target — which includes a solid cost–benefit analysis — you can run your operation effectively and efficiently by achieving a consistent service level as close to the goal as possible.

When your actual service level is too far above the target, it costs you too much in labor; if it's too far below the target, it costs you customer satisfaction, revenue, and more. You achieve cost control when service level is right on target.

You want to maximize the occupancy that you achieve while reaching your target service level. You can reach this goal primarily through better scheduling. The more closely you can match the number of agents scheduled to the actual call load requirements, the fewer periods of understaffing or overstaffing you experience.

Figure 6-5 and Figure 6-6 illustrate two ways — one bad and one good — to achieve an 80/20 service level.

Note: For ease of charting, we show time based on a 24-hour clock.

In the scenarios illustrated in these charts, at the end of the day, the call center has achieved the target service level of 80/20 (80 percent of calls answered or abandoned in 20 seconds or less):

✔ **Ineffective:** In Figure 6-5, the call center achieved a very high service level (approaching 100 percent) for 80 percent of the day, but it had a dreadful service level for the remainder of the day. In this case, occupancy would be very low for that first 80 percent of the day because the call center was way overstaffed during that time.

✔ **Effective:** In Figure 6-6, on the other hand, the call center met the service-level target by having an appropriate number of agents on the phones throughout the day, thereby maintaining much higher occupancy.

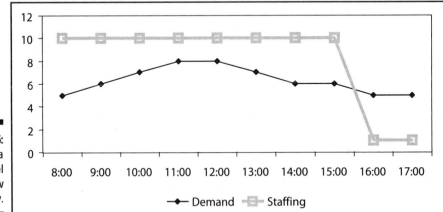

Figure 6-5:
Hitting a
service level
with low
occupancy.

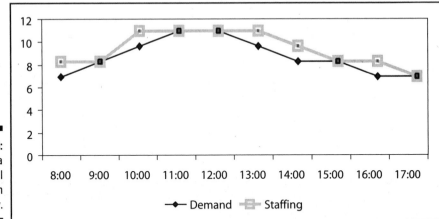

Figure 6-6:
Hitting a
service level
with high
occupancy.

Chapter 7

Right People, Right Place, Right Time: Resource Management

*I*f you're in the resource or scheduling department, you have to ensure that your call center has the right people, tools, and equipment in the right places and at the right times to support the service, revenue, and efficiency objectives of the call center, as directed by senior management. A basic understanding of simple math can help you get the job done, but with the additional knowledge of just a few key concepts and processes, you can become a call center resource management genius.

Understanding Resource Management Tasks and Concepts

The following sections provide an overview of the key concepts and tools used in call center resource management and their importance to scheduling.

Forecasting

Similar to forecasting the weather (but, we hope, more accurate), *forecasting* in call centers refers to predicting the future — specifically, how much work your center is going to have.

The key is determining your workload accurately so that you can match available resources to demand. You also have to forecast how much of different types of work you'll get and how long the work will take to do (because different types of work take different amounts of time).

Don't assume that processing calls (or e-mails) always takes the same amount of time. A very simple customer inquiry is likely to take much less time to process, on average, than a complicated, high-level technical support call. Contact length fluctuates over time, as does call volume.

Scheduling

Scheduling is the process of assigning resources to meet your demand. Whereas forecasting provides the "how much" of resource management, scheduling provides the who, what, where, and when. We talk about scheduling in Chapter 8.

Full-time equivalent

Full-time equivalent (FTE) refers to the amount of time that one full-time employee works in one day. You express staffing requirements in terms of the number of people working full-time hours. In Réal's company, in one day, one FTE equals 7.5 paid hours. (Your company may have a slightly different FTE, such as 7 or 8.) Using Réal's company as an example, if call demand required 750 total paid hours to get the work done for a day, that demand would equate to 100 FTEs (750 ÷ 7.5).

Because not all your agents work full time, you usually need more actual staff members scheduled than the number of FTEs you plan for.

Real-time management of resources

As the name suggests, *real-time resource management* refers to the process of managing call center resources immediately. We provide a more detailed explanation in Chapter 8. In essence, this term refers to making the necessary ongoing changes in your original schedule (based on real-life, up-to-the-minute changes in call volume and staff availability) so that your call center achieves the best possible results each day.

Forecasting: Timing Is Everything

Resource management is a lot easier than people make it out to be. The math is straightforward, and you can do projections for items such as department budgets and staffing requirements without using complicated scheduling systems.

 Determining how many resources your call center needs depends a great deal on the time frame in question. When it comes to forecasting, this task is done continually. Start with an annual forecast and then hone it on a quarterly basis, incorporating changes in the quarterly forecasted call volume. These changes may increase or decrease your call volume. An increase in calls may be due to a new promotion, and a decrease could occur because of a delay in communicating a promotion.

Long term: Setting budget and capital projections

Do long-term planning for requirements that expand beyond three months, up to a couple of years. In this phase, you forecast the demand on your call center and project the overall resources that you'll require: how many people and desks you'll need, how large the phone system has to be, how much data access you'll require, and so on.

You use this forecasted information to develop *operating budgets* (how much money you need to spend to run the call center) and *capital budgets* (how much money you need to spend to build the call center).

Midterm: Creating the schedules

In the long-term projection, you determine how many people and desks you need; the midterm scheduling projection tells you when you need to use those people and equipment.

Try to create a schedule over a period that ranges from three months to one year — however long you think your schedules can reliably last. Some operations have schedules that last a few weeks at most, but others can keep a schedule together for a year or more.

During the midterm scheduling phase, you attach names to schedules so that you know (generally) who's going to work when.

Short term: Making adjustments

From the time you plan a schedule to the actual day of handling the calls, changes can occur. You often have to deal with changes in caller demand and changes in the availability of staffing. In short-term projections, which you generally do approximately one week out, you adjust your schedules to accommodate any recent changes in demand or staffing availability.

Tracking forecast accuracy

You can easily track forecast accuracy by using what we call *absolute forecast variance*. The word *absolute* means that the result contains no negative numbers. When you calculate how inaccurate your forecast was, you always express the error in positive numbers because over time, tracking both positive and negative errors results in one canceling the other out, making your overall forecast appear to be more accurate than it really is.

Tracking variance with positive and negative numbers

If you're using positive and negative numbers to track how accurate your forecasts are, your forecast variance uses this formula (always making the result a positive number):

Variance = Actual calls – Forecasted calls

Suppose that you have these values for Day 1:

- **Forecast:** 10,000 calls
- **Actual:** 20,000 calls
- **Variance:** 10,000 calls (20,000 – 10,000)

Day 2 has these values:

- **Forecast:** 20,000 calls
- **Actual:** 10,000 calls
- **Variance:** –10,000 calls (10,000 – 20,000)

You get 0 when you add the variance for Day 1 and Day 2 — 10,000 + (–10,000) — so the total forecast looks entirely accurate, even though the forecast was very wrong on both days.

Tracking accuracy with absolute forecast variance

Variance tracking, which uses only positive numbers, provides a realistic picture of how inaccurate forecasts are.

Using only positive numbers, you'd change the Day 2 results in the example in the preceding section to 10,000 calls, and you'd calculate the total variance by adding the two days' variance amounts (10,000 calls + 10,000 calls = 20,000 calls).

With this information, you can calculate the error percentage by using this formula:

Error percentage = Total variance ÷ Total actual calls

So in this example, you get

Error percentage = 20,000 ÷ (20,000 + 10,000) = 0.67 (67 percent)

This calculation process does away with negative numbers to show the total error in a daily forecast. It more accurately shows how good your forecast is, compared with the approach that uses both positive and negative numbers.

Your forecaster should do this type of analysis for monthly, daily, and half-hourly calls and forecasts. Then you can use this information to reduce error to the smallest possible margin. Some forecasters use two or three different methods before they settle on the most accurate method to do their call-volume forecasting.

Using the Tools of the Scheduling Trade

In Chapter 8, we focus on the guts of doing the scheduling job — a job that can involve a lot of work, especially in large call centers. Fortunately, many tools are available (some of which we outline in the following sections) that automate the scheduling function. Although these tools can help you schedule, we believe that good schedulers should understand how basic scheduling works and know how to do it the old-fashioned way — with paper, pencil, a calculator, and maybe an Erlang table or calculator (see the following section).

Calculating with Erlang C

Erlang C is a mathematical formula that helps you determine how many call center agents you need to meet forecasted demand. We'll spare you the actual formula, but it takes into consideration the expected call volume, call length, and desired service level to calculate the number of people required on the phones. In essence, it calculates the occupancy (as defined in Chapter 6) of your agents so that you don't have to estimate the level of occupancy in any half-hour period.

We don't provide the Erlang C formula in this book, but you can find Erlang C calculators and tables on the Internet.

Planning with spreadsheets

Spreadsheets may just be the best tools ever created for the call center, and they're probably the most frequently used. A lot of scheduling systems are either professionally or home-built spreadsheet programs.

You or your scheduler can easily manage the graphs and charts that we show throughout Chapter 8 by using a simple spreadsheet program.

Using workforce management software

If you have a very large call center, which makes manual scheduling a significant challenge, you're in luck: The workforce-management-software business for call centers is alive and well. A large number of workforce management systems and providers exist (see Chapter 9), and many of them are very good.

The value of these systems is in the process of forecasting, not in the tools themselves. A great tool used by someone who lacks this knowledge doesn't do much good, but a person who has forecasting expertise can make a great tool sing.

Scheduling the Work That Your Call Center Needs to Do

Long before you create staff schedules, you need to figure out how much work the call center needs to do. The first step of the scheduling process (which we talk about in Chapter 8) is forecasting the number of contacts expected and the time required to handle those contacts for a given period (*workload demand*).

Call centers use different forecasting methods, ranging from simple to painfully complex. When forecasting, you have to forecast both the volume of calls (and e-mails, and so on) and their length, or *processing time*. When you consider these factors together, you can arrive at a forecasted demand of workload by using the following formula:

$$\text{Workload (or call load)} = \text{Call volume} \times \text{Average call length}$$

A 5 percent increase in call length has the same effect on staffing demand as a 5 percent increase in call volume.

Before you finish your forecasting activity, you need to forecast the entire planning range — from long-term budgeting right down to the half-hour-interval level (next Tuesday from 2:30 to 3 p.m., for example).

Call volume versus call load

Newcomers to call center resource management concepts often wrongly equate the amount of work to be done with call volume. This analogy explains the difference.

Imagine that you work for a company that distributes bricks. Big trucks drop off a lot of bricks that you sort and load onto smaller trucks to be shipped out to construction sites for homes, schools, hospitals, and so on. Assume that you're the team leader in charge. You know that on a particular day, your team is going to handle a total volume of 10,000 bricks. Being a good team leader, you also know that your brick distribution agents (your staff) can carry 1,000 pounds of bricks per day on average. So how many agents do you need to schedule for the day?

If you said 10 agents, guess again. You can't know because you haven't been given enough information! To determine how many staff members you need, you have to account for the weight of the bricks. Think about it: If each brick weighs 1 pound, you'll have 10,000 pounds of *load* (volume = 10,000 bricks; average brick weight = 1 pound), meaning that you indeed require 10 staff members (carrying 1,000 pounds each).

If the bricks weigh 15 pounds each, your load is 150,000 pounds, and you're going to need to call some folks in for overtime.

Determining workload in the call center is essentially the same. It's not enough simply to forecast how many calls you're going to receive. You also need to know the weight of each call — or, more accurately, the load of each individual call. The *load* of an individual call is just the average time it takes to complete a call.

So overall workload in the call center equals call volume multiplied by average call length, and you need that information to really begin the process of forecasting staff.

Starting long: The first step in forecasting call volume

One approach to forecasting involves starting with the long-term forecast and working down to the interval level. What this means is that you can forecast the number of calls you might expect down to intervals of 30 minutes or even 15 minutes.

Consider the demand that you had last year. If your call center took 1,638,000 calls last year, and you have no reason to believe that this business level will change, last year's volume is a good starting place.

You can add a little insight to this forecast if you consider the trend year after year. If volume of work has increased by 10 percent every year for the past 10 years, you can probably assume that volume will increase this year by 10 percent.

Alternatively, you can calculate the volume of calls that you receive per customer. If you've consistently received two calls per customer over the past several years, and you know that your customer base is increasing, increase your demand forecast by the expected customer base increase.

Here's the formula for calculating forecasted demand:

Forecasted demand = Contacts per customer × Customer base expected

If you know about something that may materially change your volume of work, such as a new product line or a bankruptcy, make the assumption that you will get more calls, and add a percentage of extra calls into your forecast.

Breaking the forecast into intervals

A long-term forecast usually covers a year, but the specific dynamics of your situation dictate the length of your long-term forecast. Whatever period of time the forecast covers, after you make a long-term forecast, break it down into months, weeks, days, and half-hour intervals. To do these *breakdown forecasts,* which are simply the volume of calls for any period of time expressed as a percentage, you can use historical calling patterns.

Typical breakdown intervals include

- Monthly percentage of a year
- Daily percentage of a week
- Half-hourly (or hourly) percentage of a day

Table 7-1 shows an example monthly percentage breakdown of call distribution, based on the actual call volumes from the preceding year. You base the current year's call volume forecast on these kinds of percentages.

Table 7-1 Monthly Percentage Distributions from Preceding Year

Month	Preceding Year's Call Volume	Percentage of Year
January	150,000	9.16
February	145,000	8.85
March	148,000	9.04
April	135,000	8.24
May	130,000	7.94
June	120,000	7.33
July	110,000	6.72
August	105,000	6.41
September	150,000	9.16
October	135,000	8.24
November	140,000	8.55
December	170,000	10.38
Total	**1,638,000**	**100**

The data in Table 7-1 contains the total call volume by month for the entire year. The far-right column (Percentage of Year) is a calculation of each month's percentage of total annual call volume. The call volume — and the corresponding monthly percentage — decreased from June to August. The retail industry commonly sees this type of call pattern because fewer customers tend to call for sales or service inquiries during the summer months. The call volume increases in September (9.16 percent of the total year's volume), when customers get back to school and business, and again in December (10.38 percent), because people are calling to do their Christmas shopping.

Ideally, you calculate the monthly percentage by using several years' worth of monthly call volume. If you know that your business is going to increase by 10 percent next year and that call volume will increase with the business, creating your forecast is as simple as increasing last year's call volume by 10 percent and then multiplying the new total call volume by the monthly percentages.

After calculating the percentage of volume by period (month, week, and day), you can graph the pattern, as shown in Figure 7-1, and look for any trends.

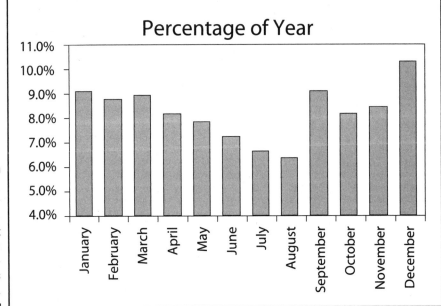

The call center depicted in Figure 7-1 is fairly busy during the winter months, gets slower in the summer, has a busy spike in September, and reaches its peak in December. These trends make sense if this call center is in the retail industry. Winter is working time for most people; vacations and breaks from school happen in the summer, September is a time of return to work or school for many people, and December is the busiest retail period of the year.

To make a forecast based on last year's results, assuming that this year's call volume will increase by 10 percent, use this formula:

Forecasted volume for this year = (Last year's volume × 0.1) + Last year's volume

In the example from Table 7-1, you calculate

Forecasted volume for this year = (1,638,000 × 0.1) + 1,638,000 = 1,801,800

So the call center has a forecast for this year of 1,801,800 calls.

If you want a forecast for the call volume of a month in this year, you use this formula:

Forecasted monthly call volume = Forecasted annual call volume × Month's historical percentage

To calculate the forecast for January for the call center in Table 7-1, you plug those values into the formula:

Forecasted monthly call volume = 1,801,800 × 0.0916 = 165,045

So the forecasted total call volume for this January is 165,045 calls.

Next, you need to determine the distribution of work over days of the week and hours of the day, following the same process of reviewing historical patterns.

When you look at trends that repeat, you can predict with some confidence that they will occur again. Update these relationships continually. Generally, the more data you use — that is, the larger the time frames, which means the broader the overview — you will be able to create a forecast with greater accuracy.

Suppose that the question you're trying to answer is "How many calls should we expect from 2 to 2:30 p.m. on Wednesdays in March if we're forecasting 1,801,800 calls for the year?" Use this formula:

Forecasted calls from 2 to 2:30 p.m. on Wednesdays in March = ([Annual forecast × Month percentage of the year] ÷ Days in month) × Active call center days in week × Day percentage of the week × Time span percentage of the day

Plug in the numbers, and you get

([1,801,800 × 0.0904) ÷ 31) × 7 × 0.16 × 0.051 = 300 calls

Following is a summary of the assumptions used:

- ✔ **This year's annual forecast:** 1,801,800 calls
- ✔ **March percentage of the year:** 9.04 percent
- ✔ **Wednesday percentage of the week:** 16 percent
- ✔ **2 to 2:30 p.m. percentage of the day:** 5.1 percent

Forecasting call length

You can use a variety of methods to forecast call length. We like to track historical call length on a half-hourly basis and use the average for a given period — such as over a rotating four-week period, as shown in Table 7-2.

Table 7-2	Tracking Average Call Length in Half-Hour Intervals				
Interval	*Week 1*	*Week 2*	*Week 3*	*Week 4*	*Average*
10:30	351	375	366	345	359
11:00	344	365	378	324	353
11:30	356	378	398	345	369
12:00	365	376	367	387	374
12:30	324	334	342	345	336
1:00	345	323	332	354	339

Accounting for unique situations

You can't always forecast future call volume predictably. Sometimes, things happen that disrupt historical patterns, and although these special situations tend to make forecasters crazy, you *can* plan for them. Simply track their impact on historical calling patterns.

Holidays, for example, disrupt historical calling patterns for most call centers. If your call center is open on Christmas Day, you probably don't get the same type of caller demand that you have on a normal workday.

A good forecaster can track the historical effect of a day such as Christmas on normal calling patterns and adjust his forecast by that effect.

Suppose that Christmas falls on a Wednesday this year. Looking at the example forecasting data in the section "Breaking the forecast into intervals," earlier in this chapter, you find

- ✔ **Forecast for the year:** 1,800,801 calls
- ✔ **December percentage:** 10.38 percent
- ✔ **Wednesday percentage:** 16 percent

This information assembles the normal forecasting data. Your forecaster knows from experience that Christmas Day has a lower call volume than a regular day; in fact, Christmas Day is only 30 percent of a normal day. So your call volume forecast for this year's Christmas Day (using the formula from the section "Breaking the forecast into intervals," earlier in this chapter, with 31 days in December and 7 days in a work week) uses this formula:

Forecasted calls for Christmas Day = ($[1,800,801 \times 0.1038] \div 31$) $\times 7 \times 0.16$ $\times 0.3 = 2,026$ calls

Now you have a forecast for Christmas Day. The forecaster may also know that call volume isn't distributed over Christmas Day in the same way that it is on other days. She would also have the historical call times for Christmas Days and use this pattern when forecasting half-hourly call volume.

You can use the same approach for other special events that disrupt normal call volume, such as holidays, storms, and promotions. Your forecaster merely tracks and applies these historical effects.

Chapter 8

Call Center Scheduling: Not As Simple As 1, 2, 3

*A*s the chapter title suggests, creating a call center schedule isn't a simple thing. It's more difficult than trying to hit a moving target. In fact, it's a little like trying to hit that moving target while you're moving, too. The mechanics don't have to be particularly complicated, however, as long as you follow a relatively specific process in your effort to ensure that you have the right people in the right place at the right time to answer all those calls.

In this chapter, we outline the typical steps of the scheduling process.

Calculating the Resources Required to Do the Job

After you forecast your call volume and average call length for each half-hour interval of the year (as we discuss in Chapter 7), determine the staffing resources that you need to handle the forecasted demand over the selected period of time so that you can develop your schedules.

Considering occupancy

The most important relationship in resource management is the one between call workload (call volume × average call length) and total staffing requirements. Not to worry — you have only to use a simple formula to determine the number of staff members you require. (We talk more about occupancy in Chapter 6.)

The formula to calculate staffing, although simple, is very important:

> Staffing required = Forecasted call volume × Forecasted call length ÷ Expected occupancy

As much as you may want (from a pure production standpoint, at least) your agents to be *occupied* — dealing with customer contacts — 100 percent of the time, you just can't make that happen. From the customer's point of view, calls are stacked up in the phone system, waiting for an agent to become available, which means lots of time spent waiting to talk to an agent. From your agents' point of view, burnout becomes an issue when there's no down-time between calls. When determining your staffing requirements, you have to account for the fact that sometimes, your agents will be idle.

After you forecast the *workload* — the total amount of time that it's going to take to handle all the calls — simply divide that number by the expected occupancy to determine the amount of staff time for which you need to schedule.

Busy versus idle time

Suppose that you forecast 150 hours of work-load for the day, meaning that you're expecting 150 hours of calls. Your expected occupancy is 75 percent, meaning that your agents, on average, will be idle 25 percent of the time they're on the phones. The number of staff hours required to handle this load is 150 hours of load divided by 75 percent occupancy, which equals 200 hours.

Confused? Look at the equation the other way around. If you had 200 hours of agents staffing the phones, and they were occupied 75 percent of the time, this equation would tell you how many hours they were occupied:

> 0.75×200 on-the-phone hours = 150 hours of occupied time

In other words, agents were busy actually working for 150 hours.

Calculating expected occupancy

To calculate your staffing requirements, you have to know your expected occupancy.

You can figure out expected occupancy in a couple of ways: You can look at the history of your operation and establish approximate benchmarks for occupancy, or you can calculate it by using a formula. We outline both of these approaches in this section.

For an established call center, you can most easily look at the occupancy that your operation typically achieves at any time when it's hitting the accessibility/service-level target. If your call center typically achieves a monthly occupancy of 74 percent when making its service-level targets, for example, 74 percent is a fair expected occupancy for the month.

In busier months, expected occupancy will be higher, and in slower months, it'll be lower. The difference isn't going to be dramatic, so don't get too worked up about it; just keep an eye on the trend so that you can collect information on it and adjust your staffing in the future.

Also, be a bit careful about the time frames you're using when working with expected occupancy. Occupancy fluctuates throughout the day. As we explain in Chapter 6, occupancy varies with demand, and because call volume fluctuates throughout the day, occupancy also fluctuates, which creates a range of expected occupancies. The good news is that monthly and daily occupancies don't fluctuate a great deal at any given service level.

Improved scheduling can increase expected occupancy, so plan for and capture the small improvements in your expected-occupancy calculations. Even a 1 percent improvement in expected occupancy can produce significant cost savings.

Another way to calculate expected occupancy is to use an Erlang C table (which we mention in Chapter 7) to calculate optimal occupancy for every hour or half hour of the day. Then you multiply the optimal occupancy that you calculate with Erlang C by your historical scheduling efficiency.

Alternatively, you can buy a good workforce management system and let it work out expected occupancy for you. While you're allowing this tool to do its job, make sure that you understand the difference between actual occupancy and optimal occupancy. Small improvements in actual occupancy can make a big difference in call center efficiency and cost control.

Calculating expected occupancy versus optimal occupancy

As we discuss in Chapter 6, *occupancy* is defined as the time agents are actively busy doing something (they're occupied, not idle), expressed as a percentage of the time they're logged into the phones. *Optimal occupancy* is the occupancy that a call center would achieve if it were staffed perfectly for every hour of the day. You'd have just the right number of people idle and just the right number of people working, so agents would answer calls within the service-level objective — no faster and no slower.

Call centers rarely achieve optimal occupancy while also meeting their service-level targets. More likely, they achieve a lower occupancy for several reasons:

- ✔ **Unpredictable call patterns:** Call volume doesn't always arrive exactly as expected. Even when your forecasts are very accurate, calls don't arrive exactly as you plan, creating an imbalance between actual staff scheduled and what you really need for optimal occupancy.

- ✔ **Disruptions in staffing plans:** Your staffing doesn't always work out exactly as you plan it, either. People often are late or absent, or last-minute demands such as training take agents away from their primary call-handling duties. These unexpected changes detract from your staffing plan, making it difficult to achieve optimal occupancy.

- ✔ **Inflexible workforce:** The biggest challenge in achieving optimal occupancy involves dealing with a workforce that isn't perfectly flexible. In a perfect world, your staff would come and go just when your callers come and go, which would allow the call center to meet caller demand precisely. In this wonderful world, your agents would work only when you needed them — a few minutes here, a few minutes there.

Although you *can* increase flexibility, you can't get the ideal amount of flexibility. Typically, the best you can do is come close to your call arrival patterns, staffing a little over here and a little under there, but being approximately right overall. This approach reduces the efficiency of your schedule, therefore reducing actual occupancy achieved and taking it further from your optimal occupancy. The first graph in Figure 8-1 shows a schedule in the perfect world, and the second graph illustrates a more realistic, imperfect schedule.

Note: To make charting easier, we use a 24-hour clock for time references in this chapter.

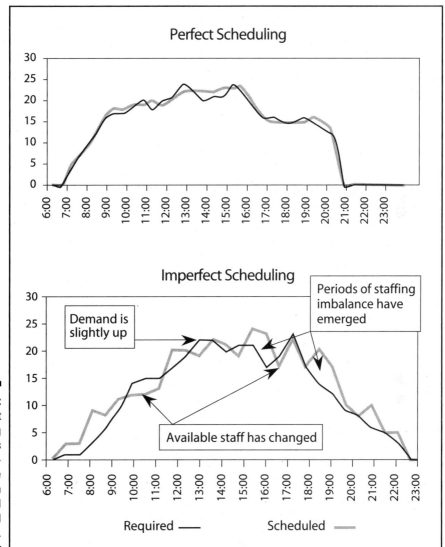

Figure 8-1: Imperfect scheduling accounts for the difference between optimal and expected occupancy.

Determining scheduling efficiency

The term *scheduling efficiency* refers to how close the call center gets to achieving optimal occupancy. If a center's optimal occupancy is 90 percent, for example, and the call center produces actual occupancy of 80 percent, its scheduling efficiency is 88.8 percent (80 percent ÷ 90 percent = 88.8 percent). About the best we see in scheduling efficiency is 92 percent.

Expected occupancy is the occupancy level that your call center expects to hit, given its existing demand and scheduling. This expectation doesn't mean that you don't want to improve and get closer to your optimal occupancy — just that you know that for the time being, you're running at 80 percent. As scheduling efficiency improves, you can adjust your scheduling efficiency forecast.

When you do this type of analysis, calculating monthly staffing requirements, you get a big-picture view of how many staff members you need, which you can use for budgeting purposes. To do this calculation, you need a forecasted call volume; a forecasted call length; and expected occupancy, which is based on your target service-level objective.

Here's an example:

- For the upcoming year, you've forecasted a 10 percent increase over last year's volume of 1,638,000 calls.

- Calls in March represent 9.04 percent of the year.

- Calls average 350 seconds in length.

- Your expected occupancy is 74 percent for the month at a service level of 80 percent in 20 seconds.

To calculate staffing requirement for one month, use this formula:

Staffing requirement for one month = (Last year's call volume + [Last year's call volume × Forecasted increase percentage]) × March percentage × Forecasted call length ÷ Seconds in one hour ÷ Expected occupancy

So for the example information in the preceding list, you get

Staffing requirement for March = (1,638,000 + [1,638,000 × 0.1]) × 0.0904 × 350 ÷ 3,600 ÷ 0.74 = 21,400 hours

To handle the forecasted call volume at the forecasted call length, you need 21,400 agent hours on the phones.

Here's a breakdown of this formula:

- **Last year's call volume + (Last year's call volume × Forecasted increase percentage):** This part of the calculation creates the new annual forecast.

- **March percentage:** Multiplying by March's percentage gives you the March forecast for next year.

- **Forecasted call length:** Multiplying by the forecasted call length determines the workload for March.

- **Seconds in one hour:** Dividing by the number of seconds in one hour expresses the workload in hours.

- **Expected occupancy:** Dividing by your expected occupancy turns the workload into total staffing requirements, in hours, for March.

Be sure to divide by 3,600 to turn the result into hours. Otherwise, you get your forecasted staff requirements in seconds (and you don't want to risk giving your schedulers heart failure when they see that number!).

Affecting occupancy

According to the immutable laws of the call center, you can affect occupancy in several ways:

- **Change how fast agents answer the phone.** Answering the phone quickly means that your agents spend more time waiting for calls. Answering quickly decreases occupancy. Answering the phone slowly means that your agents spend less time waiting for calls. In fact, the calls may be waiting for them! Answering the phone slowly increases occupancy.

- **Pool your resources.** When you increase the size of your call center (by merging sites or pooling calls from different campaigns, for example), you reduce the overall randomness of call arrivals, because callers' decisions to contact you begin to merge, and the call arrival pattern begins to smooth out. (Figure 8-2 compares call arrivals at a small center and a large one.) Because the large call center has a smaller difference between the variance in call volume compared with the average than in the small call center, it needs fewer staffing resources (as a percentage of total staff) to answer the phone quickly.

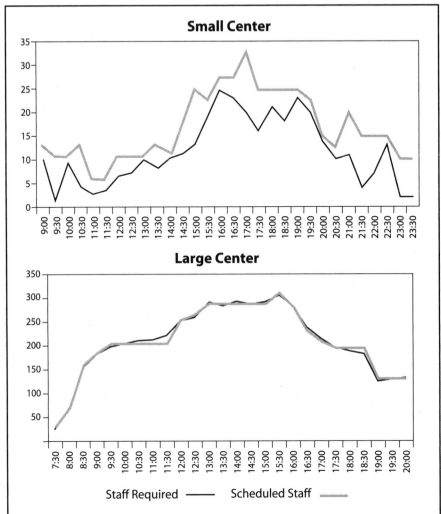

Figure 8-2:
Taking
advantage
of econo-
mies of
scale.

With a larger group of agents, your scheduling efficiency improves; the incremental staff that you need for a big call center isn't directly proportional to the increase in workload/call volume. While the operation gets bigger, you begin to realize economies of scale; the call center can answer calls with better occupancy and, therefore, at a lower cost.

To take advantage of these economies of scale, minimize the number of distinct answering groups in the call center by cross-training agents so that they can excel in several campaigns and by merging groups wherever it's possible and practical to do so.

✔ **Get better at scheduling.** If your staff schedule results in massive over-staffing for 80 percent of your operating hours and massive understaff-ing for the remaining 20 percent, overall, you have an 80 percent level of accessibility (a common target in call centers). You have a low overall occupancy, however, and 20 percent of your customers — the ones who called while you were understaffed — will be very unhappy.

✔ **Increase the flexibility of your staffing.** If you have full-time employees who start work at the same time and take breaks at the same time, your staffing won't match the way your calls arrive. You can increase your staffing flexibility by using part-time staff, varying the length of agent shifts, and using split shifts (such as agents working three hours in the morning and four hours at night). Home agents — agents who work at home (see Chapter 11) — have become popular in part because this setup gives agents more lifestyle flexibility and also helps improve occupancy.

Delivering good service costs money. Before you decide to save some costs by reducing staff and taking more time to answer the phone, check with your customers. They may have an issue with waiting 20 minutes to receive the service they're seeking.

Scheduling *close to the curve* — meaning that you match your staff schedule closely to caller demand — is a better way to achieve your accessibility target. During some times of the day, you're slightly overstaffed, and at other times, you're slightly understaffed. Overall, you still achieve 80 percent accessibility, but you have much higher occupancy, and the other 20 percent of callers probably will be less disgruntled because your agents answer their calls only slightly less quickly than the average speed of answer during the day.

The graphs in Figure 8-3 illustrate these scenarios. Both graphs show the same call arrival, and both cases achieve 80 percent accessibility, but sched-uled staff is much more in line with demand in the second chart, which increases overall occupancy.

Give 'em a break: Accounting for off-phone time

Calculating on-phone staffing requirements isn't the whole story. When people work for your company, you pay them for more than just the time they're on the phones. Your employees also get paid for training, meetings, breaks, and so on.

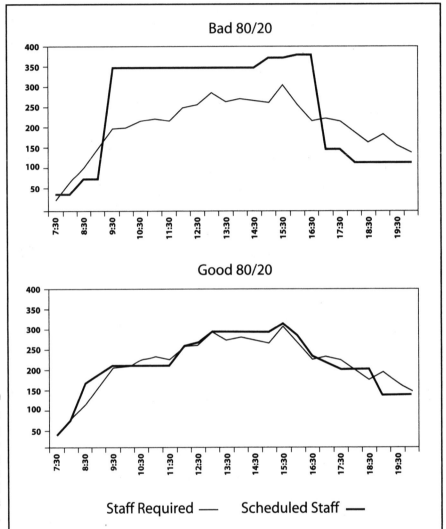

Figure 8-3:
Matching
staff sched-
ules more
closely to
demand
improves
occupancy.

You need to take *agent utilization* — a measure that tracks how much of an agent's paid time is spent processing the work — into consideration. Of the total hours that you pay your agents, what percentage of this time do they end up doing actual work — on the phones taking calls or on the computer handling customer e-mails, for example?

After you determine how much staffing you need just to handle the work, you need to think about giving those people time away for meetings, breaks, vacation, training, and the like.

If you pay an agent for 10 hours, and he spends 7 of those hours logged in working on telephone calls and 3 hours off the phone on breaks and in meetings, agent utilization is 70 percent.

Tracking, planning, and understanding historical utilization rates allow you to adjust your scheduling practices for the future. Most operations can forecast agent-utilization rates with a fair degree of accuracy.

You use a formula similar to the calculation used to account for occupancy (which we discuss in the section "Calculating expected occupancy," earlier in this chapter) to get the total paid hours required:

Paid hours requirement = Forecasted staff work hours ÷ Agent utilization

Suppose that you need 21,400 hours of staffing for March, and your forecasted agent utilization is 70 percent. You would use this formula:

Paid hours requirement = 21,400 ÷ 0.7 = 30,571 hours

So you need 30,571 hours of paid staff time to handle the forecasted calls.

After you establish the number of paid hours you need to answer the forecasted calls, you calculate the number of agents you need by using this formula:

Full-time equivalents (FTEs) required for a month = Paid time required for a month ÷ Hours per month per FTE

Now assume that a typical full-time agent in your center receives 155 paid hours per month:

FTEs required for March = 30,571 ÷ 155 = 198 FTEs (rounded up)

So you need 198 FTE agents in your office during March. (Usually, an FTE is the number of hours that a typical full-time employee works in a given period. You use this term to express staffing requirements, as we explain in Chapter 7.) You need to round up the FTEs to the nearest whole number. An FTE represents a whole person, and you generally don't schedule partial people (although you may occasionally schedule some who aren't quite all there).

Calculate the additional cost of every percentage-point decrease in your agent utilization so you understand its impact on the cost of your call center.

Just run your staffing calculations for different agent-utilization levels, and multiply each by your cost of labor (including benefits). In addition to shocking the life out of you, this information can really help you control your budget or make cost-benefit calculations.

Not long ago, Réal showed a call center director the effect of a 1 percent change in agent-utilization ratio. A 1 percent change in agent utilization was worth more than $30,000 per month to the call center. Up until that point, the center hadn't paid a great deal of attention to agent utilization. After Réal went over this number with the director, agent utilization became a hot topic in the call center and improved dramatically the very next month.

Determining When the Resources Are Required

After you figure out how much you're going to spend on staffing, you still don't know *when* those people are going to work. You have to take the forecast down to a lower level of detail to determine when your call center requires the resources — right down to the daily and half-hourly (interval) basis.

Calculating base staff requirements by half-hour intervals

Using the example from "Calculating the Resources Required to Do the Job," earlier in this chapter, calculate the staffing requirements for each interval in March to build the schedule requirement.

You use this formula:

Staff required for particular period of time = Forecasted call volume ÷ Days in month × Days in the work week × Day's percentage of the week × Interval percentage of the day × Forecasted call length ÷ Seconds per interval ÷ Expected occupancy

This information allows you to calculate the staff required:

- ✔ **Interval:** 14:00 to 14:30
- ✔ **Day of week:** Wednesday

- ✔ **Wednesday proportion of week:** 16 percent
- ✔ **Interval's proportion of day:** 5.1 percent

Plug this information into the formula:

> Staff required for 14:00 to 14:30 on Wednesday = $162,883 \div 31 \times 7 \times 0.16 \times 0.051 \times 350 \div 1,800 \div 0.77 = 76$ employees (rounded up)

So you need 76 agents on the phones from 14:00 to 14:30 (2:00 to 2:30 p.m.) on Wednesdays in March.

Here's a breakdown of this calculation:

- ✔ **March's forecasted call volume:** You take last year's volume, increase it by 10 percent, and multiply by March's historical proportion of the year (9.04 percent).

- ✔ **Call volume for the average week of the month:** Divide the monthly call volume forecast by the number of days in the month to get the average daily call volume; then multiply by the number of working days in the week.

  In this example, we divide March's forecasted call volume by 31 (because March has 31 days) and then multiply by 7 (the number of working days per week for this call center). This calculation expresses the monthly volume in terms of one week of the month, making it easy to calculate Wednesday's forecast simply by multiplying the weekly forecast by 16 percent (Wednesday's proportion of the week) — giving you 5,885 calls.

- ✔ **Forecasted interval call volume:** Multiply 5,885 calls by the time interval percentage (5.1 percent) to arrive at the forecasted interval call volume — 300 calls.

- ✔ **Staffing workload requirement:** Multiply 300 calls by the average call length of 350 seconds to get an overall staffing workload requirement of 105,000 seconds.

- ✔ **Workload by the half-hour:** To determine how many staff you need to handle the work in a half-hour interval, divide 105,000 seconds by 1,800 (the number of seconds in a half hour) to determine staff required on the phones, which gives you 58.33.

- ✔ **Factor in occupancy:** Based on the volume expected from 14:00 to 14:30, the call center will be near its peak, resulting in higher occupancy than average — around 77 percent. Divide the occupied staff requirement by your 77 percent expected occupancy, and you see that you need 75.75 total staff on the phones. Rounding this number up (unless you have three quarters of a person somewhere on staff) means that you need to schedule for 76 agents during the interval 14:00 to 14:30 on Wednesdays in March this year.

Now just go back and do this calculation for every half-hour period of the month (and year) to determine your staffing pattern. We help get you started with an example in Table 8-1, which calculates staff requirements by interval for all of Wednesday. Figure 8-4 charts the result.

Table 8-1	Calculating Base Staff Required by Half-Hour Interval			
Interval	*Call Volume*	*Call Length*	*Expected Occupancy*	*Staffing Required*
8:00	81	355	68%	24
8:30	115	357	72%	32
9:00	185	360	75%	49
9:30	265	357	76%	69
10:00	300	365	77%	79
10:30	323	367	77%	86
11:00	312	355	77%	80
11:30	300	352	77%	76
12:00	265	349	75%	68
12:30	277	376	77%	75
13:00	312	371	77%	84
13:30	312	368	77%	82
14:00	300	350	76%	76
14:30	277	354	76%	72
15:00	277	349	76%	71
15:30	265	343	75%	67
16:00	254	341	76%	64
16:30	242	338	76%	60
17:00	231	339	75%	58
17:30	196	343	74%	51
18:00	185	340	74%	47
18:30	173	335	74%	44
19:00	162	333	73%	41
19:30	138	329	72%	35
20:00	81	331	66%	22
20:30	58	335	65%	16

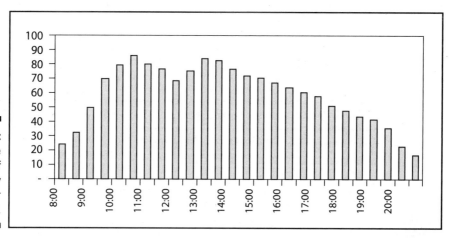

Figure 8-4:
The base
staff
required by
half-hour
interval.

Adding in the off-phone requirements

After you determine the forecasted number of staff you need on the phones for each half-hour interval of the day, you need to layer in the staffing requirements for nonphone needs, such as breaks, training, meetings, sick leave, and vacation.

First, determine what percentage of your staffing goes to each of these activities. You can use historical averages or estimate what you need. You can't exactly predict some items, such as sick leave, so you need to allow for them as percentages based on historical averages. You can plan other items, such as meetings, around peak periods.

Table 8-2 shows Wednesday's staffing requirements from the calculation of staff required for a half-hour interval (refer to Table 8-1), with off-phone allowances considered. Therefore, this table provides actual total staffing requirements for each interval of the day. The resulting chart is illustrated in Figure 8-5.

To calculate the staff required to handle calls, you use the process that we explain in the preceding section. (You can see the numbers in Table 8-1.)

Table 8-2 Calculating Total Staff Required by Half-Hour Intervals

Interval	Staff Required to Handle Calls	Sick Leave	Breaks	Meetings	Total Staffing Requirement
8:00	24	2			26
8:30	32	2			34
9:00	49	3	30		82
9:30	69	4	30		103
10:00	79	5	5		88
10:30	86	5	21		112
11:00	80	5	20		105
11:30	76	5	19		100
12:00	68	5	17		90
12:30	75	5	19		99
13:00	84	5	21		110
13:30	82	5	21		108
14:00	76	5	19		100
14:30	72	5	18	10	105
15:00	71	5	18	10	104
15:30	67	5	17	10	99
16:00	64	4	16	10	94
16:30	60	4	16		80
17:00	58	4	16		78
17:30	51	3	16		70
18:00	47	3	17		67
18:30	44	3	12		59
19:00	41	2	12		55
19:30	35	2	2		39
20:00	22	2			24
20:30	16	2			18

After you know how many employees you need to handle calls, use this formula to calculate total staffing required:

Total staffing requirement = Staff required to handle calls + Sick leave + Breaks + Meetings

If you plug in the information for the interval between 8:00 and 8:30, you get this calculation:

Total staffing requirement = 24 + 2 + 0 + 0 = 26 staff members

Continue this calculation for each half-hour interval of every day of every week of the month to find out how many actual bodies in seats you need to have at any point during the month. You can use this data in planning your call center's work schedules.

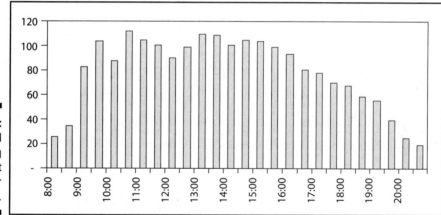

Figure 8-5:
Total staffing requirement by half-hour interval.

Don't forget shrinkage!

Did you know that 2 percent of the whiskey that's aging in kegs evaporates every year? This lost portion is frequently referred to as "the angels' share." Well, in call centers, some of your staff evaporate when they're working on the phones. Missing time comes from many sources, including breaks that go too long, extra breaks, and unplanned meetings and discussions. These situations happen, and you really can't prevent them, so plan for them. If your call center loses 5 percent of its staff's time, add that missing 5 percent back into your scheduling. Give yourself a little extra time padding so that you don't end up short-staffed.

Using your forecast to determine call center size

If you're planning to build a call center of your own (as we discuss in Chapter 4), you need a bodies-in-seats calculation (discussed in the preceding section) to determine the size of your center. Simply follow the process in the preceding section to calculate the staffing requirement for each interval of the year and then find the *peak interval* — the one that requires the highest number of staff. That number represents the maximum number of agents that you need in your center at any given time to meet your service-level targets and projected occupancy, and it tells you how many seats you need. It's a simplified method, not taking into account growth or changes in the business, but it's a first step. Then you can plan for what you believe you'll need in the future.

Scheduling Available Resources to Meet Caller Demand

After you determine the half-hourly staffing demand (which we talk about in "Determining When the Resources Are Required," earlier in this chapter), you need to plan schedules around that demand. At this point, don't worry about who, specifically, is going to work these schedules. (We go into that process in "Creating People-Friendly Schedules," later in this chapter.) Just build schedules to match staffing as closely as possible to demand.

Starting to build your schedules with full-time shifts

You can match available resources to caller demand by creating a graph that compares caller demand with total staff scheduled. In Figure 8-6, caller demand throughout the day is graphed by using the demand calculated in Table 8-2, represented by the bars.

This graph also includes scheduled shifts (the line in the graph) in an effort to match staffing with caller demand. To start building a schedule, this call center added a shift of 26 staff members working from 8:00 until 16:00.

In this figure, the staffing line isn't consistent. The chart shows that total staffing has scheduled dips at 11:00, 13:00, and 15:00. Figure 8-6 shows that this single 8-hour shift of 26 staff members can't cover the entire day's caller demand. These dips in staffing represent breaks that scheduled employees take during their day.

Not everyone takes breaks at the same time, of course, and you can stagger breaks if you want. At this point in the scheduling process, however, you're still dealing with broad strokes. When you fine-tune the schedule later, you can adjust the breaks.

Next, you need to continue to add shifts toward completing your schedule.

Figure 8-7 shows a bump of overlapping shifts in the middle of the day, from approximately 13:00 until 16:30. This bump occurs because the end of one full-time shift overlaps with the beginning of another full-time shift. As you probably can imagine, if you continued adding only full-time staff shifts, you'd likely end up with a significant amount of overstaffing — a *big* bump — in the middle of the day.

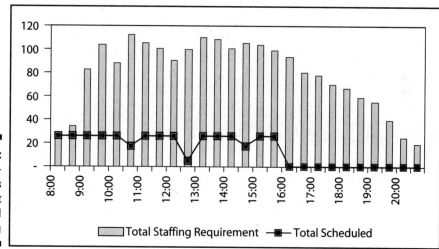

Figure 8-6: Adding full-time shifts to meet required staffing

Total Staffing Requirement   —■— Total Scheduled

If you continue adding shifts, a pattern soon emerges, as shown in Figure 8-8.

You can continue to add shifts that have different start and stop times. Aim to make the available-staffing line equal the caller-demand bars. But you can use only as many shifts as you have people to work said shifts. One shift per employee — that's it.

You're almost done; you just have to fill in the cracks. In this case, adding any more full-time shifts would create a great deal of overlap. You can accept this overlap, continuing to use full-time shifts — in which case you're probably moderately overstaffed or understaffed at various times throughout the day, which decreases the efficiency of your schedule — or you can attempt to schedule some part-time shifts in the mix, as we discuss in the following section.

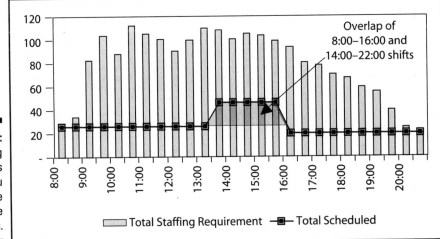

Figure 8-7: Overlapping occurs when you add more full-time shifts.

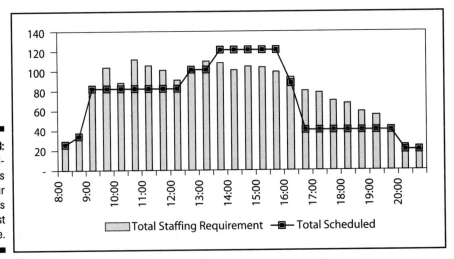

Figure 8-8: Using full-time shifts only, your schedule is almost complete.

Filling in the gaps with part-time shifts

Part-time shifts help fill the gaps in your schedule created by the overlap of full-time shifts. Figure 8-9 shows the final completed schedule for the Wednesday example from the preceding sections.

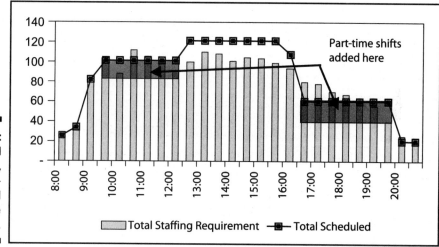

Figure 8-9: A completed schedule, using full-time and part-time shifts.

You can't make the schedule perfect — and that's okay. Ideally, you get as close to your requirement line as possible. If you have some overlap (over-staffing) during the middle of the day, you can use that time to conduct training and meetings or to assign agents to do essential nonphone work.

You can also help shore up the weak areas — where you have some under-staffing — by adjusting breaks and lunch times. Certainly, your department scheduler should make everyone aware of the weak spots in your schedule so that no one plans meetings during these times.

Part-time shifts present some problems, however. You may find managing more difficult when you have a large number of agents staffed for short shifts, and you can have problems attracting good part-time agents.

Attracting and retaining good part-timers is challenging. Compensate part-time agents at least as well as you do full-time agents on an hour-by-hour basis. The key is to ensure that you hire agents who want part-time sched-ules; otherwise, they'll find other jobs. Finding a good fit for a part-time employee's lifestyle is key, and the benefit you'll get for your efforts is increased efficiency (occupancy).

Creating a summary of schedules

When you finish creating your schedule, you actually have a bunch of shift schedules, each requiring a certain number of positions. Table 8-3 shows what the total number of schedules for the Wednesday example that we use in this chapter might look like.

Table 8-3	Shift Schedules and People Required for a Day
Schedule	**Positions**
8:00–16:00	26
8:30–16:30	8
9:00–17:00	48
13:30–21:30	20
12:30–20:30	20
9:30–13:30	20
16:00–20:00	20

After you complete Wednesday, you get to do the whole process all over again, and again, and again — for each day of the week.

Creating weekly schedules

The summary of schedules lists every schedule that you create to meet the daily demand for agents. You need to select shifts from the summary and create weekly work schedules.

A weekly work schedule includes several days' worth of shifts and days off. It's beneficial for agents to have consecutive days off (and might create a lifestyle that encourages them to remain employees for a long time).

Be sure to check that your scheduling practices meet the employment regulations of your company and your state, province, and/or country.

Weekly work schedules have more rows of shifts than the daily schedule. While you add days off to complete the schedules, you're essentially creating various five-day work weeks over the seven days, creating more rows. Use all the daily shifts created, and assign each to a weekly schedule.

Creating People-Friendly Schedules

After you create your schedule, you can attach the names of agents whom you want to work the shifts. You can most easily simply pick names and assign them to a schedule — if, that is, you really don't want people to like you.

Probably the safest (and fairest) way, especially in large call centers, is to post the schedules and allow staff members to bid on the available shifts, as we describe in the following section.

Letting agents bid for shifts

You usually determine an agent's bid priority based on seniority: The most senior agents get the highest priority. You could determine bid priority based on other criteria, such as performance: Agents who perform best over a certain period receive the highest bidding priority.

Allow the employee who has the highest bid number to pick first, and eliminate the shift that she picks so that it's not available for others. The employee with the next-highest bid number chooses next, and you continue that way until all the shifts are assigned.

Shift bids can be time-consuming. Follow these steps (and make sure that you've documented them clearly for your staff and managers):

1. **Communicate the clear criteria and process for shift bids.**

   Staff members need to know the process and the criteria every day, not just when shift-bidding starts. If one criterion is tenure, for example, does it depend on the number of hours worked or just time on job?

2. **Communicate the available shifts to all staff members.**

   The staff needs time — frequently more than a week — to review those shifts.

3. **Ask agents to submit their shift preferences in writing.**

4. **Sort the bid requests based on your established criteria (see Step 1).**

5. **Assign shifts based on these requests.**

   In bid-number order (however you assign priority), determine whether each employee's first choice is available. If so, assign that shift to that employee. If an agent's first choice isn't available, look to his next preference, and so on.

When you follow these steps manually, however, the process is complex and lengthy. Some call centers use alternatives to shift bids, including rotating staff through all shifts (essentially sharing the pain), working around employees' personal preferences, making assignments based on employee performance, or scheduling fixed permanent shifts. Also, you may need to make some special accommodations based on an employee's disability.

Many call centers gravitate toward seniority-based shift bids, because as a call center grows, accommodating the preferences of every staff member becomes increasingly difficult. Also, in large call centers, shifts can change a great deal. Rotating staff through all schedules is very effective and equitable but not always preferred by the most senior employee. In our experience, a seniority-based shift bid is the most common — and most agreeable — way to assign schedules in large call centers.

If you use performance or seniority to determine shift-bid priority, be careful when assigning schedules for newly hired staff. If several new staff members start working at the same time, you may want to assign them a temporary post-training work schedule instead of simply giving them the lowest shifts on the totem pole. Otherwise, a large percentage of new hires working at the same time (usually on night shifts) puts a strain on the management team and creates an imbalance in staffing. Keep in mind that new people usually take longer to serve customers and, as a result, skew average call length.

You might consider having a temporary post-training schedule. You can spread the newbies around on the shifts and thereby spread out the effect of their lack of experience.

Offering flextime

Admit it — many call centers have some less-than-desirable shifts. Staff can find working these shifts to be somewhat demoralizing, considering that the majority of folks would rather be working 9 to 5 Monday to Friday. You can ease their angst in several ways:

- ✔ **Rebidding:** Redo the schedule from time to time so that you can correct any problems that gradually creep in. When new staff members join and other folks move on, the seniority of those employees who remain improves. A rebid allows staff members to move up the call center food chain and get more desirable shifts, which can really improve your team's motivation.

  If your call center doesn't use a shift bid, you need to fill vacancies in your schedule with new staff in a way that your staff sees as equitable.

- ✔ **Shift-trading:** The time-honored tradition of trading shifts really is as simple as it sounds: Give your employees a mechanism for trading their shifts ("You work my 9-to-5, and I'll work your 1-to-9"). Staff members usually trade shifts on a one-day-at-a-time basis, but you can also allow employees to trade entire schedules.

- ✔ **Time bank/flextime:** In addition to regular vacations, you can allow employees the option to *bank time* (they work an extra hour today, and instead of getting paid for that hour, they bank the time). The extra hours that they have worked can be taken as time off at a future date. This approach works well if you administer and track it carefully. You need some kind of mechanism to allow employees time off one day at a time in addition to their regular vacation process. This method allows you to respond to unexpected increases in call volume or to employee absences.

Scheduling practices are subject to the employment standards of both your organization and government. Make sure that you adhere to limitations on the number of overtime hours permitted, and find out whether you're allowed to bank employee hours.

Accounting for Unique Situations

In discussions of call center scheduling, the focus tends to be on a rather typical, generic, inbound operation: one type of call coming into one site. If only life were that simple! The following sections talk about some special situations and circumstances that you may need to consider.

Scheduling for different types of work

You must plan for and schedule non-inbound-call work, based on the specific type of work.

Outbound calling is likely the most common type of other work that you need to schedule, and it's actually easier to forecast than inbound calling. Outbound call volume is very predictable (even when you're using a predictive dialer), so you can easily forecast your occupancy and average call length.

As we explain in Chapter 9, a *predictive dialer* is a piece of technology used to increase efficiency in dialing outbound calls. The dialer places more outbound calls than the available number of agents but sorts out answering machines, busy signals, and other nonhuman interactions before delivering live calls to the agents.

If you're conducting a stand-alone outbound project, scheduling is a simple matter of deciding how many calls you want to make by a certain time of day, calculating how many staff that figure equates to per hour, and staffing to fit.

You use the same math that you do for inbound forecasting, as we describe in detail in Chapter 7.

Making contingency plans

What happens when you do all the planning and still have more callers than you can handle — or you have too many staff and too few callers (in which case the boss is probably asking, "Why is everyone just sitting around?")?

A lot can change from the time that you do your forecast and create your schedule to the time that calls arrive. You can get an unexpected increase in call volume; a large percentage of the staff can call in sick; and/or systems can get slow, causing call length to go up. Success is determined by how you handle these kinds of situations. The following sections suggest some strategies.

Blending various work types

Blending refers to mixing inbound call handling with other work, preferably work that an agent can put aside or stop when inbound traffic warrants it. Examples include making outbound calls (collections, customer service, and telemarketing), answering customer e-mails, and opening regular mail. We discuss the various types of call centers in Chapter 1.

Implementing envelope scheduling

A technique that we call *envelope scheduling* is a great strategy that takes advantage of call blending to greatly increase flexibility and maximize scheduling efficiencies.

Envelope scheduling is simple. Just follow these steps:

1. **Go through your normal scheduling process for inbound calls.**

   We describe this process in "Scheduling Available Resources to Meet Caller Demand," earlier in this chapter.

2. **Add staff over and above the number necessary to cover the inbound demand, creating an *envelope* (a forecasted number of extra hours) by scheduling extra agents.**

   Add enough agents to give you the additional hours required to do work that doesn't need immediate attention (such as answering e-mails or placing outbound calls).

3. **During periods of low inbound-call volume, switch some agents to this "extra" work, which they can set aside to respond to inbound calls.**

   This practice can generate sales, thereby maximizing cost control and occupying staff with productive work other than handling inbound calls.

As Figure 8-10 shows, wherever the envelope staffing line is above the required staffing line on the chart, you switch agents over to other work.

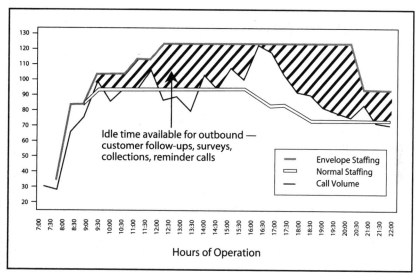

Idle time available for outbound — customer follow-ups, surveys, collections, reminder calls

Envelope Staffing
Normal Staffing
Call Volume

Hours of Operation

Figure 8-10: Envelope scheduling.

Using a combination of envelope scheduling and blending can reduce your overall cost per call by as much as 25 percent.

Extending overtime

Strategic use of overtime can help you respond to gaps in your staffing, especially during the transition between shifts. You can either extend the shifts of those agents who are already on the phones or ask agents who are scheduled for later in the day to come in early.

Allowing early leave, late start, or extended lunch

During times of lower-than-expected volume, if you give your staff the opportunity, they frequently sign up for time off without pay. You can also offer extended lunch breaks. All these options reduce staff on the phones during slower periods and thus increase the occupancy of the remaining staff. These measures can have a significant effect on cost per call.

Engaging an overflow partner

Having an overflow partner — another call center to which you can send calls when your call demand exceeds your staffing levels — can help you handle peaks and valleys in call volume. The overflow partner can be a third-party outsourcer (see Chapter 5) that specializes in this type of relationship or another call center within your own organization. In addition to providing quick access to additional staffing, the overflow partner can provide after-hours support (when your call center might be closed) or can take calls for your center in the event of a disaster (fire, a cut cable, and so on).

Scheduling for multiple-site call centers

If your company runs more than one call center, scheduling may be more complex. You can make your life (or your scheduler's life) much easier, however, if you appropriately organize your *call flow* — the kind and number of various groups of calls that particular groups of agents or call center sites receive.

If you treat each call center as an island (getting its own call volumes from its own customer base or a subset of the overall customer base), you can schedule each center independently, as though it were the only call center in your operation.

Frequently, multiple-site call centers are on the same network, so they work together just like one large center. Calls from your customer base are directed to the first available agent, wherever he or she is sitting. It doesn't matter whether the centers are separated by a few hundred feet, several thousand miles, or even an ocean: You can treat them as one call center for scheduling purposes.

Part III
Making Life Better with Technology

The 5th Wave   By Rich Tennant

"For additional software support, dial "9",
"pound", the extension number divided by
your account number, hit "star", your dog,
blow into the receiver twice, punch in your
hat size, punch out your landlord, ..."

In this part . . .

Science-fiction author Arthur C. Clarke once said, "Any sufficiently advanced technology is indistinguishable from magic."

Part III helps demystify the apparent magic that makes the call center machine hum. In this part, we review call center technologies — including basic requirements and valuable enhancements — in layperson's terms. We explain why you shouldn't implement technology unless it can advance the business causes of the call center.

In this part, we also cover the technology you need to set up a home agent program, highlight the benefits of such a program, and provide criteria to consider if you're thinking about implementing a home agent program.

Chapter 9

An Introduction to Call Center Technology

The machinery that helps manufacture great customer experiences in the call center has evolved tremendously since the cord boards that operators used in the 1950s. For many years, the phone system alone was the hub of customer communication.

Although the phone system is still in use, it's no longer alone. Modern technology is so fundamental to today's call centers that you have to know how to use it properly. Good operations blend people, processes, and technology in effective solutions that maximize efficiency, revenue generation, and customer satisfaction.

In this chapter, we explore some of the modern technology tools that can help you run your call center more effectively.

Seeing What Technology Does for Call Centers

Broadly speaking, technology does three things for your call center:

✔ It gives your customers a way to communicate with your company.

✔ It allows the call center to more readily collect, access, and edit information about customers.

✔ It provides a means for reporting on activity in your call center.

Call center technology is becoming increasingly integrated, making for improved processes that lead to increases in efficiency, revenue generation, and customer satisfaction.

Call centers themselves are a response to the demand for convenience in a world that continues to move quickly. Consumers don't have the time or desire to go to the market square to make every purchase or to receive services. Technology enables a company to meet customers' "any time, anywhere" expectations, and it's the foundation on which call centers are built.

Figure 9-1 shows the basic layout of a typical call center network, illustrating many of the pieces of technology that we talk about in this chapter.

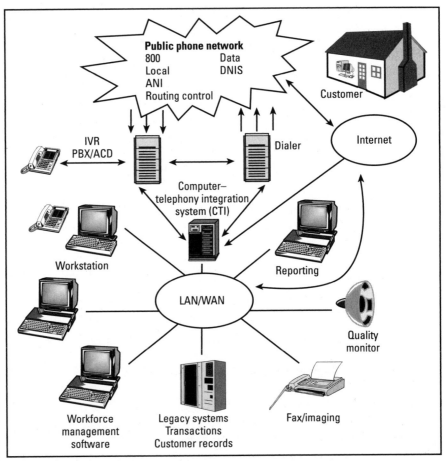

Figure 9-1:
A call center network.

Using Telecommunications Technology in the Call Center

The first piece of technology that you need must provide a means of getting customer calls to your call center. For the most part, call centers use the public telephone network — something that's such an integral part of the modern world that people don't give it much thought. Customers just pick up their phones and dial a number to connect to your operation.

Like most call center operations, yours probably uses toll-free 800 numbers. Your customer dials a number that has an area code starting with 8, and even though the call center might be thousands of miles away, he doesn't pay long-distance charges. (The bill goes to the call center rather than the customer.)

On the other side of the coin are call centers that use phone numbers starting with 9 — usually, 976. For these calls, the customer *does* pay . . . sometimes, a lot!

Today's telephone and Internet networks provide your call center valuable opportunities and services, including the following:

✔ Automatic number identification (ANI)

✔ Dialed number identification service (DNIS)

✔ Dynamic network routing

✔ Automatic call distributor (ACD)

✔ Predictive dialing

✔ Interactive voice response (IVR), including speech recognition

✔ Voice over Internet Protocol (VoIP)

✔ Hosted call center applications

✔ Web tools

We discuss all these topics in the following sections.

Automatic number identification

Automatic number identification (ANI) is a service that transmits the customer's telephone number and delivers it to your call center's telephone system.

You can use this information to identify the customer and look up her account information before an agent even says hello, maybe giving the caller special treatment. (Your best customers might be routed to an elite group of agents, for example.) Special routing allows you to boost customer satisfaction and revenue per customer. We talk more about routing in the section "Taking advantage of ACD's capabilities," later in this chapter.

On your home phone, you see ANI in action if you subscribe to a Caller ID service. The number of an incoming call appears on your phone's display, allowing you to decide, for example, whether the caller is important enough to interrupt the 12-hour *Star Trek* marathon you're watching on TV. (Maybe it's the dry cleaner, calling to let you know that your Klingon costume is ready for pickup. You wouldn't want to miss that call!)

Call centers might use ANI to pull up a caller's account information so that an agent can be ready to handle the customer's inquiry. Having this information might shave only a few seconds off average call length, but you can get tremendous savings compounded over thousands of calls.

Dialed number identification service

Because your call center probably has several 800 numbers, depending on the various services or products that the company offers, you need to know which of those numbers the customer called. Through *dialed number identification service (DNIS)*, the telephone network provides the number that the customer dialed, which tells the telephone system how to route the caller.

Dynamic network routing

Dynamic network routing is a service that goes by several names, but the basic concept remains the same. Some call centers have a computer terminal that's connected directly to the telephone company's switching office. This computer allows such a center to control the routing of customer calls at network level, before they even hit the call center's telephone system.

When call volumes peak beyond a level that your call center can service, for example, dynamic network routing can redirect calls to other centers with which you have overflow agreements. (We talk about overflow agreements in Chapter 8.) You can route calls based on various criteria, such as a predetermined percentage of calls allocated to each office. Also, because the routing occurs in the telephone network, the routing appears to customers to be seamless.

Dynamic network routing also enables you to provide an announcement to callers and route their calls depending on their responses. You might greet customers with the message "Press 1 for English or 2 for Spanish," for example, and then use the responses to route the calls to English- or Spanish-speaking agents.

Automatic call distributor

You might consider this service to be the heart of the call center. When customer calls arrive, they're delivered to the *automatic call distributor (ACD)* system — a specialized phone system designed for call centers. Unlike a regular phone system, an ACD system doesn't route calls to a specific phone set; instead, it routes a large volume of incoming calls to a pool of waiting agents. Call center operators figured out years ago that they could achieve great efficiency by lining up incoming calls when they arrive and then distributing the longest-waiting calls to available agents. (Imagine the alternative: thousands of customers calling individual agents' extensions.) An ACD system simply connects the longest-waiting caller to the first available agent.

When customers call, they're greeted by a recorded message, which asks them what language they speak (English, Spanish, and so on) and what type of service they're looking for (such as billing or technical support). Based on the customers' responses, their calls are lined up, or *queued*, to wait for the next available agent who can provide that type of service. These queues act as waiting rooms of sorts, where callers likely hear a recording similar to this: "All of our agents are currently assisting other customers. Please hold, and we will be with you shortly."

Queuing capability is a key part of call center efficiency. You can create a large number of queues within your ACD system and then route calls to various subqueues based on services required, language preference, and so on.

Taking advantage of ACD's capabilities

ACD has several important capabilities:

  - ✓ **Delay messaging:** A delay message says something like "Thank you for calling. All of our operators are currently busy. . . ." Delay messaging tells customers that they've reached the right place and very effectively gets callers to wait briefly. ACD provides multiple messages, which the call center can play at any time during a customer's wait.

Limit the number and frequency of delay messages that interrupt music on hold or recorded information. Otherwise, those "Your business is important to us" messages can become a nuisance and may drive customers to hang up quickly.

✔ **Music on hold:** This feature plays music between delay messages. The main objective of music on hold is to encourage customers to wait for the next agent.

✔ **Skills-based routing:** As a variation on routing to queues, most ACD systems can route to skills instead. As the name suggests, *skills-based routing* matches each caller's needs with the agent who has the best skill set (of those available at the moment) to service those needs.

The first step in skills-based routing is establishing a skill set for all agents. Next, you must attempt to identify the skill requirements of callers, which you can do in several ways, including these:

- Using a DNIS service.

- Collecting caller information through telephone prompts, such as "Press 1 for English . . ."

- Looking up the caller's phone number by using ANI and searching your customer database to pick up some important information about the caller. ANI might determine that a caller is one of your best customers, for example, and skills-based routing can send the caller to one of your best agents.

Skills-based routing doesn't eliminate queues, but it changes the agent queue dynamically for each caller.

✔ **Reporting:** ACD systems provide a great deal of reporting capability, both historical and real-time:

- **Real-time:** Real-time ACD reporting tells you everything that you need to know about current call center performance, such as how many callers are waiting to be served, how many agents are staffing the phones, and how long it's taking agents to process calls, as well as how many customers hung up and how quickly they hung up.

- **Historical:** You can view ACD information that spans a certain period so that you can revise your staffing plan for the next day, week, or year.

Gathering reports from ACD

The ACD component of your telephone system provides the basis of your reporting requirements. All activity starts with a customer call, and the ACD system tracks the volume, timing, and effort associated with accepting each phone call. The system can summarize and present this information in a variety of time frames, including by *interval* (time of day), day, week, or month.

You can collect reports on three general areas:

✔ **Agent performance:** ACD agent performance reports, such as the example shown in Figure 9-2, provide statistics about each individual agent, such as how long she took to service calls, how many calls she answered, when she logged in, and how long she was logged in. (We talk more about measuring agent performance in Chapters 6 and 13.)

✔ **Queue performance:** Queue performance reports can tell you how many people called, how quickly agents answered the phones, how many customers hung up, how long agents took to service the average call, how many agents were logged into the system at a particular time, and so on.

✔ **Trunk performance:** Telephone lines are frequently referred to as *trunks,* and trunk performance reports provide information about the telephone lines that deliver customers to the ACD system. You can use this information to make decisions such as when to add more telephone lines.

Trunk performance reports provide information about the use of each line and the amount of time that all lines were busy (raising the potential that callers received busy signals). They also provide information about the average time that each line was in use.

Figure 9-2:
An ACD agent performance report.

Agent Report

QTD	(All)
Month	(All)
Week Ending	(All)
Date	(All)
Team Leader	(All)

| TARGET | | | | 660 | | | | | | |

AGENT	LOGGED HOURS	OCCUPANCY	CALLS ANSWERED	AVG HANDLE TIME	AVG TALK TIME	AVG WORK TIME	AVG HOLD TIME	OUTBOUND CALLS MADE	AVG OUTBOUND TIME	AVG AUX TIME
Agent 1	285.59	59.44%	1304	458.75	458.64	0.10	8.16	32	64.66	1.76
Agent 2	149.93	65.33%	684	489.58	487.59	1.99	18.21	57	77.23	7.76
Agent 3	432.24	60.08%	1652	510.11	476.92	33.18	50.65	89	59.57	5.17
Agent 4	263.42	66.52%	1099	534.89	486.51	48.38	37.26	42	15.38	1.81
Agent 5	407.09	56.96%	1454	493.16	471.45	21.71	78.22	21	127.76	274
Agent 6	355.24	60.28%	1322	538.10	533.41	4.68	36.70	85	97.68	8.34
Agent 7	501.58	63.24%	1896	522.27	481.85	40.42	73.83	96	105.39	6.22
Agent 8	382.66	59.41%	1338	570.05	539.89	30.16	32.71	54	108.48	8.93
Agent 9	358.05	63.78%	1335	549.35	546.76	2.59	57.76	95	95.41	8.67
Agent 10	265.29	62.04%	962	583.26	580.19	3.07	25.26	46	96.37	7.43
Agent 11	202.82	69.91%	826	576.75	565.89	10.86	28.57	77	108.09	12.62
Agent 12	2.05	75.92%	9	585.67	585.67	0.00	22.89	2	57.00	14.78
Agent 13	281.71	62.77%	1019	566.11	529.52	36.59	50.88	61	102.23	7.74
Agent 14	178.06	61.54%	631	575.58	533.70	41.88	38.97	32	93.16	10.64
Agent 15	275.95	65.53%	1034	562.20	535.80	26.39	57.32	61	125.46	9.27
Agent 16	374.19	62.21%	1331	573.09	554.89	18.20	50.14	61	105.00	6.35
Agent 17	468.34	62.55%	1671	568.13	539.58	28.56	55.70	66	108.24	7.28
Agent 18	422.08	63.26%	1512	593.81	522.93	70.88	36.07	32	143.53	5.88
Agent 19	274.35	57.04%	882	592.93	580.63	12.30	37.81	62	88.48	7.95
Agent 20	194.33	70.65%	767	601.89	579.76	22.13	26.20	95	92.76	16.36
Agent 21	405.56	62.80%	1413	555.83	521.47	34.36	86.66	84	91.99	6.38
Agent 22	175.06	71.00%	686	618.23	616.19	2.04	27.16	48	53.50	6.90
Agent 23	208.52	65.54%	750	630.16	608.21	21.95	1.13	36	143.00	24.65
Agent 24	314.09	63.26%	1808	600.44	577.38	23.06	43.23	107	120.27	13.77
Agent 25	451.88	62.37%	1537	630.96	619.42	11.54	21.04	79	80.28	8.18
TOTAL	7630.07	63.74%	195195	563.25	541.37	21.88	40.10	1520	94.44	8.70

Unlike at a local bank branch, in a call center, you can't physically see the customers being served or waiting for service, but you can still get a very clear picture of what your callers are experiencing. From the ACD reports, you can determine whether your customers are waiting a long time or whether your agents aren't busy enough. With good information from your ACD reports, you can take action to correct any imbalances, such as adding staff to help waiting customers or moving agents to other work when you're overstaffed. (We talk about scheduling in detail in Chapter 8.)

ACD manufacturers have made it very easy to transfer historical data across the local area network (LAN) and into a data warehouse. (We talk about LANs in the section "Connecting agents to the local area network," later in this chapter.) After the ACD data enters the warehouse, you can mix it with information from other systems to generate some very powerful information for your management team, as we describe in Chapter 6.

Predictive dialing

A *predictive dialer* is a device that allows you to manage *outbound calls* — calls originating from your call center. Companies that place large numbers of outbound calls, such as collections bureaus and telemarketing agencies, often use predictive dialers.

This technology can increase agent productivity by 300 percent or more over manual dialing in several ways:

- It places the outbound calls, leaving agents free to perform other tasks.
- It weeds out answering machines, busy signals, and other nonhuman interactions before delivering live calls to agents.
- It reduces agents' wait time between live calls.

The call center can control how aggressive the predictive dialer is in dialing customers. If you want to keep your agents very busy, you make the dialer dial quickly. Fast dialing comes at a cost, however. In some cases, the dialer can dial so quickly that no agent is available for a customer to talk to. (That's why you sometimes hear a long delay in a telemarketing call before an agent speaks.)

Predictive dialing can lead to customer irritation when it's used irresponsibly, such as calling at unacceptable times of day.

Managing customer lists

A predictive dialer simply dials a list of phone numbers that you've loaded into its database. This list generally includes customers' names, some pertinent information about them, and (of course) their phone numbers.

You need to manage your customer list effectively if your call center does outbound calling. To maximize the effectiveness of each list, you must clean (or *scrub*) the list to remove incomplete phone numbers or numbers that the dialer has determined are fax machines or out-of-service phone lines.

Also scrub lists based on other information you may have about a customer's interest in the product or service that you're offering. You might call some of your existing customers who are now eligible for a great new product, for example. By scrubbing customers who probably don't want a product that you're promoting, you can increase the quality or effectiveness of your list and make more sales over the life of the list. As a result, you make dialing more effective.

Respecting do-not-call laws

Most countries have laws that regulate call center practices (see Chapter 1), generally dealing with telephone sales, the use of predictive dialers, and privacy. The United States and Canada have implemented *do-not-call laws,* which require call centers to scrub their telemarketing lists against government-provided do-not-call lists. By checking every list against both government lists and your own internal do-not-call list, you can be sure that you aren't calling customers who prefer not to be called for any offer.

Do-not-call lists are positive for call centers in that they provide a cost-effective way of improving lists by removing customers who don't want to talk to you — which ultimately improves dialing effectiveness.

Take do-not-call lists seriously! If you use predictive dialing and don't scrub against the do-not-call list, you could be violating the law thousands of times per day. The fine is as much as $11,000 per violation, so it doesn't take long for fines to add up to a lot of money. The governing bodies mean business; if you violate the law, you'll be paying. Using predictive dialing without scrubbing your call list also comes with hidden costs, from wasted agent time to negative effects on your company's image and brand.

Creating reports from predictive dialing

Like ACD systems (which we talk about in the section "Automatic call distributor," earlier in this chapter), a predictive dialer reports on agent productivity, office productivity, and trunk performance. The dialer reports on the results of each conversation, including sales per hour, refusals, reasons for refusals, and how many answering and fax machines the dialer encountered. Because the dialer dials more customers than it has agents to handle, you occasionally run into situations in which agents aren't available when the customer answers the phone. The dialer needs to be able to report on how many customers had to wait for an agent and how many customers hung up while waiting.

Interactive voice response

Interactive voice response (IVR) involves using automation — automated voice prompts and, sometimes, synthesized speech — to provide service to customers.

Think of an IVR system as being like a robotic agent. You encounter IVR yourself whenever you call your bank's automated account-lookup system to determine your account balance; the system reads your account balance in a computerized voice.

IVR is very cost-effective. The cost of a service provided by IVR can be less than one fifth the cost of providing the same service by using a live agent. Also, IVR systems generally provide faster and more convenient service. Rarely does a customer have to wait for the "next available agent." Because IVR is virtually always available, it's there whenever the customer is, 24 hours a day.

You should see very fast payback on investing in IVR — in significantly less than a year. You can measure the benefit in terms of inquiries and requests that live agents don't have to handle. Calls that don't make it to call center agents reduce the total calls and the cost of servicing customers.

Here are some simple keys to IVR success:

- **Provide a quick out.** Give callers who don't want to use IVR a quick way out by allowing them to press 0 at any time to get an agent.

- **Keep it short and sweet.** The IVR script should be up-tempo, clear, and to the point. Humans can interpret speech much faster than 100 words per minute, yet most IVR systems are paced slower than this, so callers get bored and opt for the quick out. Formalities aren't necessary. Callers know that they're listening to a machine, so keep the script polite, but don't bother with a lot of extra pleasantries.

- **Follow the three-by-three rule.** Try to avoid offering more than three options at a time, and don't make callers drill more than three options deep into the IVR script. If you break this rule, you may find that customers begin to drop out of your IVR service, opting to speak with a live agent.

Speech recognition

Traditional IVR systems ask customers to press a key on their telephone keypad to select an option; this keypress identifies why they're calling and directs them to the right place in the IVR system or to a live agent. With speech-recognition software, however, the IVR system can understand human-language commands. Speech recognition can range from simple ("If you'd like to reach sales, say *sales*") to sophisticated ("Please state the name of the party you are looking for"). In the latter example, the system would look up the name and provide the phone number.

Both traditional and speech-recognition IVR systems give customers the chance to get answers to commonly asked questions, get account information, or complete transactions. The benefit to your customers is that they have access to your company around the clock. The benefit to your call center and company is that removing simple requests quickly saves money.

Speech-recognition software has become more accurate at understanding what a caller says, but it's far from perfect. This software can frustrate customers when it doesn't accurately understand what they're saying, leading to a significant number of misdirected calls, which adds costs to your bottom line. Keep the design of your IVR menu simple (no more than three levels; see the tip in the preceding section), test it on your own employees first, and fix what's not working before you allow customers to use it.

Investigating speech analytics

The ability of a computer to understand what humans are saying has opened a new field of study called speech analytics. Speech analytics allows you to search recorded calls over a period of time (today, a month, and so on) for specific words or phrases, or even for the tone of the customer. Identifying trends in customer requests, issues with products, and reasons for customer calls can help you solve costly problems and, ultimately, resolve the reasons that the customers needed to call you.

Speech analytics also allows a computer to search and group recorded calls in a specific category (such as sales calls). By listening to these calls, you can identify why products are popular and spot missed selling opportunities. Instead of scratching your head and wondering why your sales are down, now you can use technology to target and analyze specific calls. All these capabilities allow you to bring more revenue and a better customer experience to your company.

IVR reports

The IVR system provides reports about calls received, the options that customers selected, the length of time customers spent using IVR services, and the time when customers used those services.

Figure 9-3 shows an IVR report for a customer-opinion-survey application. The report shows how many calls the call center received, the average call length during each half-hour interval of the day, and IVR selections made by the customers who completed the survey. The detail in the IVR report can tell you about the success of the applications that the system is running.

IVR Report

Responses Results

How satisfied were you with the amount of time our representative took to process your request?

Interval	Calls Received	Avg C.S.T. (Customer Service Time)	1 — Very Dissatisfied	2 — Dissatisfied	3 — Neutral	4 — Satisfied	5 — Very Satisfied	Grand Total
10:00	11	153.14				1	10	11
10:30	14	142.01					14	14
11:00	10	100.90			1		5	6
11:30	17	105.79	3			2	12	17
12:00	11	142.53			1		17	18
12:30	15	162.77		1	1	3	13	18
13:00	14	124.01	2			1	23	26
13:30	15	151.68	1				17	18
14:00	11	147.48					7	7

Figure 9-3: An IVR report.

Voice over Internet Protocol

The abbreviation of this system's name doesn't mean "hello" in an alien language. *Voice over Internet Protocol,* or *VoIP* (pronounced *voyp*), is the name of a communications technology that changes the meaning of the phrase *telephone call* by transmitting speech over a computer network. Just as many people have switched their home phone service to high-speed VoIP access, companies also use VoIP. Unlike consumers, however, businesses have VoIP options that can improve the quality and reliability of call center services.

Potential benefits of VoIP

VoIP service offers several benefits to call centers:

✓ **Cost savings:** Because VoIP allows you to carry all calls through your computer network and out over the Internet, you don't need expensive phone lines (also called *trunk lines*). If you support international calls into your call center, you can avert per-minute costs (but still incur 800-number charges for domestic callers). Also, the point-and-click administration of VoIP saves you money on maintenance and management charges.

- ✔ **Multiple-site capability:** VoIP has enabled call centers of all sizes to employ home agents (see Chapter 11) and integrate mobile workers. (The fellow in the plumbing aisle at Home Depot can now offer support to professional plumbers when they call from their clients' basements for help!) VoIP also can enhance multiple-site coordination, routing calls between two or more call centers and balancing call volumes.

- ✔ **Benefits for the rest of the company:** This technology includes some very cool features and applications that can help improve productivity and solve challenges throughout your business. You can use VoIP to seamlessly connect physical offices with mobile workers, such as technicians or salespeople, for a low cost.

- ✔ **Energy savings:** On top of the financial and customer benefits of VoIP, the move to home agents reduces your call center's carbon footprint, which is good for the planet.

Potential drawbacks of VoIP

Despite what VoIP can do for a call center, deciding whether your call center should use it isn't a no-brainer. You need to consider the following potential problems:

- ✔ **Effect on current systems:** You and the person in charge of information technology need to discuss the effect of VoIP on your current phone, computer, and network systems.

- ✔ **Cost:** The cost of implementing a VoIP system might require you to analyze the benefits (see the preceding section) to determine whether the implementation would be worth the price.

- ✔ **Physical vulnerability:** VoIP requires electricity, so a power outage knocks it out of service. Also, because calls are transmitted over the Internet, the sound quality may vary.

- ✔ **Security vulnerability:** VoIP introduces a new kind of security challenge because (like a Web site) your network can be hacked by intruders if you don't protect it properly.

Make sure that you do your homework, understand the issues, have service-level agreements in place with your VoIP provider, and establish a Plan B for use in case problems arise.

For a further look at VoIP, check out *VoIP For Dummies,* by Timothy V. Kelly, or *VoIP Deployment For Dummies,* by Stephen P. Olejniczak (both from Wiley Publishing).

Hosted call center applications

You can actually have call center technology tools hosted at another location and maintained by another company instead of buying and installing them in your company's computer room. In essence, you can rent technology and access it remotely (by using the Internet, for example).

Hosted technology tools, which you may hear called *Software as a Service (SaaS)* or *application service providers (ASPs),* have several attractive benefits:

- ✔ **Low up-front costs:** Instead of buying an expensive tool, you can rent it, which means that you can be up and running more quickly. You can also decide to buy the tool later, after you try it out.

- ✔ **Low maintenance costs:** Maintaining hardware and software requires upgrades and patches, so you need a person at your company who knows how to support the tools. If you use a hosted tool, you don't have to worry about these costs.

- ✔ **Redundancy:** Hosted-system suppliers usually have multiple servers in multiple locations that include backup generators to ensure availability.

- ✔ **Flexibility:** Hosting has given small and midsize call centers access to tools that only large call centers could afford before. You can rent what you need today and add new tools or grow the number of agents or locations in the future.

No matter what capability you want technology to deliver to your call center, you probably have an option to host instead of buy. A few of the most popular hosted applications are

- ✔ **Hosted IVR:** You can easily route calls to different locations, based on area code or time of day, for example. If your customers mainly want to look up account balances, or if you want to use enhanced speech recognition (covered in the section "Speech recognition," earlier in this chapter), you might want to use a hosted IVR system.

- ✔ **Home agents:** Technology-enabled hosting allows you to have agents working remotely from their homes. We cover this topic in detail in Chapter 11.

- ✔ **Support and management tools:** Whether you want better scheduling, call recording, reporting, or customer-satisfaction surveying tools, your call center can rent them.

- ✔ **Call center in a box:** Some applications offer an all-in-one solution for a call center. You may want to use this approach if you're just starting an operation or want to expand your call center slowly.

Hosted applications also have drawbacks. You need to understand exactly what you're buying, as well as the risks that come with the new setup and the company that offers the hosted application. Be sure to build a service-level agreement that guards against risks, both now and in the future.

Web tools

Several tools can help you support customers through the Web. If your company has an online Web presence, it may offer a self-service system in which customers can find answers to their questions. Offering this kind of Web support can make life easier for your customers and reduce your company's costs of providing service, but keep these factors in mind:

- ✔ **Delayed versus real-time responses:** Handling e-mail (to which the customer might expect a response within 24 hours) is very different from handling real-time chat (in which the customer expects a response now!). A good example of real-time Web-based response is the Call Me button that businesses place on their Web sites. After a customer enters his phone number on the Web page, this information immediately routes to the call center, and the system initiates a phone call back to the customer with a live agent ready to answer that customer's question.

- ✔ **New processes and skills:** Handling e-mail, text messaging, and real-time online chat is very different work from talking to customers on the phone. Don't assume that your processes, training, or even current staff can deliver just because you installed a new technology.

- ✔ **Customer support in a social-media world:** Blogs, product forums, YouTube, and Facebook (to name just a few media) allow people to publish information and ideas online easily. In this environment, customers can express whatever they want about your company (or your products or services) in a very public way.

Web tools allow customers to interact with one another to solve problems and answer questions, and if they can't get the help they need from the online community, they can submit a request for someone in your call center to resolve the issue. (See how to connect your agents to your online presence in the section "Connecting agents to the local area network," later in this chapter.) You can also use these tools to give customers information about what your business offers.

When your company declares the need to reduce costs by pushing some customer calls to self-service (such as to the Web or an IVR system), establish a strategic plan so that you know what this change means for your call center. When your marketing team decides to move aggressively toward new online and social-media marketing, you should have a plan that outlines the effect on your call center. Usually, the easy part of putting customer support on the Web is installing the technology; the hard part is preparing your agents and changing your processes.

Getting Information to Agents

The two most important devices for call center agents are the phone and the computer. The phone routes a call from the customer's house, cellphone, or office to one of your skilled agents. Without phones, you obviously wouldn't have much of a call center. Without computers, agents can't easily (or quickly) respond to customer questions, retrieve information, and complete customers' requests.

In the following sections, we discuss these and other tools that give your agents access to information.

Giving agents the tools they need

Recruiters and trainers can put a very skilled and motivated person on the phone. But after the call is routed to him, that agent needs the best possible tools and resources to provide quick and accurate customer service. Today's networked computer systems are the means by which your agents access these capabilities, which include (at minimum)

- Customer accounts
- Product and service information and prices

More sophisticated environments also include access to the following:

- Company knowledge bases, including problem-solving guidelines, policies, and procedures
- Controlled Internet access (meaning limited or no access to certain areas of the Web, such as offensive sites) so that agents can research and respond to customers
- Call guides and scripts, sometimes including dynamic scripts that customize call-handling recommendations based on customer characteristics and preferences
- A personal performance dashboard, which provides agents critical information about their job performance
- Communication tools that allow agents to contact other departments, peers, and members of management
- Software to respond to e-mails or handle online chat

Make each workstation very neat and relatively spacious. The computer should use an industry-standard operating system (such as Microsoft Windows) that includes a graphical interface so that the agent can navigate easily by using a mouse or keyboard.

There's no tool like an old tool

Not long ago, Réal was working with a call center for a travel agency. Call length had always been long, but it was getting longer; as a result, costs were out of control, customers were becoming dissatisfied, and management was becoming concerned. Réal quickly determined that the number-one reason for the long calls was that agents needed to call other travel companies to book travel packages. In some cases, his client's agents were waiting 40 minutes or more to get through to the other company's agents.

Réal and his client set about to find an online travel-reservations system that would allow agents to bypass the other company's call center. After more than a week of research,

Réal described what he was trying to find to one of his client's agents. This agent knew what Réal was talking about immediately — an application called Vacations Online, which allows a company to deal directly with all of its suppliers' data. As it turned out, the client even had Vacations Online but simply hadn't implemented it because the person who purchased it had left the company some time ago.

To make a long story not so long, the client immediately began using the software and chopped more than 100 seconds off its average call length. We probably don't need to tell you the financial effect of this reduction (but in case we do, see Chapter 6).

The more easily agents can access anything that they need to serve callers — including account information, troubleshooting tips, call strategies, and phone services — the more successful they can be on every call.

Providing specialized call center applications

The world is full of packaged workstation tools and applications, many of which were built especially for the call center industry or even for specialties within that industry. Following are a few examples of specialized call center applications:

- **Contact management software:** Tracks customer contacts, reasons why customers are calling, and how issues were resolved; also books any follow-up actions that may be required

- **Help-desk software:** Records, tracks, and allows for the analysis of support requests within an organization

- **Knowledge-management software:** Provides call center agents a question-and-answer path that leads to a solution for a customer request or problem

- ✓ **Sales and marketing software:** Helps call center agents maximize their sales efforts by providing product and pricing information, as well as by *cross-selling* (suggesting new products based on customers' past purchases) and *upselling* (suggesting related products or services in addition to the original purchase) while talking with customers

- ✓ **Billing and order system:** Gives agents access to your company's customer-account information and the tools that they need to process a customer request

- ✓ **Reservations system:** Provides industry-specific tools that agents may require, such as travel-industry tools for booking flights

Connecting agents to the local area network

A *local area network (LAN)* is an internal network that delivers online services across the organization to anyone who has a computer. You can connect services such as customer billing systems to the LAN, making those services readily available to anyone on the network without dramatically changing the look and feel of the billing system.

Examples of other services that you can connect to a LAN include

- ✓ Fax and imaging servers
- ✓ E-mail and chat servers
- ✓ Scheduling software

We discuss these services in the following sections.

Fax and imaging servers

In the past, whenever a customer needed to fax information to the call center, the fax arrived at a local machine and went into an agent's inbox. Then the agent would process the fax and file it. The process created a lot of potential problems, because faxes could be misplaced or misfiled, and creating them wasted a tremendous amount of resources.

Installing a fax server on the LAN can prevent these problems. When customers need to fax your call center, the faxes are stored electronically on your fax server, and agents can easily retrieve faxes from their workstations with no worries about filing. This process can save a significant amount of time and reduce errors.

This same server can store images (that's the *imaging server* part), giving you the ability to scan any document and store it electronically. Your agents have network access to the stored documents through their workstations. If a customer writes a letter or sends documentation regarding warranty claims, for example, an agent can scan, store, and retrieve the documents when they're needed.

E-mail and chat servers

Increasingly, customers want to contact call centers electronically, such as via e-mail and online chat. In a call center, the e-mail and chat server routes electronic customer communications to agent workstations and manages the contacts in an organized fashion, much the same way that an ACD system manages phone calls (refer to the section "Automatic call distributor," earlier in this chapter).

The system coordinates which agent receives the next contact in a large pool of customer contacts and collects statistics on how quickly an agent handled the customer's request. The system also allows you to build and reuse templates to answer common customer questions quickly and consistently.

Scheduling software

Workforce management software can do all your scheduling work for you. (We talk about scheduling in Chapter 8.) This software forecasts call volume and length, determines staffing requirements, creates and organizes work schedules, automates shift bids, and tracks where your employees should be.

Today's scheduling and workforce management systems are integrated into the call center's computer network, making it possible for the system to share data with other systems and for users anywhere in the center to take advantage of its capabilities. The systems can also provide other services, such as quality control, agent-performance management, payroll, and reporting.

Probably the biggest benefit of workforce management software is its ability to keep track of all the thousands of bits of information required to prepare a call center schedule.

Generating Reports

Routing calls to your center (see "Using Telecommunications Technology in the Call Center," earlier in this chapter) starts the process of providing service to your customers. Keeping a well-designed set of tools and information at agents' fingertips (discussed in "Getting Information to Agents," earlier in this chapter) helps ensure that you're providing that service with a decent level of efficiency and accuracy. If you don't have reporting capability, however, you can't figure out how good you are, whether you're improving, or whether you're actually getting worse.

To be effective, reporting must be timely, complete, and accurate — all a lot easier said than done, but good reporting systems are worth the great deal of time and diligence required to build them. Call center systems put out many kinds of reports that provide vital feedback on business measures, making continuous improvement possible. Check your management reports to ensure that you're making fact-based decisions about your operations and how you service your customers.

Using multiple systems to generate reports

Your call center can get reports from the following systems:

- ✔ ACD (discussed in "Automatic call distributor," earlier in this chapter)
- ✔ Predictive dialer (which we talk about in "Predictive dialing," earlier in this chapter)
- ✔ IVR (check out "Interactive voice response," earlier in this chapter)
- ✔ Scheduling (flip back to Chapter 8 for the lowdown)
- ✔ Workstation applications (dive into these applications in "Giving agents the tools they need," earlier in this chapter)

Not enough data for you? You can also conduct surveys with customers and get data from your order management system (as well as your e-mail and chat server) to help you understand your call center's interactions with customers.

Other systems can provide useful reporting data. The payroll system, for example, can provide information on the number of hours for which the company paid your agents and the cost of paying these agents for their time.

Pulling the data together

These systems provide a lot of reports containing huge volumes of data. By themselves, they give you bits of information but don't paint the complete picture. In fact, looking at one piece of information without the benefit of other data can be very misleading. An agent who has very high call length, for example, may appear to be unproductive until you realize that the same agent has the highest level of sales and customer satisfaction in the company.

Combining data from the various systems can create meaningful information about your drivers and business performance. But don't get carried away. Your goal isn't to create a ton of metrics and reports; it's to obtain clear and actionable information.

The process of combining data manually is labor-intensive, slow, and not very sophisticated. (In some call centers, pulling reports together amounts to printing out daily results from a variety of systems and then retyping this data in a formatted spreadsheet.) Many call centers have made dramatic strides in their reporting capability by automating the collection of reporting data through the creation of a data warehouse attached to the LAN. The data warehouse performs automated processes called *routines* — often during off hours for the call center — that place data in prepared reporting templates. The reporting team checks to ensure that the reporting data has been entered correctly before sharing that data for use in the operation. In addition to saving time (because no one has to print reports and type the information into other reports), consolidating the data allows managers to create a complete picture of how the call center is operating.

These kinds of reports can actually improve results instead of simply reporting on them. The less time team leaders have to spend preparing performance reports, the more time they can use the reports to coach their agents.

Being able to report with this level of detail, speed, and accuracy helps a call center manage processes and key performance drivers. The adage "If you can't measure it, you can't manage it" proves to be very true in the call center industry.

Chapter 10

Technological Enhancements: Getting the Newest and Coolest Stuff

- -

In This Chapter

▶ Establishing communication between your computers and telephones

▶ Creating a data warehouse to monitor agent performance

▶ Checking on quality and customer satisfaction

▶ Working with customer relationship management technology

▶ Drawing on a knowledge base

▶ Showing how technology pays for itself

- -

*A*s part of a strategy of continuous improvement, call centers are always looking at cool new technologies that may provide improvements in their business practices. Okay, maybe those technologies aren't all that cool, but they definitely make things work better!

In this chapter, we provide some examples of technological enhancements.

Integrating Phones and Computers

Computer–telephony integration (CTI) refers to a system of hardware and software that allows for communication between the telephone system and the computer system. With this communication, you can instruct these systems to work together to produce some interesting and powerful applications.

CTI is kind of like call center superglue. After years of using it, we're still amazed by the magic that this technology can perform in a call center; it's ideally suited for creativity and continuous improvement.

In the following sections, we describe a few common CTI applications.

With a good CTI team, management can use this technology to improve customer service and create efficiencies in the call center.

Screen pops

One popular CTI application is the *screen pop,* in which the phone system collects the caller's telephone number — either through automatic number identification (ANI) or interactive voice response (IVR), both of which we discuss in Chapter 9 — and passes this information to the CTI system, which looks up the customer's information in the database. When it finds a customer account, the CTI system coordinates with the telephone system to send the call and the customer information simultaneously to an agent's telephone and workstation. The agent doesn't have to look up the account; it arrives on his computer screen at the same time that the call arrives on his telephone.

Our experience has shown that the screen pop saves 10 to 15 seconds in average call length, and this time savings directly reduces the cost of running a call center.

Mandatory data entry

You can use CTI to require agents to enter critical data before they take the next call. Are you frustrated, for example, that some agents forget to ask the customer what prompted her to call? Make completing the Reason for Calling field a mandatory task before the agent can move on to another call.

Soft-phone functionality

A *soft-phone application* houses an agent's telephone on his computer, which gives the agent easy access to a phone function by using that computer's mouse. Agents no longer need physical phones on their desks; all the tools they need are now housed on their computers.

Using a software-based telephone increases the amount of information that the call center leadership team can collect about how an agent uses her time. Whenever an agent leaves her desk, the soft-phone application can prompt her to account for her time. She might make an entry such as **Lunch Break** when she's away for 30 minutes, for example.

Enhanced reporting

The CTI system tracks a customer call from cradle to grave — from the moment that the telephone system recognizes a customer call through the call's entire life cycle in the call center. The CTI system knows how long a customer waited for service, what he selected in the IVR system, his phone number, which agent he spoke to, what actions the agent took by using company applications, whether the agent transferred the customer, and to whom the customer was transferred.

This incredibly rich source of information makes for very detailed reporting and analysis. You can report not only on call length, but also on how long an agent spent using each part of the company's applications.

Idle-time training

CTI can monitor how busy the call center's phones are at any point in time. When it identifies a lull in caller demand, it can route training information to idle agents. Better still, it can identify individual agent weaknesses and route the most appropriate training materials to each agent. You get customized agent training with no loss in agent utilization. That's what we call a killer app!

Coordinated screen transfer

This function enables an agent to transfer customer data on his computer screen to another agent's or team leader's computer. This way, customers don't have to repeat their names and account information after the transfer. This type of information transfer not only saves time, but also represents good customer service.

Call routing

You can use CTI to control the routing of calls to agents, essentially taking this function away from the automatic call distributor (ACD). You can use CTI to control call routing and gain the added benefit of CTI's sophisticated logic in making routing decisions. When a customer calls, CTI may look up the customer's account history, her preferences and likely behavior, and her selections in the IVR system before deciding which agent to route the call to and what information to present to the agent.

See Chapter 9 for more information on ACD and IVR.

Dynamic scripting

After it routes the caller to an agent, CTI may prompt the agent with a customized script or call-handling approach to serve the specific customer. In doing so, CTI refers to a customer's analytics database, which predicts the customer's preferences and suggests the most appropriate call-handling strategy.

Call blending

Call blending occurs when CTI switches agents among different types of work at any time. The system might blend an agent between inbound customer service calls and outbound collections, for example. CTI can control this process by monitoring inbound caller demand and dynamically moving agents between inbound and outbound calling.

Call blending greatly increases the efficiency of inbound call handling and gives you an effective way to move occupancy closer to optimal levels. (We discuss optimal occupancy in Chapter 8.)

Web-enabled call centers

As we discuss in Chapter 1, call centers are increasingly being called contact centers because companies have added multimedia contact methods to inbound and outbound telephone calls. Other methods of contact can be woven into the call center through CTI integration and blending. In these cases, the CTI system routes other forms of contact (such as e-mail, online chat, and scanned letters) to agents who possess the skills needed to handle these methods of contact.

Again, the CTI system controls the routing of these contacts. CTI can also blend these other forms of contact with inbound calls, creating more call-blending efficiencies. Presto! Your call center just became a contact center.

Warehousing Data to Track Agent Performance

Many call centers have agent performance data in various computer systems. Your phone system has all the productivity numbers, such as average handle time and the number of calls taken in a day. Your order-taking system or your customer relationship management system has the number of sales or orders that an agent has taken or perhaps the number of complaints or problems that he has resolved.

To get an overall view of agent and team performance, many call centers move data from different systems into a central database called a *data warehouse*. This data can be organized so that team leaders can access it for any interval (daily, weekly, monthly, the year to date, and so on). Also, the data warehouse presents the same information about all agents, which allows team leaders to do some analysis by comparing agents on their teams and in their departments.

You want to collect data on performance drivers and report on individual agent performance relative to these drivers so that you can target improvements in operational effectiveness to meet the business goals and mission. Without a tool to summarize all the reporting information and report on individual agent performance, it's virtually impossible to produce consistent, timely, and reliable reports.

Monitoring Quality

Most call centers randomly listen to, record, and grade agent telephone calls by using call-recording software.

Most call centers can benefit from using an automated call-monitoring system and integrating it into their local area networks. Such a system automatically captures complete agent phone calls, recording both the voice conversation and a video picture of how the agent navigates screens within the computer system while she solves the customer's issue. To review agent calls, team leaders simply log into the system from their workstations, retrieve sample calls for the agents they want to evaluate, and begin scoring. This software application has many benefits:

- ✔ **Team leaders don't need to wait for a call to come in.** A team leader can go to a library of recorded calls, choose one randomly, listen to it, and evaluate it. Then the team leader can attach comments to the call and show those comments to the agent. This feature increases team leaders' personal productivity.

- ✔ **The agent and team leader can stop the call's recording at any point to discuss it.** In the coaching session, they can talk about what the agent did well and whether he might do something differently in the future. You can find more information on specific coaching best practices in Chapter 13.

- ✔ **A team leader can target specific agent challenges** such as high call length, low customer opinion, poor sales, or high returns. The team leader can look for the root cause of a particular challenge by sitting side by side with the agent, as well as by listening to calls through a call-monitoring system.

- ✔ **The agent can listen independently.** Then she can complete a self-assessment of the quality of the call.

- ✔ **The team leader can gather great calls.** He can add these calls to a library that demonstrates best practices, which any agent can listen to.

- ✔ **The team leader and the agent can evaluate the agent's use of the call center's computer systems.** Because the software also records the agent's computer screen during the call, the team leader and agent can determine whether the agent used the most efficient navigation path.

Many agents perform perfectly during a side-by-side evaluation with their team leaders, but when the team leaders listen to calls remotely through a call-monitoring system, the agents don't give the same high-quality performance. This difference in performance can occur for a variety of reasons, including lack of motivation or lack of practice.

If you want to use a call-monitoring system, keep these points in mind:

- ✔ **You have options.** You can find hosted services, for example, if your center can't afford the expense of this type of technology. If you use a hosted service, your call center doesn't have to buy the technology outright; instead, it pays the technology company for what it uses.

- ✔ **You must determine how much to record.** Because housing all recorded calls can be costly, many companies record a percentage of total daily calls. If you work for a financial institution's call center, however, specific regulatory and risk-mitigation requirements force you to record all calls. Even if you don't work for a financial institution, not recording calls means that you don't have as many agent calls to evaluate. You have to weigh this need against the cost factor of storage.

Using Customer Relationship Management Technology

Customer relationship management (CRM) is a business term that refers to the process of relating to your customers in a way that allows you to maximize the length and value of that customer relationship. It involves collecting and analyzing data to better understand your customers' needs and wants. It also includes creating customized strategies to address unique customer needs. The whole point of CRM is to get new customers, keep the customers you have, and maximize the value of the relationships you have with those customers.

Putting CRM to work

You can gain benefits from CRM by using a diverse range of technologies. You don't have to use overly complex or uncommon technology, though, especially in the beginning of your implementation. CRM technology tends to involve three components:

- ✔ Data collection, management, and analysis
- ✔ Creation of business rules
- ✔ Onscreen presentation of the correct data to agents

Companies collect data about their customers from a variety of sources, including legacy customer information and billing systems, call center customer contact systems, Web-based contact information, and all other points of contact where the company can collect customer information. Marketing and sales use this information to build the CRM database, which is stored in the data warehouse. The call center uses a subset of this database, accessing specific customer data.

Marketing uses the data warehouse to analyze customer information and anticipate your customers' needs and intentions. A bank, for example, could determine from analyzing the data warehouse that if a customer is in his early thirties and renting his home, the bank should offer him a mortgage. Therefore, if this type of customer contacts the call center, the CRM application may suggest to the agent that she offer this customer a mortgage.

CRM applications have many functions, such as searching for customers; updating customer information; merging duplicate accounts so that the database is up to date; linking one customer to another within the same family; accessing a customer's call history, purchases, and preferences for products and services; tracking the status of a current inquiry or complaint; and taking orders for products and services. All points of contact from the customer (e-mail, online chat, phone, and so on) access the same CRM application.

You can use your CRM application to produce a daily list of the customers who are most likely to stop using your products. This evaluation allows you to make a service call to these customers to see whether you can do anything to enhance their use of your product or service. This proactive initiative greatly reduces customer cancellation rates and keeps those customers actively connected to your company.

Developing a CRM strategy

In our opinion, CRM is first and foremost a strategy, not just a technology. The core of this strategy involves how you want to treat your customers, what you want to get from your customer relationships, and what you plan to give customers in return. All parts of the organization should coordinate in the execution of your CRM strategy, from marketing to call center operations.

The execution of the CRM strategy includes three components: people, process, and technology. You can easily purchase technology in the hope that it can solve your problems and achieve your strategic goals, but even with the best technology, the people in the call center need to see the value in pursuing the CRM strategy.

Call center agents, who for a long time have been concerned primarily with call length and keeping the customer happy, must come to believe that collecting customer information and offering each customer new products and services — that is, selling to customers — helps the company, the customer, and the agent.

Changing old behaviors may take some time. Call center managers need to believe that the extra time agents take to collect data is worth the investment in longer call length and increased cost per call, and senior managers need to give the call center time to adapt.

The CRM process doesn't spring to life overnight. Companies may spend millions of dollars on CRM applications, training, and consulting, and they reap the benefits of CRM only many years later. It takes time, trial, and error for all the components to come together in a successful and profitable solution.

The technology component of call center CRM addresses handling each customer contact. What does your customer data tell you about a customer's needs and preferences? How should you handle her? Does marketing route her to the IVR system because her history shows that she typically calls to complete a transaction and has a history of refusing your product offers?

After the call reaches an agent, CRM applications give the agent the means to access information about the customer (including recommendations developed from data analysis) and to collect new information provided by the customer.

Employing a Knowledge Base

Agents live in a world in which new and sometimes confusing information comes at them quickly every day. Call center managers expect agents not only to know this information, but also to weave it into natural conversations with customers. Some agents think that they have to memorize all existing and new information, but they really need to retrieve this information quickly, understand it, and respond to the customer without missing a beat.

You can help agents by giving them access to a *knowledge base* — an organized library of your company's products, services, process, and procedures. This library includes a search engine that presents options to the agent to ensure that he has the right information at his fingertips. Good knowledge bases contain images of your products and processes, which can help agents understand the information quickly. If you think about the customer experience and the pressure on the agent to provide the right answer at the right time, providing a robust knowledge base that has good search functionality can pay dividends not only in customer satisfaction and workplace productivity, but also in employee satisfaction.

You can also help your agents by increasing what we call their *think, type, and talk* proficiency: *Think* about what the customer is asking, *type* the right request to find the appropriate information, and *talk* to the customer to deliver a response seamlessly. This type of proficiency grows with practice, and as we describe in Chapter 13, you can accelerate an agent's skill only by providing that agent coaching at her workstation right after she completes a call with a customer.

Surveying Customer Satisfaction

In the section "Monitoring Quality," earlier in this chapter, we talk about quality-monitoring applications. If you use these types of applications, you can get some specific benefits in improving the customer experience, but you can't get much information about what the experience felt like to the customer. The call center industry spends a lot of time doing *calibration exercises* — meetings in which team leaders spend time with quality analysts listening to an agent's call, evaluating it, and determining how the call quality compares with those of other calls within a specific group of agents. These exercises aim to have less than a 5 percent deviation in the call-quality scores of agents in the group.

A calibration exercise creates consistency within the group, making sure that team leaders and quality analysts understand the specific components of what the center thinks makes up a good customer experience. These sessions can go awry, however, if the team leader discusses how the agent made the customer feel. Only the customer can give that type of feedback (which you can get through customer-satisfaction surveys).

To get this type of customer feedback, many centers implement postcontact surveys. You can get immediate customer feedback by conducting the postcontact survey right after the customer's interaction with an agent. You can conduct these surveys in several ways, including using an e-mail–based survey with which you reach out to customers to get their rating of the experience. You can also conduct postcontact surveys through IVR technology. (We talk a bit about the many uses of IVR in Chapter 9.) When a customer calls a call center that has a postcontact survey set up, an automated voice asks the customer whether he wants to participate in a survey. If the customer presses the number for Yes, after he speaks to an agent who services his request, the IVR system presents a short survey to the customer. (If the customer presses the number for No, he's simply routed to an agent, and the call has no follow-up survey.)

If your technology can accrue the results in real time, you can review the responses and scores daily, which allows you to recognize when your agents do excellent work. If specific agents have consistently poor responses and scores, you can prioritize your time to coach these agents first. Real-time results let you take action when a call is still fresh in an agent's mind.

Your quality analysts can look for department-level trends in this data and dig into the root cause of your results, whether those results are positive or negative. This analysis feeds directly into your continuous improvement process, which we talk about in Chapter 15.

Getting Approval for Technology

Okay, you're a technology genius, and boy, oh boy, have you found some technology that's going to make a big difference in improving your customer experience. So what's next? How do you go about getting approval so that you can start saving the call center money?

Our first piece of advice is to keep it simple. The simplest, most appropriate, and most effective way to submit a proposal for technology enhancements is to prepare a one-page cost–benefit analysis that you can use to create a case for change if you need to. You can create this kind of analysis easily, and Réal suggests that you follow two specific rules:

- ✔ The analysis must fit easily on one page of 8½- by 11-inch paper.
- ✔ Express your argument for spending money on new technology in one minute or less.

You can most easily meet both of these rules by using the business model that we outline in Chapter 2. The model says that all business activities go toward the key goals of generating revenue, minimizing cost, or satisfying customers. To make the case for new technology, you have to define the benefit of new technology in terms of those key business goals.

To make your case for a new technology, you have to show that it can affect at least one of the drivers in a manner that substantially adds value (increases revenue or reduces cost) to the company, thereby justifying the cost of the new technology.

Chapter 11

Using Home Agents

*I*magine that one of your best agents is moving to the other side of the city. She comes into your office to tell you that her commute is more than an hour, and she's thinking of resigning to find a job closer to home. She has a young family and doesn't want to spend two hours a day driving in big-city traffic. This scenario repeats itself across North American call centers every week.

Or maybe next year's call volume forecast, based on new programs that your organization is planning to roll out, contains both good news and bad news. The good news: Sales will be up. The bad news: Your operation is at capacity, and you don't have any room for more desks and people. (You already have three agents working next to the coffee machine!)

If you find yourself in one of these situations, consider a home agent program. Over the past four years, we've helped many of our clients start home agent programs. All of them started their programs for different reasons, but all of them enjoy many benefits from using these programs.

In this chapter, we discuss why you might want to go the home agent route, the key planning issues that you need to consider, and how to go about starting a program.

Seeing Reasons for a Home Agent Program

Also known as *virtual agents* and *at-home agents, home agents* (the most commonly used industry term) take calls and do their work from their homes; they don't regularly come in to the call center to work. They're a group of agents connected to your systems, customers, and call queues through what's known as a virtual private network (VPN), via the Internet or a supplier that provides this type of platform. (Although we don't go into the details of VPNs in this book, you can find information about them on the Internet.) If you execute a VPN well, to your customers, it sounds and performs the same as — or better than — agents in your call center operation.

In the United States, industry studies predict that the number of home agents will grow from an estimated 150,000 in 2008 to 330,000 in 2011 — a remarkable growth rate of more than 35 percent per year. In Canada, according to an April 2009 study by Triad Services, Inc., about 25 percent of call centers currently use home agents, and 50 percent of companies say that they plan to be using home agents within two years. The trend looks unstoppable.

The following sections provide a few reasons why companies start home agent programs.

Making your business run more efficiently

You probably could use a few extra advantages to make your operations more efficient and productive; everyone could! Using home agents is one more way to keep improving your business. We've identified four key ways that home agent programs improve companies' operations:

- ✔ Smoothing out service-level peaks and valleys
- ✔ Reducing turnover of skilled agents
- ✔ Attracting new talent
- ✔ Reducing costs while the company grows

We discuss those benefits, and others, in the following sections.

Smoothing out service-level peaks and valleys

You may experience variation in your call center's service level, and you need to smooth out those differences, especially if your call center experiences large swings through the course of a single day. (In Chapters 7 and 8, we talk about forecasting and scheduling.)

Home agents allow you to switch from a fixed labor pool of 9-to-5ers to a variable labor pool of flex workers whom you can schedule in relatively short time blocks and multiple times per day. This scheduling works because home agents find the lack of a commute and the freedom to use time between shifts for personal activities attractive.

Home agents can quickly sign in when unexpected peaks in call volume appear and queues back up. They get extra hours exactly when you have extra customers — a perfect win–win scenario. We can't make you a workforce expert in this chapter, but moving from fixed schedules to flexible schedules is just common sense, right?

Be careful about starting with the same scheduling model for home agents that you currently use in-house and then trying to make the change to flexible short shifts later. Some of your agents might feel betrayed if you shift the rules after they decide to work from home. Be honest about setting and managing expectations.

Reducing turnover of skilled agents

With employees looking for more flexibility (so that they can achieve that coveted work/life balance), home agents give you a viable option in your employee retention strategy. Many companies that SwitchGear surveyed about why they launched home agent programs mentioned that their number-one reason was keeping agents who otherwise might leave, for any of several reasons:

- ✔ A family relocation (in the case of an on-the-move military spouse, for example) or life change (such as a new baby)
- ✔ Dissatisfaction with a large, stressful operation
- ✔ An expensive and stressful commute
- ✔ Environmental allergies (perfume in the next cubicle causing an allergic reaction, for example)

Attracting new talent

You can gain access to new workers outside your labor-pool area (sometimes in other cities) by using vendors that specialize in home agent recruiting and have access to labor pools in multiple markets.

You can use home agents if you're recruiting for multilingual agents whom you can't find in your hometown. Small call centers that struggle to compete for multilingual talent can find home agents to be particularly helpful.

Reducing costs while the company grows

While your company grows, you can expand customer service without incurring the additional costs of creating a new bricks-and-mortar work area. By using home agents, you can scale up your operations quickly for peak buying seasons (such as Christmas), new product and service launches, or major campaigns, and you can scale them down again just as quickly. You can much more easily increase the hours of a large pool of flexible home agents than build more capacity in a building and recruit under duress.

One recent industry study estimates that the fully loaded cost of an agent in a bricks-and-mortar operation decreases by 30 percent when that agent works from home. (We explain fully loaded costs in Chapter 6.) Another report estimates a similar 30 percent decrease — $21 per hour for home agents, compared with $31 per hour for agents in bricks-and-mortar operations.

You may see an even more dramatic savings if you have an expensive unionized environment and can transition over time to less-expensive independent workers.

This calculation might make your eyes pop: If you can send 20 percent of your agents home and save 30 percent on that group, you can improve your expense line by 0.2×0.3, which equals 0.06, or 6 percent. That's a big savings from one initiative.

Reaping other rewards

Additional benefits reported by our clients that use home agents include

- ✔ **Business continuity:** Power off in one site doesn't affect 50 dispersed agents in their homes (as long as you have your call center operation's phone switch on a backup power source).

- ✔ **Environmental benefits:** If you have 1,000 agents commuting for 12 months about 40 minutes each way twice a day, having them work at home could save 125,000 gallons of fuel and emit 170 tons less air pollutants. That kind of environmental consideration will make ice-cap watchers very happy!

- ✔ **Lower absenteeism during extreme bad weather:** When it snows heavily and in-house agents might not make it to work, your home agents can simply walk down their hallways with coffee in hand (and maybe in pajamas).

Graham Kingma, vice president of customer service for a television shopping channel, had his home agent program in place for 12 months when an incredible snowstorm hit the city. As he told us, "It took most people more than two hours to get in. I knew it was going to be a very challenging day. I made it in after a two-hour drive, and when I saw our operations supervisor, I hesitantly asked him how things were going. He said, 'Well . . . we have 21 agents absent for the day.' I shuddered. He then said, 'The good news is we got 19 home agents to come on, so there is no effect on the service levels.' That's when I realized all the effort of building our home agent program was worthwhile."

Providing an attractive work option for your agents

You can provide two ways for your agents to work from home: They can be home-based employees, earning their current pay and benefits, or they can work for your company as subcontractors for an outsourcing firm. (We discuss outsourcing in Chapter 5.)

Your agents might want to work at home for several reasons:

- ✔ **They don't have to commute.** Not having to get to work (because they work from home) saves many home agents a lot of time and fuel costs.

- ✔ **They may enjoy more personal time.** Home agents like the integration of their work and their personal lives, where pajamas and computers can work together.

- ✔ **Their workday has more flexibility.** Many home agents prefer to work three two-hour shifts with an hour in between rather than seven straight hours in the call center.

- ✔ **They can save money.** Home agents have no costs for commuting, and they may save on clothing and lunches. If they work as subcontractors, they can also enjoy tax write-offs on home-business expenses.

Is working at home perfect for every agent? No. The at-home option works best for agents who can handle a relatively isolated work environment that provides little face-to-face contact with other people. Also, home agents need to be self-directed enough to work on their own without hourly supervision.

You may want to create a self-assessment questionnaire to help agents determine whether working at home suits their personalities and lifestyles. See the nearby sidebar "Home agent interview" for a sample questionnaire.

Home agent interview

1. Do you have a private work space with a door you can close to minimize noise during work time?

2. Do you have the following items in your work space?

   a. Desk

   b. Reliable computer with a Webcam that meets the company's requirements and that can be used for coaching sessions and meetings with your boss

   c. Phone that has mute, hold, and conference features or a software-based phone that has similar features

   d. Headset outlet and headset

   e. Broadband Internet connection

   f. (For traditional phones only) Two phone lines — one dedicated to call center calls (usually paid for by the company) and one for personal calls

   g. Router and firewall/antivirus software

3. (For traditional phones only) Can you access the Internet and use the phone at the same time?

4. Can you ensure that customers won't hear sounds that tell them you're at home (such as a doorbell ringing or baby crying)?

5. Can you set up and install the hardware and software required for your job?

6. Can you troubleshoot your basic home agent technical setup so that the company doesn't have to send tech support for very minor issues?

7. Can you work at least the minimum number of hours per week required?

8. Are you willing to train for the position via online courses and phone or Webinar sessions?

9. Are you comfortable communicating with a supervisor via a company chat line?

10. How will you handle the isolation of working alone?

11. Do you have (or can you set up) a bank account for automatic payroll deposits?

12. Do you have any experience working at home or for a remote manager?

13. Are you a highly motivated self-starter who enjoys working by yourself?

14. Can you pass basic and criminal background checks (where required)?

Deciding Whether a Home Agent Program Is Right for You

This list gives you the most important questions to ask when you decide whether to launch a home agent program:

- ✔ What are your main objectives for going the home agent route?
- ✔ Why aren't you outsourcing the calls instead?

✔ What calls and queues do you plan to send to home agents?

✔ Will you use an *employee model* (run it yourself) or a *contractor model* (use a vendor)? How does this decision support your objectives?

✔ What does your organization need to invest to set up a home agent program, and when can it achieve a payback?

✔ What do you expect to save in costs, and does using home agents fit into your overall business goals? (Assume that establishing home agents gives you a reduction in agent attrition rates and an increase in productivity.)

✔ What risks does this change come with, and how do you plan to deal with them? Risks might include upset customers going to the competition, upset employees leaving, decreases in productivity, union grievances, or hidden costs of technology or networks. We talk about mastering change in Chapter 16.

Include facts and data that support the opinions and insights that you offer in your recommendation to the executive decision-makers. You may be convinced based on talking to your peers for years, but facts help make the case.

Figuring Out the Technology

Whether you decide to go it alone or use a hosted solution, the following sections cover various technology considerations that you need to address with your technology advisors, which can help you speak their language.

Deciding where to host the network

Your first (and major) choice is whether to set up and run the technology yourself (with your tech team) or outsource the network and security to a hosted vendor that will deal with the headaches associated with technology.

Hosting the network yourself

Mario Perez, chief executive officer of Telax, a hosted call center solutions provider, advises that you use the following criteria to decide whether to keep the network in-house. According to Perez, if the following elements are in place, you can host and manage the network yourself:

✔ A *private branch exchange* (PBX) that allows you to run a Voice over Internet Protocol (VoIP) phone system.

✔ A tech team that can manage the remote setup and maintenance of a large number of agents. Your team may be able to handle 5 to 8 agents, but can it keep pace with 100 agents?

✔ Relatively low security-level needs (see the nearby sidebar "Levels of security") and a security setup capable of protecting you across the Internet. You can't have any high-end security requirements that need dedicated data lines or a complex network design that separates voice and data.

If you don't have all those elements in place but your call center has 200 to 300 seats, your company can afford to invest in new equipment and software for hosting its own network.

Using a network provider

According to Perez, you may want to consider using an experienced provider to host your network if your call center doesn't have any one of the elements listed in the preceding section. Also, if your call center has fewer than 200 seats, a hosted solution is probably more cost-effective.

Setting up a network in-house

Figure 11-1 is a simple diagram that shows you how your tech team will set up your network. In the figure, *PSTN* stands for *public switched telephone network,* which involves good ol' dial-up phones; *ACD* stands for *automatic call distributor;* and *IVR* stands for *interactive voice response.* (For more information on ACD and IVR systems, see Chapter 9.)

Here's what your tech team needs to set up (and what you need to include as costs in your business plan):

✔ **IP-enabled phones at home:** Each phone added requires the equivalent capacity at the switch in the call center. The type of PBX and security setup existing in your call center may dictate the type of phones your agents need.

✔ **A router in each agent's home:** You can purchase phones that have routers included or have a separate router at each location.

✔ **A computer data line into the house:** If the agent already has a broadband Internet connection, you don't need to add this line (but you might assume the cost).

✔ **A dedicated phone line:** Unless you're sending VoIP calls, which would travel on the existing broadband data line, each agent needs a dedicated phone line.

Calculating installation time

Setting up your home agents can take as little time as 4 weeks or as much time as 12 weeks, depending on these factors:

✔ Whether the phone vendors are responding quickly to your requests and have available inventory of phones, routers, and PBX cards

✔ Whether your tech team has the resources to get the job done and you've finalized the technical requirements

✔ Whether the telephone company can provide added bandwidth and dedicated lines

✔ Whether the back-end PBX switch is IP-ready and requires upgrades to card slots or security

✔ How far your agents live from a tech team, which dictates how far tech teams have to travel to agents' homes for setup

Protecting your data

Here's a starter list of security and data protection tasks for your tech team to carry out:

✔ Remove home agents' ability to cut and paste data, print confidential reports, or copy data to their hard drives.

✔ Ensure that home agents have up-to-date operating systems and firewall protection for their computers (and that their firewalls are turned on).

✔ Install the latest security software, and give enterprise security software to all home agents.

✔ Set up agents with strong passwords, and train them to lock their computers when they're away from their desks.

✔ Enable remote access for tech support personnel so that they can both support and observe agents' computer behaviors.

✔ Allow home agents to see only the last four digits of customers' credit-card numbers.

Levels of security

Here's a summary of security levels:

✔ **High (most expensive):** Dedicated data and voice lines that only your data passes through

✔ **Medium:** Virtual private network over the Internet

✔ **Low (least expensive):** Internet access with minimum security standards

Premises-Based Solution

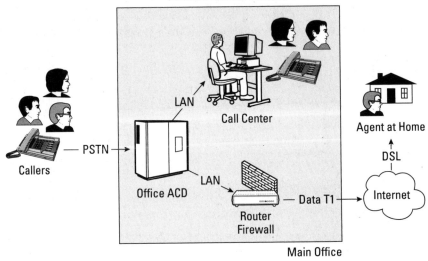

Hosted Solution

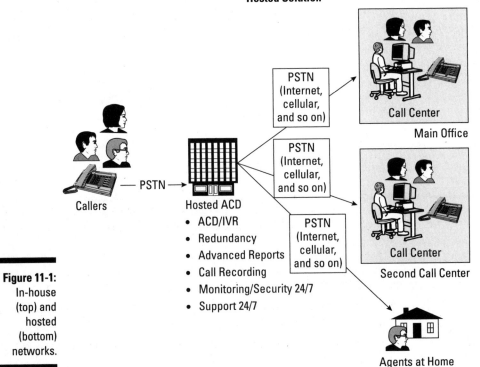

Figure 11-1:
In-house
(top) and
hosted
(bottom)
networks.

Making home agents secure

With a little bit of thought, you can ensure that working at home doesn't mean more downtime, more data risk, or lower productivity. You can manage these risk areas, if you know how:

- ✔ Have each home agent sign in and out by using biometric fingerprint scanners to prove that it's really the agent who's logged in.

- ✔ Provide home agents technical support whenever they need it to eliminate viruses and fix other computer problems so that those agents can keep working (and feel supported).

- ✔ Educate home agents about security risks and how to protect against them.

- ✔ Ensure that each home agent knows the most serious compliance guidelines — the ones that can lead to dismissal if not followed.

- ✔ Require agents to block or stop all other Internet traffic (games, downloads, and so on) while they're working, because this traffic reduces bandwidth and affects the sound quality of a call.

Implementing the Program

After you figure out whether home agents can fit into your call center's structure, you can create an *operating plan* (sort of like a checklist of tasks that you must do to get a home agent program going) and determine what type of work and leadership support agents may need.

Creating an operating plan

An operating plan follows the principle of the skilled handyman: Measure twice, cut once. Do thorough planning so that you can avoid making costly mistakes later. You have plenty of issues to consider. Here are a few important ones to start with:

- ✔ **Business specifications:** Your operating plan needs to have a list of business specifications that can help support your strategy, including

    - • Types of calls that you route to home agents and optimal periods of time during which you schedule home agents

    - • Whether you're going to build your own program or outsource it (see Chapter 5)

- Security measures and what expectations you set for your agents with respect to security and privacy

- Home agent technical setup

- Whether to use proven in-house agents or combine newly hired agents and existing agents

✔ **Selection process for home agents:** How can existing agents apply for these positions? How do you select candidates?

✔ **Selection process for team leaders:** How do you select the right team leader for these home agents? What's the right ratio of team leaders to home agents? How are you going to help your team leaders coach remotely?

✔ **Training:** What type of training do you plan to provide to existing agents? You might have them trained in troubleshooting simple technical issues with their computers, for example, which can save you downtime and money when an agent's equipment isn't working.

Planning the work

You have to make the same decision — which calls you want to send to home agents and how much ramp-up you need per call type — regardless of whether you outsource or manage your own home agent program. Going the outsourcer route might involve many new agents who work remotely and aren't experienced in your business. If you're in pizza delivery, and your operation has relatively simple transactions and huge swings in call volume (pizza companies see a threefold to sixfold increase in calls starting Friday night into the weekend), using home agents makes loads of sense, because you can easily train many folks remotely. It's difficult, however, to train home agents to support complex financial products or services.

You might also consider using home agents when you need agents who have highly specialized skills, so you have to look in a larger geographic area to find and recruit enough quality agents who have that specific skill. Such specialized areas include technical support, insurance, travel agency, and health care. You may have a longer ramp-up, however, because of complex scenarios, the kind of decision-making and judgment required, and the need for formal certifications (or very thorough security checks).

Building a management team

Depending on the scale and speed of the growth of your home agent program, you need to determine in your operating plan (refer to "Creating an operating plan," earlier in this chapter) whether you need to make the following management roles full-time, dedicated, or part-time.

Whatever time you think you need, add 50 percent until you test it. During planning, people have a tendency to underestimate (a lot!) the actual effort required.

The core team includes

- ✔ **Team leader:** Oversees the home agent program. This person needs training in the specifics of remote management — how to monitor, motivate, communicate, coach, and train.

- ✔ **Tech-support liaison:** Needs great rapport and patience with home agents who have technical challenges. (You don't need this liaison if another company looks after your computers and network.)

- ✔ **Home agent training specialist:** Knows how to deliver training online and across virtual networks, and can lead the occasional in-house class.

Explaining the program to your staff

Touch on these key points to help sell the idea of working at home to your agents and management team:

- ✔ **A flexible workforce is important for success.** Both the company's and the call center's long-term success may depend on home agents as part of the mix, for reasons including business continuity and employee retention. You can cite the reasons that we discuss in this chapter to explain why companies go this route.

- ✔ **This is only a test.** Let your staff know that you're starting a pilot only to test the concept. You'll share with the team along the way what's working and what's not working, and together, you'll keep improving the program. (For more details on pilot programs, see the sidebar "Launching a pilot home agent program.")

- ✔ **Home agents aren't going to replace in-house agents.** In-house agents can become home agents, if necessary, but the company doesn't plan to force anyone to work from home.

- ✔ **Managers can expand their skill sets.** In our research of home agent programs, we've found that managers who are involved in these programs acquire new skills from leading both in-house and at-home agents, and many enjoy the new challenges. Those who work with home agents say that the program helps them understand how to measure and motivate, as well as focus on results, without having the face-to-face advantage.

See "Providing an attractive work option for your agents," earlier in this chapter, for a good benefits list that you can also use in this discussion.

Launching a pilot home agent program

You get many benefits from using a pilot home agent program, which reduces risk and helps persuade current team members to sign up. You can start with, say, six agents working from home; test the issues; and get the pioneers through a phased transition. Use the pilot results to make your business case to the executive team, other managers, and other agents. Here are a few things you can try:

✔ Start the agent guinea pigs in-house in isolation pods so that they work alone and become accustomed to seeking support only through the channels they'll have as home agents. Dedicate a team leader to manage your home program, giving these agents full attention and documenting the issues that arise. Run this isolation program for one to three months until all six agents say, "We're ready to do this!"

✔ Send the six agents home, and repeat the pilot. By now, you've addressed some of the differences caused by isolation, so you have to deal with only the new considerations that come from working at home. Again, your dedicated team leader documents and solves new issues when they arise. Run this pilot program for three to six months.

When you use this slow and steady approach, only a small percentage of calls will involve a negative customer experience (barking dogs, remote systems down, and so on), so you can manage your customer risk.

Selecting and/or recruiting agents

You might hire in-house (select) or from external sources (recruit). If not enough internal employees sign up or meet the requirements to work at home, you may need to recruit.

When selecting current in-house agents to move into home agent positions, use an interview process and a self-assessment to check for the following:

✔ Do they have 12 to 18 months on the job and know your products and services well? (You may decide to drop this criterion if you have a very short training cycle and a simple product line.)

✔ Have they had strong, consistent performance evaluations?

✔ Are they willing to work part-time shifts and short time-interval shifts? Can they work shifts that allow you to have the most flexible workforce?

✔ Are they self-motivated, getting the job done without supervision?

✔ Do they have better-than-average time-management skills?

✔ Do they have sufficient computer skills to handle downloads and computer fixes?

Make your interviews behavior-based, asking your potential home agents how they'd respond to different scenarios (such as isolation, technical problems, or stressful calls).

Setting up the agents at home

We recommend that you consider the following factors when you get agents set up to work at home:

- ✔ **Employment contracts:** Companies provide employment contracts that outline technology and Internet use, customer privacy rules, procedures for adapting and maintaining the work environment, security, required performance levels, and types of shifts. Home agents must understand that if they don't follow some of these guidelines (such as security), they may lose their jobs, and other violations (such as preventable background noise) can lead to your recalling them to work in the call center.

- ✔ **Employment guidelines:** Develop a consistent set of guidelines, and build them into a contract. In union environments in which new contracts aren't allowed, make it clear that these guidelines don't qualify as contracts but still set the working relationship. Have all home agents sign a copy of these guidelines.

- ✔ **Technical setup:** Take the time to set up each home agent's work area properly. You may want to use an ergonomics checklist to assess the safety of each home office.

- ✔ **Employee expectations:** Set clear expectations, refresh your home agents on existing expectations, and make sure that agents know the new expectations that working at home impose.

- ✔ **Paperwork:** Don't underestimate how long you may have to wait for 20 to 50 agents to send back accurate paperwork.

Integrating Best Practices into the Program

You can follow several best practices to ensure that your program runs successfully and that home agents stay motivated and productive. Many of the best practices for home agents are similar to best practices for your call center. Use the practices that we discuss in the following sections to better your chances of managing and growing your home agent program.

Delivering uniform customer service

Delivering consistent customer service doesn't change dramatically when you use home agents. The same criteria that apply to in-house agents apply to home agents; agents have different customer-handling proficiencies, motivations, temperaments, and so on.

Focus on these criteria for success:

- ✔ **Select the best-skilled agents who can work independently, know the products well, and can navigate the online systems competently.** Skill and experience are more important for complex operations (such as telecommunications or insurance) and less so for operations that handle calls such as offering billing information, answering retail shoppers' questions, or taking food-delivery orders.

- ✔ **Set clear expectations, and monitor home agents against their results.** Make sure that the home agents have the same key performance goals as your internal agents, and communicate with your home agents often if they're not meeting your expectations.

- ✔ **Give home agents ongoing coaching.** Put a specific focus on customer-handling skills, listening skills, and content knowledge (especially on the most frequently asked questions). Use a dedicated home agent team leader to stay on top of this ongoing coaching. (For more information on coaching, see Chapter 13.)

- ✔ **Provide subject-matter experts for the same hours that home agents work.** If you do this, when customers need specialized information, an expert is able to provide it quickly.

- ✔ **Provide virtual chat rooms.** These chat rooms can provide real-time agent support and allow home agents to contact managers or senior agents about nonurgent issues.

- ✔ **Give home agents the authority and training to do the right thing for customers.** You should also establish this policy in-house.

- ✔ **Include home agents in incentives and contests.** You want them to feel that they're part of the team and are rewarded the same way.

- ✔ **Give home agents the same tools and system stability that you provide in-house** (if you have good tools and stability in-house, of course).

- ✔ **Give home agents regular performance feedback.** Make this feedback a coaching opportunity.

The best service is provided by happy and energetic agents. If home agents are happier than they would be as in-house agents, they provide better service.

Aligning the workforce and quality teams

For a home agent program to work successfully, you must explain to your call center's support teams what processes will change and what processes will stay the same. Quality assurance, which ensures agents' call consistency and obligations, and the workforce team, which schedules the home agents' work hours, play important roles in a home agent program:

- ✔ **Quality assurance:** Most of our clients who use home agents make no big adjustments in their quality-assurance programs, although they may listen for background noises such as doorbells and dogs barking. You can use the same monitoring process as long as your tech team can provide remote real-time or recorded-call capability. You use the same ratio of quality-assurance staff to home agents as you do for in-house agents. You may want to increase the monitoring in the beginning, however, to ensure that customer service doesn't go off the rails.

   Make sure that your home agent team leader can take agents through their quality-assurance scores, and use those scores as a coaching opportunity. Don't have quality assurance toss scores over the fence to the agents (with no feedback loop) and hope that they land softly.

- ✔ **Workforce:** Smooth workforce scheduling improves vastly if you closely match work shifts to customer volumes. If you have very high short-term intervals — mainly, hourly swings — you can greatly benefit from having agents who are willing to work by the hour or (better still) by the half hour. Some home agent outsourcers that employ subcontractors (meaning self-employed home agents) contract those agents for 30-minute increments and guarantee them a minimum number of hours per day. This setup doesn't work for all companies, but you may want to use it if you have high interval swings.

All programs are set up differently, but if you want a highly flexible staffing pool, you want many part-timers working very short incremental shifts. Many programs have home agents working 10 to 20 hours per week, so you need to think about a 3 to 1 ratio when recruiting — that is, you need three part-timers working 12 to 13 hours per week to cover the same shifts as one full-time agent working 35 to 40 hours per week in-house.

If you don't achieve maximum scheduling flexibility, in which staffing matches your call volume spikes, you might ask why you're using home agents. Make sure that your home agents are willing to work more variable shifts as a trade-off for working from home.

Helping Agents Deal with In-House and At-Home Differences

To set up a successful home agent program, you need to ensure that agents who move from in-house to at-home work don't lose productivity or can't focus on delivering great service. Home agents sometimes have trouble transitioning because they feel isolated working at home, don't feel that they're part of the company, and don't have in-person supervision. The following sections look at some strategies you can use to remedy these kinds of problems.

Training

If you rely on a virtual training model, plan to add 15 percent to 25 percent more training time. Without face-to-face contact, people can find it more difficult to quickly grasp what they're being told, and instructors can't easily watch those people navigate the online systems.

If you're providing online training, do you already have the content developed? Preparing this content can take a long time if you have to start from scratch. If the training team takes four weeks to train in a classroom, you have to manage a lot of content and transpose that content online. Part of your operating plan (which we talk about in "Creating an operating plan," earlier in this chapter) should include your training strategy and the people who will implement that strategy.

Isolation

The home option works best for agents who can handle a relatively isolated work environment because interactions occur via phone, chat, and e-mail. The following practices can help you keep home agents from feeling isolated:

- Allow home agents to chat online or blog to create a community of home agents who experience similar issues.
- Include home agents in all the contests, annual parties, and awards in your call center.
- So that they can connect to your company culture and to coworkers, allow home agents to visit the call center whenever they want. (Some companies even require home agents to work on-site at regular intervals — typically, two times per month.) If your home agents visit your call center each month, they feel that they belong to the company, they can bond with the support teams, and they can meet their team leaders for some one-on-one coaching.

Provide a dedicated support system

When Arlene King and Ian Cruickshank from TELUS started their home agent program, they tried different operating models to determine what would work best for their agents and front-line managers. Home agent feedback quickly revealed that those agents had different support needs from in-house agents. Team leaders needed to develop new skills and processes to enable them to better support the unique needs of home agents.

King and Cruickshank switched direction, consolidating all their virtual teams into teams comprised mostly of home agents. From their existing pool of managers, they selected those who best demonstrated the ability to work with virtual call center employees to lead the home agent teams. Those managers were specially trained in the unique processes, communication, recognition, and coaching tools for managing home agents.

This team system generated very positive results. The home agents improved their customer service and productivity results, and they felt happier and more engaged in their jobs. The managers could provide a broader range of coaching, training, and process support to their home agents in these specialized teams than in the previously blended teams.

> Set up some temporary workstations, and create well-structured schedules for each visit. Make these visits worth the home agents' while; they didn't drive across town (or from another town) for a group hug. Plan to help them hone their skills, connect with others, and leave their visits inspired (not tired).

✔ Have a home agent team leader, if possible. Home agents understand the needs, wants, and challenges of being a home agent better than anyone else.

Part IV
Creating High-Performance Teams

The 5th Wave   By Rich Tennant

CUSTOMER PHONE SERVICE AT DISNEY CORP.

In this part . . .

We cover recruiting, job expectations, training, coaching, and feedback. We also provide a simple framework to help you manage the performance of the most important resource in your organization: your agents.

In this part, you can also find out about the concept of employee engagement and discover some strategies to motivate your agents.

Chapter 12

Hiring and Training

• •

In This Chapter

▶ Reviewing the primary components that contribute to agent success

▶ Introducing a step-by-step process for managing agent performance

▶ Understanding the importance of employee evaluation in hiring

▶ Setting clear expectations for employees

▶ Providing effective training

• •

*E*very agent is a miniature version of your call center. Each efficiency achieved or sale made, or each customer gained or lost, by an agent directly affects the overall productivity, revenue, and customer satisfaction of the entire operation. Moreover, variation in performance among agents highlights opportunities for improvement in both agents and processes. All too frequently, however, call centers don't manage agent performance well or don't do it at all.

After you build a high-performing team (we discuss call center roles in Chapter 3) and understand the basic principles of optimizing performance (see Chapter 14), you can use a simple process to manage your agents' performance in a way that improves results for your operation.

Recognizing the Key Components of Optimal Performance

In virtually any human endeavor, the three primary components that contribute to success are skill, motivation, and opportunity. Only when your agents can optimize all three factors can you maximize call center performance and results.

Here's a brief overview of these important components:

- ✔ **Skill:** Skill is ability or aptitude to do the job. It includes what the agents bring to the party and what you provide them after they arrive.

- ✔ **Motivation:** Motivation is behavior that directs agents toward a goal. What your company does to arouse, maintain, and direct agents' motivation also affects agents' performance.

- ✔ **Opportunity:** No matter how skilled or motivated your agents are, they can't find success without opportunity, and they can't control opportunity on their own. The environment that you put your agents in shapes their opportunities. Tools, marketing, company policies, work processes, competition, media, economy, customers, and scope for growth within your organization all affect opportunity.

  Generally, all agents have the same level of opportunity. You can do a lot of things to increase opportunity for your agents, however, such as improving tools like customer relationship management applications (see Chapter 10), improving your product, and improving work processes and company policies.

Think about how these elements of performance relate to professional athletes, who need a certain level of skill and an appropriate amount of motivation. The best players tend to have a natural, inherent desire to succeed. But athletes can't play if they don't have an opportunity. Without fans buying tickets, no games are played — and no games means no opportunity to show off all that skill and motivation.

Managing agent performance involves managing agents' skills and motivation in an effective and ongoing manner. If you manage agent performance well, skill and motivation improve continually. If you manage poorly, at best nothing happens; at worst agents become disenchanted.

Managing Employee Performance in Five Simple Steps

Managing agent performance boils down to following these five steps:

1. **Hire the right people.**

2. **Tell them what to do and why.**

3. **Show them how to do it.**

4. **Give them feedback on how they're doing.**

5. **Make supporting them your number-one mission.**

We cover the first three steps in this chapter; Chapter 13 talks about the final two steps.

Recruiting the Right People

Hiring the right people to work in your call center is very important. Perhaps you're thinking, "In a call center, who's the right person? Someone who can speak?" But if you hire a person who isn't a good fit, especially from a skill and motivation standpoint, your call center's performance suffers. We discuss the skill and motivation aspects of recruiting in the following sections.

Evaluating skill

Testing for skill is the easy part. You can take many approaches to evaluate skill level, several of which we discuss in the following sections.

Résumés and interviews

You can't find a better predictor of future success than past success. If candidates have done well in the past on jobs similar to the one you're considering them for, they're seemingly ideal candidates. Making this determination is easier said than done, however. To ensure that you can weed out those candidates who might have exaggerated past successes, use these behavioral questions to determine just how well they did:

- ✔ What steps did you use to perform a relevant activity?

- ✔ What challenges did you face when you had to deal with a new aspect of your work?

- ✔ What results did your former employer measure you on? Which measures did you excel in, and which did you struggle with?

- ✔ What are some of the techniques you used when you were performing your job function? What did you say to be successful? What techniques did you try that weren't successful, so that you stopped using them?

✔ What do you do first when you have an upset customer on the phone? What do you do next?

When interviewing potential call center agents, you may want to consider doing the first interview over the phone. A phone interview gives you an excellent opportunity to see how the candidate sounds and handles himself in a live-call situation. Tell the candidate that you want to record the interview, and be sure to ask for permission first.

Reference checks

Reference checks are becoming more difficult to do, because previous employers may face legal liability if they give a bad reference and the candidate doesn't get the job. Also, candidates never give you references from places that fired them, so you have to read between the lines. If a former employer is gushing and enthusiastic, she's likely sincere. If she mumbles, refuses to answer direct questions, and makes vague statements, she may be trying to avoid a lawsuit.

Here's some key information to get from a candidate's former employer:

✔ Confirm the candidate's employment record, dates of work, position and title held, and so on.

✔ Describe your job, and ask whether the former employer feels that the candidate may be suitable for it.

✔ Find out what the candidate did exceptionally well and what he would require some coaching to improve.

✔ Ask whether the former employer would rehire the candidate if given the chance.

Aptitude tests

If you can't predict a candidate's likelihood of success in the job by looking at her résumé, interviewing her, and checking references, you can use employment testing. Online testing and case studies (including sample calls) are becoming the industry standards. You generally offer these tests after screening a potential employee but before offering a formal interview.

Here are some of the tests that we find most valuable in determining a candidate's fitness for the job:

✔ **Customer service aptitude testing:** Indicates whether the candidate can handle different customers' styles, emotions, and issues in a professional, calm, and empathetic manner.

✔ **Sales aptitude testing:** Indicates whether the candidate has the aptitude and listening skills to diagnose customer problems and offer solutions that can make money for your company. Sales aptitude includes confidence and assertiveness, as well as a positive attitude about selling.

✔ **Computer skills testing:** Indicates whether the candidate has the analytical and logical skills to use multiple systems.

✔ **Call center aptitude testing:** Indicates whether the candidate can sit in one place for an extended period and handle the routines and repetitiveness of the position successfully.

You can find these tests by contacting recruiting agencies or searching the Internet.

Make sure that your human resources team has thoroughly validated a test to prove that it accurately predicts success on the job. Using a test that hasn't been validated may expose your organization to lawsuits filed by people who feel discriminated against.

Reducing recruiting time through technology

If you run a call center that has a large number of employees, you're probably recruiting new agents continually to keep up with staff turnover. Some large call centers use interactive voice response (IVR; see Chapter 9) to manage large volumes of applicants so that a limited recruiting staff can focus on the personal-interviews stage.

When a call center uses this method, interested job applicants simply call a toll-free number. Typically, the IVR system asks the applicant to enter a telephone number and other identifying information for potential callback by recruiters. Then the system gives the applicant a brief introduction to the business; lists available positions; and interviews the caller about his education, qualifications, and other job requirements. At the end of the automated interview, the applicant receives a reference number, and the call ends.

The IVR system uses the data collected to create reports that your recruiters can search or filter based on their preferred criteria. You can select only those candidates who have customer service experience or a certain education level, for example, thereby eliminating those who don't qualify for a live interview. This system reduces the number of live interviews conducted and allows your recruiting team to focus on those applicants who are qualified for the job.

Do your own in-house validation to see which methods work best for your call center's needs. You could collect data about agent performance, for example, and then compare your employees' success on the job with their employment test results to see whether your employment tests accurately predicted ability. You probably have a math whiz in your office who remembers how to do correlation analysis; if you want to be really precise, let him have at it, and see what he uncovers. He could amaze you!

Evaluating motivation

Predicting skills and *aptitude* (the ability to develop skills) is fairly easy, but you also need to understand a candidate's motivation, which can be much more difficult.

You can uncover some of this information at the interview and reference-check stages, assuming that the candidate's previous job was call center–related. Did she like her previous job? How was his attendance? Did she advance? Why did he leave?

If the candidate's never done a call center job, have her listen to some calls — maybe for a few hours. Ask the candidate specific questions, such as these:

- ✔ What do you think of the job?
- ✔ Does it interest you?
- ✔ Can you see yourself being in this role for five years?
- ✔ How would this job help you achieve your life goals?

Levels of interest and motivation in past jobs give you a good indicator of future motivation in the new job.

In the same way that skills testing tells you whether a candidate can do the job, motivational assessment indicates whether he *will* do the job. Some form of motivational testing helps supplement interviews and reference checks. You can build a motivational analysis into the skills test, or you can give a separate test for each of the factors. Either way, a motivational analysis can greatly enhance your hiring success. Go online and search for *job motivational tests* to get a look at your options, or ask your human resources department for recommendations on motivational testing.

Frequently categorized as personality profiles, good tests include a mechanism for detecting any attempt to manipulate the test.

Integrate whatever testing you do into your overall recruiting plan or model. (Figure 12-1 illustrates a sample recruiting process, including all the points at which you can weed out a candidate.) Also, assess your recruiting process against your employees' success on the job from time to time. If you aren't getting consistent results, you need to change the process.

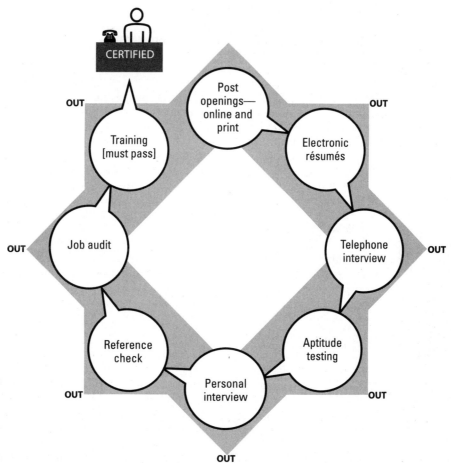

Figure 12-1:
A sample recruiting process.

Setting Agent Expectations

One of the primary reasons why people don't succeed on the job is that no one told them what to do, let alone provided specific, clear expectations. Make your expectations for agents clear on their first day of work. Agents need to know what they have to achieve to keep the job and what they need to do to excel. In this section, we provide pointers on setting expectations for your agents.

Setting performance goals

Most experienced leaders agree that at minimum, you need to make performance expectations specific, measurable or observable, and realistic. Typically, call centers have no problem setting specific and measurable expectations; making expectations realistic is more of a challenge.

Frequently, call centers set expectations at the level where management wants to see performance, rather than what's achievable but a challenging stretch for the majority of agents. If you set expectations unrealistically high, agents either ignore them or become frustrated and demotivated in attempting to achieve them. If you set expectations unrealistically low, agents may ignore them because those expectations aren't challenging. In both cases, the expectations fail to motivate employees.

A minimum expectation gives clear direction to your staff on the minimum they need to achieve. Because the expectation is based on the average performance of the group, minus an acceptable percentage near that average range, most employees will eventually achieve it without too much concern. Perhaps 15 percent to 20 percent of your staff will be conscious of the minimum expectation at any time.

Establishing bonuses

To really motivate your agents and promote continuous improvement, consider setting a bonus level of performance.

Set the bonus level the same way that you set minimum expectations, except that for the bonus level of performance, you calculate the group average performance and add one standard deviation. At any time, approximately 13 percent of your staff will achieve this bonus-level expectation, making the expectation realistic. Some employees will perform just below this bonus level, and because they're close to achieving the bonus, they'll feel motivated to do just a little better. This motivation results in improvement for both the individual agents and the group as a whole, pushing up average performance, the minimum expectation, and the bonus-level expectation.

When you set minimum and bonus goals by team each quarter, you create gentle pressure on the entire organization to improve. Periodically, you need to change the goals to reflect improvements in process and agent performance.

Doing the math on agent performance

To create agent expectations that are specific, measurable, and realistic, you can use the historical performance of the agent group. Use one standard deviation from the average performance of the group to set the minimum, as illustrated by the control chart in Figure 12-2.

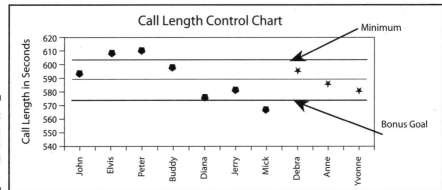

Figure 12-2: Tracking call length on a control chart.

A *control chart* sets high and low expectations, and maps where each agent falls in comparison to those expectations. In the preceding figure, the minimum expectation is set at approximately 603 seconds — one standard deviation above the team average of 589 seconds. The bonus target for call length is approximately 575 seconds — one standard deviation below the average. So 87 percent of your staff will achieve this minimum. You can target those who don't achieve the minimum for extra help.

For more information on standard deviations, control charts, and other topics that are beyond the scope of this book, see *Statistics For Dummies,* by Deborah Rumsey (Wiley Publishing, Inc.).

Balancing your expectations

If you concentrate your expectations on any one measure, you get what you ask for — great results in that one measure, perhaps to the detriment of other areas of performance. You need to take a balanced approach to setting expectations.

Every call's a sales call

In Chapter 2, we mention that improvement in your call center's revenue generation can have a greater effect on results than improvements in cost-control measures. In large call centers, small improvements in *retention rate* (maintaining customers who call to cancel service) can represent hundreds of thousands — or even millions — of dollars in saved revenue. Similarly, small improvements in selling and upselling (see Chapter 6) can represent hundreds of thousands of dollars or more.

Because every interaction with a customer gives you a chance to enhance your business relationship, you need to set the expectation that agents will treat every call as an opportunity to increase revenue, now or in the future.

In compiling agent performance data for a rock-and-roll call center (where people called to answer trivia questions), management noticed that no one measure told the complete story about which agents were contributing more than the others, as the following examples show:

- John had the lowest call length, but when management combined this measure with other measures, he came out fourth in the overall ranking. He should focus on improving his first-call resolution. Maybe he tries to get through calls too quickly.

- Mary made the most sales, but her average revenue per sale needed some improvement.

- Peter was the highest-performing agent because he had a high customer-opinion rating and high average revenue per sale. Even though he had a longer call length than the others, his overall contribution translated into the highest overall performance index.

Consider the measures that you want to weigh in your call center's overall performance index to reflect their importance to the call center and the company.

Giving specific directions

When you tell your agents specifically *what* you expect of them, you're ahead of the game. When you tell them *why*, you're adding an extra level of motivational turbocharging that can kick-start continuous improvement.

Here are two good reasons you can give your agents for achieving their minimum expectations and stretch goals:

✔ **"Our department will meet its goals if we pull together."** Too often, the front line is left out of the big picture. Most people want to be part of a successful team. What's more, people want to know that their department and company are doing well and that their jobs are secure. Sharing department goals, how they work, and how individual results contribute to the overall goals can empower and motivate your agents.

✔ **"I'll reward you."** Raises, bonuses, commendations, or opportunities for advancement — whatever the reward structure is, you need to tie it to agents' achieving their objectives.

Providing Appropriate Training

After you hire very motivated and skilled people, and tell them exactly what you expect of them, don't stop there. If you do, you'll have some very frustrated high-performing people. (We wouldn't be alone in a room with a group of them.) Next, you have to show people how to perform the jobs that you're asking them to do. Many companies train, but not all of them train in a manner that shows people how to excel at what's expected of them.

You can find plenty of material on effective training. Online searches can give you many good options to explore. In the following sections, we focus on a few basic rules.

Make sure that you target training to your agents' job performance goals by asking these questions:

✔ How can this training help agents meet and excel at their job expectations?

✔ How can this training help agents get ahead in their skills and knowledge?

✔ How can this training help agents help the company?

Keeping the training simple

Research shows that shortly after training ends, trainees forget a very high percentage of the information that was delivered during training — maybe as high as 85 percent.

You have to stop fighting for retention of information and focus instead on a few critical things that you can get agents to remember, such as how to get a raise and what to avoid doing if they want to keep their jobs.

Also, focus on the development of critical skills for the job, such as how to use the database (which houses thousands of pieces of information that can help agents do their jobs well) and how to handle calls.

Focusing on a few critical policies, call-handling skills (call control, customer service, sales, and difficult situations), and knowledge tools can take your agents a long way toward getting the skills they need.

Covering the basics

Your call center's training should cover these key components:

- **Individual goals and expectations:** Provide a recap of what's expected of your agents, how their goals affect the department and the company, and how the training can help them achieve their call center goals.

- **Key policies and procedures:** Provide the critical information that agents need to know, and tell them how they can access information on policies and procedures in the future.

- **Product knowledge:** Make sure that agents know what products or services they're supporting and how to look up information about those products or services. (Agents who work in the call center of a major retailer, for example, probably can't remember details about all 53,239 products that the company sells, so they need to know how to access the relevant information.)

- **Call handling:** Demonstrate the skills that agents really need to do the job, and have them practice those skills. Agents can't achieve mastery in the training class, but good skill development in key areas can help them through difficult situations — especially during the challenging first few days or weeks on the job.

  Call-handling skills include

  - Call control
  - Defusing anger and dealing with difficult situations
  - Customer service
  - Sales strategies

  Also make information and tutorials on call handling accessible to agents through department systems.

- **System navigation:** Show your agents how to navigate all the various systems that they need to do their jobs. (See Chapter 9 for examples and explanations of the call center technology that agents may use.)

Systems in today's call centers are becoming increasingly integrated and user-friendly. Still, some operations continue to have a hodgepodge of older and newer systems. In these environments, agents may find remembering all the codes, toggles, back doors, and tricks to be very tough. New agents need a tutorial to help them along.

Keeping the training short

The sooner you get your agents on the phones, the sooner they can start developing the seeds that you planted in training. Even the best trainers don't plant fully developed crops, however. Give the new agents enough training to ensure that their lack of proficiency won't negatively affect your customers, test those agents to make sure that they understand what to do, and then get them out there (with support and coaching, of course). Training is a process, not an event.

Encouraging continued training

Jack Nicklaus, one of the most successful golfers of all time, once told an interviewer that he was still learning about the game of golf, even though at the time he was in his mid-50s.

You can look at training for a job in the same way. You can give your agents a great start by providing new-hire training, but the process of actually figuring out the job never ends. With this philosophy in mind, you can build in procedures to encourage continuous training, such as these:

- **Weekly quizzes:** Quizzes can test for ability in a specific area and, in the process, develop skill in and awareness of the subject.

- **Regular coaching sessions:** Conduct side-by-side sessions with agents to build their confidence and proficiency in interacting with customers. Specific areas include closing knowledge gaps; helping them think, talk, and type (multitasking); and further developing their *soft skills* in dealing with customers, meaning how those agents constructively communicate. Make these sessions short, sweet, and to the point. We provide more details on coaching in Chapter 13.

- **Mystery calls:** *Mystery calls* are mock calls that the phone system sends to an agent, in which a trainer or team leader plays the part of a customer incognito. You can use this approach to develop agents' problem-solving skills quickly and effectively.

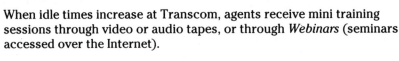

✔ **Team meetings:** Team meetings allow you to get new information (nothing too complex, though) or updates out to the entire team, and you can also celebrate successes. Use team meetings to develop some team bonding with recognition, idea generation, and fun activities.

✔ **Updates training:** When your agents need complex skill development, you may need to use classroom training. Again, keep the training simple and as brief as possible. Agents need to know the critical components of the new information — why it's so important and how it affects their job performance. Make sure that they also know where to find procedures and policies on the subject.

✔ **Idle-time training:** You can even inject training events between an agent's calls. Because you actually use the agent's idle time, you lower your cost, and because you tie the training to individual needs, that training is very effective.

When idle times increase at Transcom, agents receive mini training sessions through video or audio tapes, or through *Webinars* (seminars accessed over the Internet).

Chapter 13

Creating a Coaching Culture

● ●

In This Chapter

▶ Understanding the benefits of coaching

▶ Following some basic principles of coaching

▶ Training your call center's coaches

● ●

*Y*ou only need to look at the professional (and amateur) sports model to see the impact of coaching. These multimillion-dollar businesses have managers and administrators, as is typical in any business. The core position, however, is the coach, whose role involves the development of the human capital — that is, the players — to their full potential.

Call centers that have a similarly high human-capital component don't always take advantage of coaching. They often relegate the job to managers and administrators instead of doing what sports teams do: Remove the administration and management duties from the coach so that he can focus on people performance.

In this chapter, we show you how to make training a top priority for your team leaders. Yes, training! You may have promoted your best agent, but that doesn't necessarily make her the best coach. Coaching is an art and a science that uses specific techniques and methods to help you maximize your agent potential. This chapter also includes the recipe for the secret sauce: the top ten applied coaching principles that set you up for success.

Don't think of coaching as just a nice employee-centered activity. It *is* a nice activity, but we do it because it's the surest path to minimizing costly repeat calls; optimizing revenue opportunities; and delivering a consistent, high-quality customer experience. With 65 percent to 75 percent of your costs being driven by agent wages, benefits, and incentives, coaching is a critical tool to improve the retention and overall performance of your agents. It also corrects a common problem of noncoaching organizations: Despite the expense and effort, classroom training fails to produce a performance return on investment.

Seeing the Benefits of Coaching

Selling an investment in coaching to your organization isn't very different from persuading the organization to buy a piece of technology. Whether you're trying to get approval from your boss to invest in training for managers or to purchase a resource that can streamline administration, be sure to quantify the financial returns from any investment.

Financial benefits

Focused coaching can give you a significant number of measurable benefits, such as lower average handle time, improved sales, and increased first-call resolution. Moreover, coaching takes advantage of existing operational expenses (such as wages and benefits), so unlike technology solutions, it doesn't require new capital expenses.

Rather than plead for assistance, build a business case on why investing in your managers or the right support structure makes sense. Senior managers are more likely to see exactly why they need to invest in coaching when they can see the financial benefit. (See Chapter 10 for insights on building a business case.)

Here's one impressive statistic about good coaching that may sway senior managers: Industry statistics consistently indicate that a rigorous coaching system returns an 8 percent to 18 percent reduction in operational expense or increase in revenue.

Performance benefits

If your call center uses coaching, agents can benefit by figuring out how to do their jobs more effectively and quickly, which makes them feel confident and relaxed when they perform those jobs. Very often, top performers get more money and promotions. Also, agents who know how to do the job want to improve their performance. High anxiety in call centers often stems from coming to work every day and not knowing whether you're doing the job correctly.

Companies can quickly get a good result from time spent coaching their agents. The following sections talk about five areas of positive effect.

Operational efficiency

Coaching enables each agent to minimize the time spent on each call on a call-by-call basis and over each shift worked. It has a direct and immediate effect on profitability because constant improvements in efficiency mean that you need fewer agents (and fewer support roles around them). Reducing agent head count by even 5 percent provides your organization significant savings. (In Chapter 6, we talk about where agent time goes and how to make agents use their time more efficiently.)

Operational effectiveness

Coaching helps agents handle the reason for a customer's call during that first call, without errors and with high customer satisfaction. These effectiveness elements together reduce expense by reducing repeat calls. Many non-coaching organizations experience a 40 percent repeat call rate on the same issues, which dramatically drives up their operating costs.

Revenue generation

Coaching supports and improves the advanced selling skills of agents, including how to identify customer needs and offer additional products to the customer. An agent's ability to sell, especially on service calls, allows organizations to transition from cost center to profit center, which can easily pay for the investment in coaching effort. With a lot of companies pushing many contacts to self-service (such as interactive voice response or the Web), every live contact with the customer needs to provide an opportunity to sell, as well as to service.

One of SwitchGear's clients is a small technical support center that handles inbound support calls from consumers. In response to the center's potential outsourcing, the director of the center decided to initiate a specific revenue opportunity. We identified a specific call driver tied to an additional product offering that could prevent problems from arising in the future. Focused coaching over a six-month period produced enough revenue to cover 18 percent of the call center costs, which made the executives decide against losing that revenue source by outsourcing.

Customer satisfaction and retention

With the high cost of customer acquisition, you have to retain the right customers if you want to succeed. Exceptional customer service is the only sustainable competitive advantage in businesses. Ongoing coaching helps keep the importance of every customer interaction front and center in every agent's mind.

Employee engagement and retention

You want to keep proficient agents and team leaders engaged and in the organization for a long time. Often, agents leave your call center because they feel stressed, unsupported, and inefficient. Sustained coaching can easily produce a 25 percent to 50 percent reduction in the number of agents leaving your call center for jobs elsewhere.

If your call center spends less on recruiting, training, and lost productivity related to agent turnover — by adding as little as two to four months to the time an agent stays with you — you can potentially save hundreds of thousands of dollars.

Understanding the Principles of Coaching

Overall, organizational culture helps determine potential for success. A building block of a coaching culture is the ability to establish trust and engage people in meaningful work. You can manage employees without trust, but leading and coaching them require that they trust you.

Coaching can succeed only if it becomes a top-priority job responsibility for the team leader. Often, an organization assigns too many duties to team leaders, which spreads them thin, taking them off the floor and away from their agents.

In the following sections, we explain ten key principles that can help you and your organization focus on active coaching in your call center.

Get the coach on the court

Get the coach (meaning the team leader) working side by side with the agents she supervises and the team she leads. A team leader can't establish the foundational credibility that she needs to be an effective coach if she has a superficial knowledge of the business and is more comfortable being a spectator than a competitor.

Prioritize ruthlessly

A team leader absolutely needs to focus. Nothing is more valuable than the team leader's ability to motivate his agents and accelerate their performance. Assign the task of writing reports and doing other administrative work to someone else so that team leaders can focus on their teams.

Distinguish among management, leadership, and coaching

Be clear about the differences among management, leadership, and coaching, which are completely different disciplines that may not mix:

- **Management** is about policies, procedures, projects, and administration — the "what" of the business.
- **Leadership** is about inspiring people — the "who" of the business.
- **Coaching** is about helping people develop skills and improve their ability to do their jobs better — the "how" of the business.

Often, team leaders are caught in a reactive approach to the business that focuses on reports, new ways to control agents, and what happened yesterday. Coaching, by contrast, is proactive, affecting the team's ability to produce results in the future.

Ask, don't tell

Managers need to focus on getting information from their agents, rather than judging their agents. In this knowledge-based world of contact centers, the old command-and-control approach to management fails. An operation is destined to fail if the people who know the least about the processes, systems, and issues (meaning management) tell the people who know the most about the operational details (that would be the agents) what to do without seeking input. Managers need to ask, not tell.

Put energy before value

If agents don't trust management, those agents probably don't trust team leaders or welcome them on the call center floor. A team leader first needs to bring positive energy and then bring value that improves the performance of team members. If agents can't stand having the team leader side by side with them in the business, that team leader can't truly add value to the way agents do what they do.

Build on strengths

Don Shula, the former coach of the Miami Dolphins, said, "Build on people's strengths to engage them early in the process and have them partner with you to deliver results." Leaders must inspire and build on strengths instead of tearing agents down. A decade of employee satisfaction research shows that the number-one reason people leave an organization is because they have a poor relationship with their direct boss. If an agent is doing her job well 75 percent of the time, why isn't 75 percent of the feedback that she receives positive?

Focus on one skill and one step at a time

A weekly or daily approach that first focuses on specific behaviors can really help an agent improve his job performance. Conversely, if you give an agent a monthly list of results that you want him to improve on without offering daily support on how to make those improvements, the agent typically fails to improve his results.

In call centers that heavily manage their agents' performance, you typically find 5 percent to 15 percent of employees (the ones who perform poorly) on performance improvement plans. In coaching organizations, by comparison, you have 100 percent of employees using action plans so that those employees can continually improve performance and develop essential skills. Everyone should be on a plan to improve performance.

Be specific

If your summary notes from coaching say that agents must build better rapport or ask more questions, agents find this coaching hard to implement. They ask themselves, "How do I build better rapport? How many questions should I ask?" If an agent and manager don't know exactly what to work on after meeting, coaching hasn't happened.

An employee needs to leave a coaching session with a specific and actionable commitment that helps her develop her job skills.

Follow up

If an agent can't use the coaching that he receives on the next customer call, and therefore doesn't start implementing this new information immediately, he probably won't implement the new technique weeks from now. Team leaders need to follow up with agents after coaching sessions as soon as the agents have had a chance to put the new skill into practice. Usually, this follow-up should happen the same day.

We're not suggesting that team leaders micromanage their agents' performance, but if agents don't trust their team leaders, they may feel that they're being micromanaged. The objective of coaching follow-up is to provide support and positive reinforcement, not to make agents feel smothered.

Practice consistency, repeatability, and results

Start the wheels in motion by focusing on a repeatable approach that works every day. As Stephen Covey says in *The Seven Habits of Highly Effective People* (Simon & Schuster), the main thing is to keep the main thing the main thing! World-class leaders and coaches all have the ability to focus on improving the call center's results by working with their agents every day — not once a month.

Coaching the Coaches

Many call center organizations believe that they have an effective coaching program in place when they really don't. They can find many clues, if they want to look: poor or inconsistent service and sales results, increasing operational costs, poor attendance, and high agent attrition, to name a few. Few companies have a sustainable and successful coaching system that can fundamentally change the company culture to a high-performance coaching culture, in part because very few companies invest in the most important positions: the coaches.

Although organizations push for improvements in performance and encourage change, they often focus on the agents directly by offering a lot of training. Usually, they ignore the team leaders. This small group of resources in your call center determines the performance ability of *all* your agents and the call center's culture. They can either enable positive change or prevent it from occurring. Yet most of these managers used to work as agents, and the company promoted them without training them to coach and lead people. Being great agents didn't prepare them for being great team leaders.

A coach who can help improve the performance of her agents by continually becoming more skilled herself provides a huge asset to the business. Your organization probably promoted the current team leaders because they performed well in the role of agent. Now you need to train them to be great coaches.

Chapter 14

Creating a Motivated Workforce

In This Chapter

▶ Recognizing the importance of employee motivation

▶ Finding out about agents' needs

▶ Motivating and rewarding your agents

Keeping your agents motivated and engaged doesn't happen by accident. You need to make thoughtful and deliberate decisions about how you want to treat your agents. *Growing engagement* within your call center, which means motivating the agents who work there, should be one of your key strategies; it not only creates an enjoyable and fun work environment, but also increases your customer satisfaction and fosters innovation so that you can improve constantly. The icing on the cake is that you can save a lot of money too.

In this chapter, we define what it means to have truly engaged employees; explain why you should be interested in motivating employees; and offer specific programs and ways to recognize, value, and motivate your agents.

 To motivate agents, you need to establish an environment of trust in your center, especially between your agents and team leaders. If your call center has poor relationships, you end up with the proverbial treadmill of agents leaving, which means you have to deal with an endless cycle of recruitment and training. Before you take the time to create programs to survey, reward, and develop your agents, take the time to build trusting relationships (see Chapter 16).

Knowing What Motivating Your Employees Involves

In many call centers, after an agent has gained knowledge and mastered most of the job, she can find it routine and repetitive. For this reason, many call center leaders want to know how to motivate their agents — especially when those agents have been doing the same job for years.

When unmotivated agents — and, more important, your top performers — walk out the door and never come back, that absence has an enormous effect on the organization because it quickly translates into higher cost (cost of replacing employees) and possible loss of revenue (often as a result of new hires who have less knowledge and lower proficiency). Knowledge- and service-based centers are hit the hardest by employees leaving because of the challenge of finding good talent in large numbers within the short recruitment time frames that those call centers often require.

Monetary reward programs, agent appreciation days, and other motivational programs can get agents excited but often fail to sustain a high-performance culture. A key reason for this failure is that programs alone don't create motivated agents. The leadership team needs to figure out — and take actions to address — the root causes of agent dissatisfaction.

In the call centers that we visit every month, some leadership teams focus on keeping their agents happy by not creating conflict or avoiding actions that may cause employees to disengage. This type of management behavior is called *employee appeasement.* Employee appeasement doesn't necessarily make the work environment happier, because it leaves employee performance issues unaddressed — and it leaves those who are working hard and performing well wondering whether they actually need to bother. Therefore, employee appeasement can drive a culture of declining performance.

On the other hand, true *employee engagement* occurs when the executive leadership team builds a partnership between the employees and the organization. The leadership team creates an environment in which employees are passionate about the vision of the call center and committed to live by its values. Agents go beyond the basic job responsibility to delight customers, are proactive and persistent, and make decisions that are consistent with the company's strategic goals and objectives.

If you search for the phrase *employee engagement* in an Internet search engine, you can find a lot of articles that point to a direct correlation between high employee motivation and high customer satisfaction (not to mention company growth and profitability). You can find an equal number of articles that dispute this claim, of course, saying that these aspects of a business aren't necessarily affected by motivated employees. But common sense says to us that if your agents are happy, this enthusiasm and energy come across on the phone and in e-mail, providing a great start to creating a memorable customer experience. Customers who receive consistently good service develop loyalty to the organization that treats them well, and those loyal customers come back for more, often referring other customers.

Also, highly motivated agents provide stability to your call center. Fewer agents leaving your center means less time devoted to hiring and training agents and to making newly hired agents proficient in their jobs — and more time devoted to helping your seasoned agents improve your customers' experiences and your call center's operational efficiency. The time associated with replacing agents who know the job very well with newly hired, inexperienced agents carries a significant cost.

On average, annual agent attrition rates range from 25 percent to 40 percent for most call centers. A call center that requires a high degree of knowledge and skill — such as a health-care or technical-support center — tends to have a relatively low attrition rate.

Seeing the benefits of motivating agents

Based on our estimates, the cost of replacing an agent ranges from $6,000 to $20,000, depending on your industry's salaries and training time. Also, you may have to offer extra benefits to attract the talent you want, based on the supply and demand of the skills you need.

An easy calculation can show the magnitude of the savings that you can experience if you reduce employee attrition. To keep our example simple, we've included only the typical cost of hiring and training. We don't include other costs (such as cost of errors made and coaching time) in the calculation.

For a call center that has 100 agents, a 30 percent annual attrition rate, and a cost of $10,000 to replace one agent, you can calculate the cost of replacing an agent by using this formula:

100 agents $\times$ 30 percent (0.3) $\times$ $10,000 per agent = $300,000

100 agents $\times$ 20 percent (0.2) $\times$ $10,000 = $200,000

Savings = $300,000 − $200,000 = $100,000

If this call center reduced its agent attrition to 20 percent, it would save $100,000! Then it could redirect this money to offer better training, which can improve the customer and agent experience. So in addition to creating a positive working environment, keeping your agents motivated has a definite monetary benefit for your call center.

Identifying why agents leave

When an agent leaves your call center, have an objective party conduct a brief exit interview with the departing agent. Some companies outsource this task to an agency that specializes in these types of interviews. A single interview doesn't tell you much, but if you can consolidate information from several of these interviews, you can see trends and patterns.

If you're lucky, an agent may tell the truth in an exit interview, but in most cases, no one wants to burn a bridge by saying bad things about his former employer. Departing agents often give these kinds of reasons for leaving:

- ✔ I wanted to go back to school.
- ✔ I got a job in the field of my studies.
- ✔ I found a job that pays more money.
- ✔ I found a job that gives me a promotion from what I do currently.

Based on our experience, answers like the ones in the preceding list suggest that the call center job didn't challenge the agent and that she didn't see any potential for personal or career development in your company. Often, agents leave because they find jobs that offer more money — but money can be an emotional factor, compensating agents for something that they feel they're not getting from your company. You need to create a trusting environment that focuses on learning from mistakes, helping agents grow and develop in their job, providing agents the opportunity to try different roles within your center, and creating a career path that has specific outcomes — recognizing, supporting, and ultimately achieving the agents' ambitions.

Many organizations have exit interviews in place, but you need to analyze the results so that you know what changes you need to make.

Figuring Out What Motivates Your Agents

You can do many things in your organization to keep the environment positive and enjoyable, but you have only so many hours in the day. By surveying your agents, you can pinpoint exactly where agent dissatisfaction exists and then use your time effectively to work on initiatives that matter to your agents.

Understanding what agents want

Agents, like any other employees, have certain needs. If you can satisfy the needs of the majority of agents, you set yourself up for success. Don't feel limited by the following list; try to determine specific needs that your agents have.

Agents want to be

- ✔ Led by a capable team leader who has a clear sense of direction
- ✔ Heard and acknowledged

✔ Able to use their skills and abilities to their fullest potential

✔ Able to find meaning in their work

✔ Recognized and given credit for good work

✔ Treated fairly

✔ Appropriately compensated

✔ Able to grow their skills and to develop as individuals

Surveying your agents

You can most effectively measure how engaged your employees are in their work by asking them. Some companies do it once a year, and others do it four times a year. If you survey your agents too frequently, you may not be able to implement some changes that you make based on the results fast enough, so the agents may think that you're not making any change or taking any action based on the feedback they give. Whatever frequency you choose, be consistent in surveying, and look for improvement from one survey to another.

Here are some practices to consider when you survey your agents:

✔ **Communicate openly.** Each time you conduct a survey, tell your agents

- Why you're doing the survey

- What you want to achieve

- Which company goal this survey supports

- What you plan to do with the results (what changes you want to put in place)

✔ **Assure your agents that the survey is anonymous.** That way, they feel comfortable giving you honest feedback.

✔ **Encourage everyone to participate.** Explain how agents can make a difference, and give them time to complete the survey during their work day. You want to get a good sample size so that not only vocal agents direct your actions. Check with an expert in research and surveying to determine the right sample size for your call center.

✔ **Analyze the survey results and formulate a plan based on those results as soon as possible.** If too much time elapses, the initiative loses steam, and the agents think that you didn't take their feedback seriously.

✔ **After you analyze the results, communicate face to face with your agents.** Make sure that they understand what the results mean, what next steps you plan to take, and why you're choosing to make those specific changes.

✔ **Keep your commitments visible by using posters or bulletin boards.** You don't want these displays to look like wallpaper, so update them continually to show progress on the changes you're making.

✔ **Meet with your agents three to four months after the survey results have been published.** Provide agents an update, and show them how their feedback has positively affected their work environment, their job, and the company. Survey again to see whether your changes improved agent satisfaction.

Comparing your call center with others

Compare your call center with other call centers by participating in a regional or national employee-satisfaction survey. This comparison can help you understand how your call center ranks against others. Ranking higher than other companies in the following areas can ensure that you have a bountiful supply of talented candidates to draw from for agent positions. Here are some characteristics of well-led call centers:

✔ **Trust and integrity:** Do your team leaders communicate expectations and demonstrate the same expectations within their role? If you expect agents to get to work on time, for example, your team leaders have to get to work on time every day.

✔ **Good agent–team leader relationships:** Do agents value their relationships with their managers?

✔ **Link between employee performance and company performance:** Does each agent understand how her work contributes to the company's performance?

✔ **Professional development opportunities:** Is the company making an effort to develop the agents' skills and knowledge?

✔ **Personal growth opportunities:** Do the agents have future opportunities or a clear path for growth?

✔ **Coworkers/team members:** Does the work environment offer support, recognition of work, and collaboration, and does management encourage ideas?

✔ **Pride in the company:** Are agents proud of being associated with the company? Does your company have a great reputation for being a service leader or a community leader? If not, what steps are you taking to make changes, and how can your agents contribute to making improvements?

Motivating Your Agents

When you can motivate and engage agents, you create a positive working environment. Agents have an enjoyable time doing work that gives them a sense of satisfaction and accomplishment, and that allows them to work with people who are genuinely interested in their job success and personal growth. We talk about what makes agents engaged in their work and within your center in "Figuring Out What Motivates Your Agents," earlier in this chapter. The following sections outline specific actions that you can take to create that atmosphere of engagement.

Making agents feel valued

Inspiring others starts by communicating very clearly about specific behaviors that support your call center's vision and values. Agents need to understand what's expected of them, but team leaders must first demonstrate these behaviors. Reinforcing the importance of your agents' role and contribution when you roll out strategies and changes can help agents understand how they fit into the bigger picture of your call center's mission and vision.

Because your agents talk to your customers and have firsthand knowledge of what your customers experience each day, they can give you input and feedback about your products, customers, processes, and systems. You can get useful information in several ways:

- **Conduct focus groups.** You can conduct regularly scheduled focus groups or impromptu ones based on need. Bring together a small group of agents, and ask them specific questions such as these:

    - What obstacles prevent you from providing great service?

    - What are customers saying about our new product?

    By asking more in-depth questions based on the answers you receive, you can come up with the top three pressing issues for agents. To keep these ideas and feedback coming, you need to communicate progress to your agents and show them that changes are being made.

- **Sit with a few agents at their workstations every month.** You can see firsthand the agents' point of view and the challenges they face. This activity also shows that you're interested in and value what agents do: work hard every day to satisfy customers' inquiries and requests.

- **Encourage employee involvement by establishing committees.** If you find yourself wondering whether agents would approve of changes you've planned, you can take the pressure off yourself by creating an agent committee. That committee produces new ideas and plans how to implement incentives effectively — information that it passes along to a team leader. Committee involvement gives agents a voice in something very near and dear to their hearts: their pay!

✔ **Design a process to capture, acknowledge, and implement agent suggestions and ideas.** These suggestions can relate to improvements to your products, processes, and overall customer service. After you commit to the employee suggestion process, you have to build a structure within your department to keep suggestions active and ongoing. A group of people or one person in your call center should be assigned the job of acknowledging and reviewing each idea and then determining whether the call center should implement the idea immediately, later, or perhaps not at all. This group or person also needs to communicate decisions back to the agent who suggested the idea so that she knows what happened to it.

✔ **Give your agents some control of their jobs.** Allow them to make certain decisions. When you give agents some information about the effect of their decisions and some guidelines about what they can do, they can gain a sense of confidence and control by solving customer problems without having to get approval from their team leaders.

✔ **Understand agents' personal situations.** Make good decisions that balance employee needs with business needs. Many new team leaders think that they have to treat all agents the same way, but agents and their situations are unique. When appropriate, involve agents in coming up with solutions to their individual problems. An agent may not be able to work overtime because he has to pick up his child from day care, for example. By brainstorming possibilities with the agent, you can try to come up with a solution that works for both the agent and the call center as a whole, such as giving your agent notice when the call center may need him to work overtime so that he can make alternative arrangements to pick up his child that day.

Taking time to recognize agents

Call center leaders constantly look for ways in which agents can improve. When team leaders and quality analysts listen to calls, everyone looks for ways that the call could be better. But if you praise a job well done, you reward the positive outcomes that agents create for your business, and you reinforce the actions and behaviors that you most want those agents to repeat. If you focus only on what an agent can improve, that agent may think that she doesn't do anything well and may become demoralized.

Recognition can seem shallow and uninspiring over time if you limit it to generic encouragement, such as "Good job!" or "Well done." To make recognition meaningful, be specific in your praise of what the agent has done well, and give your feedback soon after the impressive behavior occurred. You could tell the agent that you liked how he acknowledged the customer's situation and built confidence when he said, "I'm sorry to hear that you had so many problems, but I'm glad you came to me, because I can help you solve your issues today!" With this specific feedback, the agent can understand what you liked and what he should do again in a similar situation.

To build and celebrate behaviors that you want to see repeated, you can establish programs that recognize agents who

- ✔ Are consistent every day in meeting all the criteria for good performance.
- ✔ Go the extra mile to help customers or other agents.
- ✔ Give suggestions that create benefits for the call center, such as saving money or improving customer service.
- ✔ Are the most improved in building their skills or working toward a goal. This kind of recognition helps encourage those agents who aren't always at the top but are trying hard to improve.

Recognizing individual agents

A call center's leadership team can take myriad actions and offer all kinds of rewards that cost very little and energize agents. Here are a few examples:

- ✔ **Encourage peer-to-peer recognition.** The leadership team encourages agents to recognize teammates who go above and beyond the call of duty.
- ✔ **Offer a handwritten note with detailed praise.** This kind of personal recognition can make anyone feel special.
- ✔ **Give a personal acknowledgment and a small token.** You can give gift certificates for small items, such as coffee at your local coffeehouse or lunch at your company cafeteria. You can even have the agent pick her certificate from a bag to ensure fairness and add to the fun.
- ✔ **Allow the agent to work a preferred shift.** Recognizing achievement in this way delights agents because they can work a shift that integrates better into their lifestyles.
- ✔ **Point out the agent's accomplishment to the senior leadership team.** Drawing attention to that agent not only gives him recognition, but also allows you to showcase the type of talent you have in your call center.
- ✔ **Create a "smile team."** This team schedules random, fun events that recognize agents for good quality of work, best sales, or significant improvement.

Recognizing the whole department

You can even recognize the whole call center department for a job well done. Maybe everyone worked hard during a seasonal time to help the company meet customer demand for its services or products, or maybe the call center's daily effort helped your company exceed its profit targets. You can use these activities to show the entire call center that the company appreciates all the work:

- ✔ Have the head of the call center cook for the agents by holding a company barbecue onsite or in the parking lot.

- ✔ Arrange for high-performing agents, or even one select agent, to have lunch with the executives or leaders, whom they typically wouldn't meet. Giving agents direct access to executives in a casual setting helps agents and leaders understand one another better.

- ✔ Offer an unexpected perk — such as pizza, chocolate, or ice cream — for everyone in the center.

Recognition programs can fail if you single out a few mysteriously selected agents, thereby sapping the morale of those who don't understand the criteria. Don't use personalized, subjective criteria to determine winners.

Paying agents appropriately

You can easily say that compensation programs must be fair, but you have to work to find out what the going rate is in your area and what you should pay to attract the right talent. Make sure that you can show your agents how their compensation is related to the expertise required in the job. Various companies provide compensation surveys and research relevant to your industry and area; you can find this information by doing an Internet search.

Good compensation programs match your business goals and, therefore, drive the right behaviors and results, compensating agents for good work. Regardless of the type of call center, you have two types of compensation plans to consider, each with its own merits:

- ✔ **Fixed salary:** To drive higher sales or another specific behavior, you can introduce random incentives as a minor part of an overall compensation program.

- ✔ **Pay-for-performance:** This compensation program uses a relatively low fixed salary and a relatively high variable component called a bonus. You base this monthly program on the agent's ability to realize three to four specific performance targets.

    Pay-for-performance programs are becoming very popular, particularly in sales call centers, where performance can be measured easily through sales achievement.

Offering incentive and bonus programs

Whichever path you take, the following sections provide some best practices for incentives and performance bonuses.

Introduce the program properly

Your top goal in rolling out a new program is communicating with your agents about the program early, telling them how you plan to help them succeed in this program. These activities can set you up for success when you introduce new targets or a new program:

- ✔ **Determine which agents can receive bonuses if you use the new targets, compared with the current program.** If the same agents benefit after the change, reevaluate your change, because it doesn't provide enough challenge for your agents or enough benefit for your company.

- ✔ **Design a gap analysis for each agent.** A *gap analysis* examines how much money an agent is making today and how much she'll make if you establish the new program. If fewer agents would get bonuses in the new program, determine what support you'll provide through the team leaders to bring these agents up to the same earning bracket as before.

- ✔ **Give your agents time to adjust.** While you're still using the current program and before you start the new program, show your agents how much bonus they'd receive in the new program and whether that bonus is less than what they earn today, and work with them to find ways to get to the same level of monetary compensation — or to a higher level.

Keep your measures simple

Pick three or four key measures that have specific targets — not ten measures. Choose targets that your agents can attain, and make sure that those targets can drive the desired long-term behaviors you want. If you choose to measure productivity, for example, you need to balance it with quality. Choosing one without the other encourages wrong behavior, such as rushing through a call and not giving the customer good service. Some call centers use customer-satisfaction survey scores as a qualifier for the program, meaning that even if an agent hits his productivity or sales target, he doesn't qualify for a reward if the customer doesn't give the call a high score.

Maintain accurate performance data

Keep your data accurate, and ensure that one person is responsible for gathering data, validating it, and producing a report based on the results in a timely manner.

Keep the program flexible

We recommend that you run your bonus program on a monthly basis and not run any incentive for more than two months. Agents experience fatigue and loss of interest if an incentive goes on too long. By reviewing the targets monthly or bimonthly, you can tweak (not completely change) the program to include seasonal or promotional differences, or include specials that the marketing department dreams up.

Support company goals

We've seen programs in which companies encourage agents to get sales without thinking about what happens in the after-sales process, so those companies end up with orders that they can't process because the orders contain incomplete or inaccurate information. Let your agents know that ensuring the accuracy and completeness of an order are as important as taking the order itself. To do so, include order information in the structure of the incentive or pay-for-performance program (see "Paying agents appropriately," earlier in this chapter).

Measure against company goals

If you reward your agents for meeting the targets, but your company isn't doing well, you may want to rethink your program. The acid test for a good program involves determining whether your call center is meeting targets. The call center needs to contribute very specifically to the overall goals of your company. If your program's targets don't lead to this contribution, go back to the drawing board.

Seek input from agents

You may find raising the bar on performance to be tough because you have to get your agents excited about a new program each year. Don't just say to your agents, "Thank you, but now you have to do 10 percent more." Let them know why you want to raise the bar, and include them in finding a solution so that you can implement that solution effectively. Incorporate their suggestions on ways to improve the program.

Also, discuss the changes that you plan to make with other company employees who will be affected to ensure that all employees recognize and agree with the importance of those changes. You want everyone to be on the same page regarding sales strategies and corporate goals, understanding how compensation can support these strategies and goals.

Add a benefit for everyone

Establishing a pay-for-performance program means that you pay bonuses only to those who meet the performance targets. Agents whose performance sits just on the borderline of meeting targets may challenge you for that compensation. Unfortunately, you have to draw the line somewhere and can't change the bar after the fact. Consider creating a program to acknowledge effort and to reward those agents who almost reach the target.

Successful programs reward good results and recognize effort through a point system. This point system encourages those agents who tried hard to meet a target but fell short, because they can redeem the points that they did earn for rewards. This type of program needs to have a minimum acceptable level of achievement as a qualifier for agents to earn points. Suppose that your sales target is $10 of revenue per call, and for each $1 of revenue that your agent brought in, she earned 2 points. Your agent didn't qualify for the bonus because she got only $5 of revenue, but you can still encourage her because she earned 10 points, which she can redeem for gift certificates or merchandise.

Rewarding and recognizing performance

An executive with a large financial services company once approached us with a typical sales scenario. Only 10 percent of his sales team — the same high performers every month — were being recognized through his organization's rewards and recognition (R&R) program. This left the rest of the team, particularly those agents who performed at a medium level relative to their peers, demoralized and unmotivated to improve their sales results. This medium-tier group represented about 70 percent of agents — a huge opportunity to improve sales performance and team morale.

To address this motivational issue, our client decided to move from an R&R program focused purely on sales numbers to one that included reward for positive behaviors. His team identified the key behaviors that led to the best results. One example was doing the right thing for the customer, which meant that in case of problems, an agent referred the customer to an internal party who could better address the customer's needs instead of trying to close the sale himself. The agent "lost" the sale, but the action created a better experience for the customer and higher revenue for the organization. This positive behavior was reinforced through weekly coaching by team leaders.

Implementing the new R&R program had a big payoff. Performance improved at every level.

among high, medium, and low performers. Because of the focus on positive behaviors, the whole team was able to improve results and be recognized for both big and small successes.

Building on the success of the new program, our financial-services client sought to improve the sales performance of his overall team. He found that the way sales objectives were being set demotivated most members of his sales team, because targets were being met by only the top 10 percent of the group. Rather than set a fixed target that only a few agents could achieve, he set objectives based on a ranking system that compared individual sales results with a weighted team average. He called this system a "peer-to-peer" system because objectives were set based on peer performance. The system created targets that agents could buy into — results that their own peers were achieving, not top-down objectives set by management.

Implementing an R&R program that blended sales results, positive behaviors, and peer-to-peer ranking to set targets produced a dramatic improvement in sales results. The client's team achieved a 32 percent lift in gross sales in one quarter, and he improved sales results and team morale without increasing his R&R budget.

Helping your agents make career choices

One of our Canadian clients, Scotiabank, has call center agents who have limited knowledge of other areas of the company, as is common in call centers. To give agents a broader understanding of the business, the client created a career Web site where agents could look at job descriptions by department to find what each department does and the type of jobs that it has available. The Web site also includes a skills self-assessment form, which an agent can use to compare the skills that he has today against those he needs for a job that he's interested in. Agents can also find opportunities on this Web site to attend a panel discussion with former agents who have moved to other departments, where those former agents can share experiences and tips. Agents can use this Web site and the opportunities it offers to discuss with their team leaders how they can develop their skills most effectively.

Developing agents' careers

By creating a development path or a plan of action to help your agent build his skill and knowledge, you can clearly show that agent where he is in terms of his personal development and where he can progress.

Dangling that proverbial carrot of a promotion to get your agents to accelerate their performance can backfire very quickly. You easily lose the most important part of the relationship — trust — when an agent doesn't get the promotion. What if the company doesn't have any positions available to which the agent can move? What if your agent doesn't get the job because she isn't as qualified as other candidates for that position? Any of these situations may leave you with a very demoralized agent.

To develop an agent's skills, you first need to convince him of the importance of sharpening the skills required for his current role, as well as how he can easily use these skills in other types of roles. Skills such as decision-making, judgment, thinking on one's feet, multitasking, managing conflict, and effectively selling are great skills to have in most jobs, including leadership roles, and an agent has hundreds of opportunities (otherwise known as calls) to practice and develop these skills. We talk about the value and importance of coaching in Chapter 13.

Developing, succession planning, and mentoring

It may all sound the same — development, succession, mentorship — but it isn't. Every employee in a company should have a development plan that leads her to improve her knowledge and skill. This improvement then earns her participation in succession planning and mentorship programs:

- ✔ **Development plan:** A sort of map that your agent can use to get to a higher skill level as it relates to his current job. This plan could include observing or shadowing employees in other roles while they do their jobs within your center or even other departments. This process helps an agent develop understanding of the role, which helps him decide whether that role is a possible next step in his career.

- ✔ **Succession plan:** A plan that starts with the team leader's vision of how the call center will support the customer in three to five years, and what skills and key people can help the team leader reach that goal. Succession planning involves ensuring that the call center has the next line of leaders in place, ready to take the next step when they're needed.

  A succession plan includes ways to further enhance the skills required by specific people in new roles. Your three-year vision could require another ten team leaders, for example. You can hire them from outside the company, but developing the skill and knowledge of your agents for this next role can benefit all parties: Agents have a path to further their opportunities and income, and you can benefit from internal candidates' existing knowledge of company products, processes, and systems.

- ✔ **Mentoring:** Actually part of a succession-planning program. Mentoring pairs an agent who has a consistent and proven track record of high performance with a team leader, a manager, or even the head of the call center so that the agent can gain knowledge and experience.

ANECDOTE

Tapping the real experts

Karen Jensen of Assante Advisor Services, an associate of Afshan's, told us about a challenge that she faced in her call center: keeping phone representatives knowledgeable and up-to-date on changes in products, processes, and procedures. Because of the company's full range of complex products, ever-evolving regulations, new products, and taxation information, her staff members were overwhelmed by the amount of information they had to know.

Jensen decided that her call center needed subject-matter experts (SMEs). The SME initiative involved assigning specific agents to deal with a specific area of the business (one product, for example), rather than requiring everyone to understand all of them. This approach allowed the SMEs to provide knowledgeable support to financial advisers and customers who needed assistance in that particular area.

Jensen saw significant results from her SME effort. The center increased first-call resolution, so customers got their issues resolved the first time they called. Also, the agents who were responsible for a specific area of knowledge felt very motivated, had a sense of ownership, and found their roles more challenging.

Creating a great career-development program

Whether you want to implement a development or succession plan, you need to consider some key factors:

- ✔ **Understand your agents' motivations and aspirations.** By using this knowledge, you can link the skills that an agent uses or the work that she does to her aspirations. If your agent loves to help others but doesn't feel comfortable selling, for example, you can show her that building competency in selling can allow her to train and lead others to improve. This approach might pique her interest in improving her own selling skills.

- ✔ **Talk to agents about their demonstrated strengths and behaviors.** What does an agent need to do to enhance his potential for advancement, and where does he need to spend time to close the gap in his weaker areas?

  Suppose that you have an agent who's interested in training and who's taken many techniques-and-facilitation courses. Taking a course only builds knowledge, however; it doesn't necessarily provide opportunity to apply that knowledge. Therefore, the agent lacks training experience. If she wants to be a trainer, give her an opportunity to put a small training session together for your team so that she can apply her knowledge in a real-life situation. This training time supports her goal and provides you the benefit of a better-trained team.

- ✔ **Let the agent know where he is in his development.** Make it visual, just like a map at the shopping mall: You are here, and you want to go there. Depending on where your agent is in his development of the skills that he needs in his role as an agent, you can design this path to move within your call center or to other areas of the organization outside your center. If the agent has mastered his job and now wants to do more, for example, he can pursue many paths. Center your discussion with this agent on the option that interests him most and what benefit that option offers him, and design a plan to help him build the knowledge and skills that he needs for that role.

- ✔ **Agree on specific next steps, and establish frequent check-in points with the agent.** Each agent needs to take responsibility for her own development. The team leader can coach, provide advice, mentor, and suggest possible opportunities, but the agent has to do the work to build skill and demonstrate that she really wants to advance.

Part V
Ensuring Continuous Improvement

The 5th Wave   By Rich Tennant

In this part . . .

*M*ost call centers can benefit from establishing a plan for continuous improvement. In this part, we explore call center operations, including a method for consistently delivering an outstanding customer experience; examine policies and procedures; review the importance of understanding employment laws that affect call centers; and discuss quality and certification trends in the industry.

In this part, we also talk about recognizing the need for change, improving your personal change leadership style, and overcoming resistance to change.

Chapter 15

The Power of Process Improvement

*M*any call centers have fallen prey to what W. Edwards Deming called "instant pudding." Deming, a management guru whose theories led to the development of *total quality management* (a management philosophy that focuses on process and controls to ensure continuous improvement), was referring to the act of installing the latest technology or implementing the latest management fad in the hope that this addition alone would result in operational success. Ongoing improvement and excellence, however, don't come without internal examination and innovation.

Many organizations have realized that improving processes is one of the necessary steps to improving the customer service experience. In this chapter, you can find a framework that starts with customer experience and then finds ways to improve processes and ideas about how to continually improve the experience for your customers.

Managing Complexity through Process Improvement

Because call centers have a significant effect on their organizations in terms of revenue, cost, and customer relationships, bad results get quick attention. In fact, in response to corporate and customer dissatisfaction with call center performance, subindustries and government watchdogs sprang up during the past decade.

Call-handling process improvements generate big wins

A few years ago, Réal was helping a telecommunications company improve the cost of running its call centers. He focused on the process of handling various types of calls, which involved mapping out how agents handled the most common types of customer inquiries. Up to that point, the call center had offered no standardized approach for handling various call types.

While Réal and his team identified and documented the general approach that agents used to handle customer inquiries, the agents began making their own suggestions for improvement, with two major results:

✔ Réal's team developed several new call-handling processes that went into effect almost immediately.

✔ The agents defined a process for making ongoing improvements in the call-handling process.

Within a month, call length had declined by 15 percent, and the total cost per customer of running the operation fell by a similar amount. Also, the leadership team reported that the number of errors and callbacks had decreased. Months later, the improvements continued.

Considering complexity in call centers

Call centers are struggling with the growing complexity of delivering service to customers. This complexity arises from several factors, including these:

✔ The breadth of products and constant changes in information about these products

✔ Changes in the processes and procedures that support the products

✔ The number of systems and ways to reach companies, such as phone, fax, e-mail, and Web chat

As a result, your agents need a lot of knowledge and skill to listen, think, talk, and type, conducting a natural, positive conversation with your customers. Your agents have to be product experts who can solve a broad range of customer requests through multiple computer systems (either by talking on the phone or by writing in e-mails and Web chats) and must continually upgrade their knowledge and skills.

Complexity always creates challenges, but by putting a method in place to clean up the fallout from your complexity, you can provide an excellent experience for your customers. The best byproduct of putting this kind of discipline in place is that improvements in customer service often translate into cost savings for your organization. If you want to streamline a process so that customers receive their product faster, you can reduce the time it takes your company to send off an order by reducing the number of people involved in the process. If fewer people are involved, you reduce labor hours, which means cost savings for your organization.

Benefiting from process improvement

Process improvement is a systematic way to make steps or actions in a process better. Think of process improvement in terms of what it does for the drivers of performance. If a process improvement positively affects a driver, you can enhance performance (and results) — often, in a very quantifiable way.

Here are some examples of typical process improvements that you can make in your call center and the potential benefits associated with each improvement:

- ✔ **Redesign your call-handling process.** This improvement reduces average call length, cost per call, the total expense of running your operation, and the number of seats needed. It might also improve customer satisfaction because customers receive quick resolution of their needs. (We talk about call length in Chapter 6.)

- ✔ **Create a new schedule.** Try to match your scheduling and caller demand as closely you can. This improvement speeds answers and can increase customer satisfaction. (See Chapter 8 for more information on scheduling.)

- ✔ **Improve off-phone or overhead work processes.** Improving the processes that don't directly affect agents on the phones can result in a reduced need for total support duties and a corresponding reduction in the average cost per hour of call center services.

- ✔ **Design a new interactive voice response (IVR) system.** Create new automated voice prompts that provide service to customers who call your center, which can reduce the number of callers who need to speak with a live agent, contacts per customer, total cost, number of staff, and equipment needed. (You can find more on IVR in Chapter 9.)

- ✔ **Develop an effective way to present customer data to your agents during calls.** Agents can present purchase options to customers, resulting in a higher percentage of calls that lead to sales or higher average value per sale.

- ✔ **Analyze why customers call.** Determine the number of simple inquiry or transaction calls for which the customer could use the company's Web site to get answers or conduct the transaction. Developing a strategy to help customers serve themselves allows the customer to seek information independently in a way that's easy and convenient for him. For the company, this strategy provides cost savings because each question or transaction costs significantly less over the Web than it does through the call center.

Developing a Culture of Improvement

Process improvement can provide the greatest benefit when everyone involved in the process being improved is also involved in the improvements. Many organizations often overlook one group of potential contributors: their customers. Your customers can tell you what's working and what's not while they do business with you.

The other key contributors to improvement are the people who work with a process every day, because they can best tell you how employees actually perform tasks as opposed to how they're supposed to perform those tasks. Your agents are a gold mine of ideas and suggestions, and they can point out duplication of work (when too many people or departments are involved in the same process) or situations in which a specific task or action takes longer than necessary. All these ideas should help you streamline or stop activities that don't add value for the customer or the company.

Seeing your company through the customer's eyes

Developing a culture of improvement starts with everyone — from your agents to those who run the company — understanding what type of experience your customers want. After you determine how to treat your customers, you can integrate that experience through your processes and train your agents in what to do and how to do it so that your customers feel satisfied. Then you have to improve the experience over time, for several reasons:

- ✔ Your customers' expectations change over time, and you have to keep pace with their needs.
- ✔ Your agents may use approaches that worked yesterday without understanding the value of those approaches to the customer or the company. To figure out whether your agents know why they do what they do, ask them. When an agent takes a particular approach, ask him, "Why do you do that? What value does this step provide for the customer and for the company?" If he can't explain it, the approach likely doesn't serve its original purpose.

 You can use what we call a customer-experience blueprint to establish the way that you want to treat your customers. This blueprint gives your agents a guide to satisfying customers and creating a consistent experience that goes above and beyond customers' expectations.

The customer-experience blueprint guides the agent from the time she says hello to a customer to the time she says goodbye. This blueprint helps agents consistently handle the customer requests and the customers' emotional state by clearly articulating the key steps, knowledge, and skills required at each stage of the client experience.

When you create a customer-experience blueprint model, break the interaction into the key phases of the call, as in this example:

- ✔ **Phase 1:** This phase is the beginning of the call, during which the agent connects with the customer and discovers what he's requesting.

- ✔ **Phase 2:** The agent provides a solution to the request and confirms next steps to solve that request, if needed.

- ✔ **Phase 3:** The agent adds value by providing information that the customer may find helpful in his future transactions with your company, or perhaps by discussing products or services that are relevant to the customer's situation or needs.

A company has service expectations of its agents at each phase, and each phase requires an agent to demonstrate a specific set of skills.

In the first phase of the preceding example, the first step involves greeting the customer. The guide for this step might ask the agent to

- ✔ Answer within a certain number of seconds with a friendly greeting.

- ✔ State her name, the department in which she works, and the company's name.

- ✔ Make the customer feel welcome by offering assistance.

After you create your own unique blueprint, you can train your agents and your leadership team in the steps, knowledge, and skills required to create an outstanding experience for your customers.

Checking the internal view

Many call centers don't have a customer-experience blueprint; instead, they rely on their quality analysts to identify what aspects of a call effectively lead to the desired results and what aspects need improvement (such as broken processes, quality issues with products, or poor customer service from agents). We recommend that you start with the blueprint because it reduces the number of opinions about what good customer service looks like.

Ceridian's customer-centered approach

Ceridian Canada, a human-resources and payroll management company, significantly improved customer satisfaction by tapping into customer feedback. After a thorough analysis of that feedback, management realized that the organization was defining the overall customer service experience, not the customers.

The management team conducted a series of customer interviews to get more specific feedback about what customers really wanted. Then, based on this feedback, the company implemented a few customer-focused practices:

✔ Analyzing key call types and surveying customers to simplify internal processes

✔ Training managers and agents to understand the meaning of certain metrics and the opportunities that those metrics represented so that agents could modify their behaviors to use those opportunities effectively

✔ Constantly considering what customers want and developing strategies to deliver the desired products or services

By following the simple approach of ensuring that the service experience reflected the voice of the customer, Ceridian saw great improvements in overall Net Promoter Scores to exceptionally high levels while reducing service costs and motivating its agents — a win–win situation!

We also recommend that your quality analyst receive agent suggestions and customer feedback, integrating her own observations. As we discuss in Chapter 3, quality analysts also listen to agent calls and provide feedback about service-related negative and positive trends so that they get a well-rounded view of the biggest issues in your call center, which allows them to make well-founded recommendations.

After you figure out what issue you want to fix, you can most effectively find gaps in the handling process by mapping out the process related to the issue and identifying points of failure. Then analyze the root causes of the failures, brainstorm solutions, test the most promising solution, and implement that solution.

Mapping your processes

You can use *process mapping,* a project management method, to design and analyze business processes. Literally, you graph a business process in a *flowchart* — a diagram that shows the sequence of operations in a process, such as the steps involved in a successful customer call — so that everyone can understand the steps involved in producing a result. Figure 15-1 shows a call center recruiting and hiring process chart that you can use as an example.

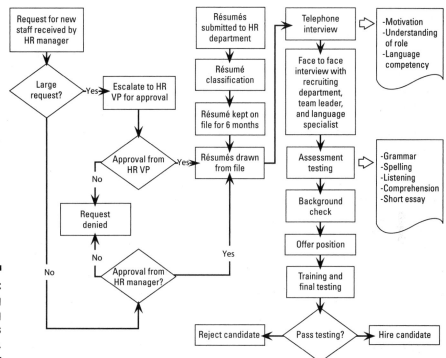

Figure 15-1:
A recruiting
and hiring
process
flowchart.

With a little time, some common sense, a pot of coffee, and a bunch of dry-erase markers, your management team can put together some homegrown process charts that can really help your call center manage and improve processes.

Involving the team

You can most effectively use process mapping as a collaboration tool, so get everyone involved, including managers at all levels and your call center agents. Aside from the process-improvement outcome, the process-mapping . . . well, process, also provides a wonderful team-building exercise.

Although process mapping is fairly straightforward, spend some time with your team reviewing how it works and why it's important. A bit of up-front training can help prevent blank stares at the beginning of your process-mapping exercise. Also, be sure to share the spoils of your process-improvement success. You don't have to do anything elaborate. Just offer some form of recognition — a party, a platter of fine imported cheeses, whatever.

Involve members from all parts of the call center team in process mapping. Any and all input can help the process-mapping exercise while increasing employee commitment and improving the quality of the results.

The act of charting the steps of a process helps simplify the process and clarifies potential problems and inefficiencies, or places where you need to rework the process. At some point while process-mapping, we bet that you'll laugh out loud and ask, "What idiot designed that?" (On second thought, you may want to keep that thought to yourself. The idiot may be *you!*)

Charting the Flow: An Amateur's Guide to Process Mapping

In its simplest form, creating a flowchart involves drawing a picture of what happens in your work process, starting with inputs; identifying all actions and decisions associated with a process; and then finalizing your diagram with the output or goals.

Follow these basic steps to construct a process flowchart:

1. **Determine the process beginning and ending points.**

2. **List each step involved.**

   Here are a couple of things that can help you stay focused and consistent when listing steps:

   - Use action verbs to describe steps.
   - Decide whether you want to provide a general overview or list every discrete step.

3. **Write down an approximate order for these steps.**

   Relationships and parallel steps begin to emerge.

4. **Place each step in the appropriate symbol.**

   In Figure 15-1, for example, the diamond-shaped items represent a step in the process in which the human-resources manager makes a decision — usually, yes or no — and the rectangular items illustrate an activity.

5. **Add arrows.**

   The arrows show the direction of the process flow.

6. **Check for redundancy.**

   Follow the steps in the flowchart to identify steps in the process that seem redundant or repetitive. If you identify redundancies, eliminate them, and work through the steps again to ensure that you have a complete process.

7. **Check for missing elements.**

   Also make sure that you've captured all the steps in the process. If you're missing steps, add them to the flow.

8. **Have a second and third person review the flowchart.**

You diagram a process so that you can understand it and ask yourself, "What do customers expect of us? What should we do to provide better customer focus and satisfaction?" The process map can identify the best practices that you need to incorporate and locate appropriate benchmarks to improve your services.

As American scientist Dr. George Washington Carver put it, "It is simply service that measures success."

Doing a root-cause analysis

After you map the process and identify the points of failure within the process (which customers, agents, and your operational data told you about), take the time to find the root cause. A *root-cause analysis* is a class of problem-solving methods aimed at identifying exactly what leads problems or events to occur.

Don't let finding the root cause become overcomplicated. Keep it simple by asking why until you can't ask that question anymore; then investigate further by asking "what" and "who" questions, such as "What caused this to happen?" and "Who is responsible for this step of the process?"

Suppose that customers are waiting a long time to get a response from their e-mail inquiries. When you map the process related to e-mail response, you find out that after an agent receives the e-mail, he responds and sends that e-mail to another person, who checks all e-mails for proper grammar, tone, and accuracy before finally releasing that message to the customer. Here are the questions you should ask:

- ✔ Why do the e-mails need a check for accuracy? You may find out that customers used to receive many e-mails containing mistakes and poor grammar, so the call center put this step in place.

- ✔ Why did e-mails contain so many errors before the call center put the proofing practice in place? You may figure out that several new agents were working in the call center at that time.

- ✔ How many errors are occurring today? The answer to this question may tell you two things: Preformatted e-mail templates now help agents create their responses, and the agents are now more knowledgeable and skilled.

Knowing the answers to the questions in the preceding list allows you to come up with possible solutions to reduce the turnaround time for e-mails. You could

✔ Add more people to do the quality check, if that check gives you a sense of security about the quality of e-mail accuracy.

✔ Take out the quality step because you currently have a low error rate and put in spot checks instead.

You have to identify the right solution for your particular call center, but by mapping your process and figuring out the root cause, you can come up with an informed and educated decision about which solution can eliminate the problem most effectively.

Documenting policies and procedures

If it isn't written, it isn't real! Whether your call center's processes are effective or not, write them down, and formalize them into some kind of procedures document. You can create and agree to the most efficient and effective set of processes and procedures in the world, but if you don't write them down, your agents probably will stop using them.

By documenting your procedures and making them accessible to everyone in your center, you create a reference guide and training tool that people can use to judge their actions. Written documentation also becomes a standard against which you can audit work processes. Probably the biggest advantage is that it serves as a baseline for future improvement. Put the information that agents need right at their fingertips by using a knowledge-base software application (see Chapter 9 for more information on knowledge bases).

You need to take some specific actions to ensure that your knowledge base is user-friendly. Make sure that it

✔ **Provides visuals:** A picture paints a thousand words. The documentation in your knowledge base should contain primarily words, of course, but it should include a lot of photos, diagrams, and flowcharts as well.

✔ **Communicates changes in processes:** Many call centers are in a constant state of information overload. After you identify the improvements that you want to make, you need to communicate those changes to your agents. Explain why you made the change, what kinds of calls the change affects, and what the agents have to do differently to integrate the change into their calls.

Have a process in place for updating and changing your knowledge base, and assign one person to this task. This person needs to understand what agents like and don't like about the knowledge base. Agents need to be able to use the knowledge base easily, and the person assigned to update the knowledge base must make it as agent-friendly as possible.

Overall responsibility for improving processes and ensuring that the changes are well integrated must be assigned to a senior person in the call center — ideally, the most senior person.

If you don't have the top person in the call center involved, you run the risk of losing momentum in making the change — and making it stick — because you need her support to get the green light from executives, approval for resources, and so on.

Staying Informed: Legislative Considerations

In addition to improving processes, you need to establish procedures and stay abreast of legislation that affects your call center. In your knowledge base, include a section on policies about complying with legislation.

What's the difference between policies and procedures? *Procedures* are the steps you follow to perform tasks; *policies* are rules that govern your behavior. Call centers write a lot of policies, which are designed to protect the agent, the customer, and the company. Policies related to agent safety, for example, outline what agents need to do to prevent accidents in the workplace.

Law and order: Creating appropriate policies

In your knowledge base, include policies for any legislation that someone in your call center would need to adhere to so that the center can avoid the risk of violation because the employee doesn't know about the law. Include the policies that your leadership team should know in a separate section of your knowledge base. These policies might relate to

  ✔ **Labor laws:** These laws are related to recruiting, working conditions, working hours, labor relations, discipline, termination, layoffs, compensation, harassment, and employment equity.

✔ **Call center–specific legislation:** This legislation directly or indirectly affects how your call center can operate — hours of calling for outbound projects, telephone solicitation of new business, do-not-call lists, privacy of personal information, and so on.

✔ **Legislated service levels:** Call center operations in certain industries have minimum service-level targets that their local government establishes. In some U.S. states, for example, the cable television industry has minimum speed-of-answer requirements for call centers. Failure to meet these minimums can result in substantial fines for cable operators.

All these obligations are very serious, and you need to incorporate them into your operations. Create policies that address these legislative requirements; then filter your procedures through the policies, and train the affected staff members in the policies and underlying legislation. Failure to comply could land your call center in a heap of trouble, incurring hefty fines and risking reputational ruin.

Knowing the laws

If you want to know the laws that apply to your call center, start by hiring a good lawyer or two. You need a labor lawyer and a lawyer who specializes in the laws affecting call centers and/or telecommunications.

Give your lawyers copies of your policies and procedures, and ask them to review and comment on those policies and procedures. Then ask them to identify the areas of legislation that your policies and procedures don't adequately address. They'll find a lot of stuff — that's what lawyers do — and you can amend your policies and procedures to ensure compliance.

Periodically ask your lawyers to review any updates or provide you information about new legislation that affects your operations.

Wherever you live, be aware of and compliant with all your local laws and — equally important — the laws of the countries with which your call center does business. The following sections give you an idea of the kinds of laws that affect call centers.

If you have a large call center, or if you run an outsourcing call center, you may want to consider creating a compliance-officer role in your operation. The compliance officer is responsible for making sure that your company complies with all the legislation affecting your call center. The best part of having a compliance officer is that he's the person who has to talk to the lawyers!

U.S. laws

The United States regulates telemarketing through the Federal Trade Commission (FTC), which enforces a variety of federal antitrust and consumer-protection laws and is responsible for taking action against practices that are unfair or deceptive. The FTC's authority extends to the Internet, which (like other media) can be used to deliver fraudulent content.

In addition, the Federal Communications Commission (FCC) regulates interstate and international communications by radio, television, wire, satellite, and cable in the United States. Here's some legislation that affects call centers:

- ✔ **Telemarketing and Consumer Fraud and Abuse Prevention Act:** Under this law, the FTC adopted the Telemarketing Sales Rule, which prohibits misrepresentations and calls to a consumer after that consumer has asked to not receive telemarketing calls, sets payment restrictions for the sale of certain goods and services, and requires that call centers keep specific business records for two years.

- ✔ **Telephone Consumer Protection Act:** The FCC places restrictions on unwanted telephone solicitations, automatic telephone dialing systems, artificial or prerecorded voice messages, and the use of fax machines to send unsolicited advertisements.

- ✔ **Do Not Call Implementation Act of 2003:** This law gave the FTC the authority to create and enforce a National Do Not Call Registry, which the FCC has also adopted. After consumers place their names on the National Do Not Call Registry, telemarketers can't make unsolicited sales calls to those consumers. If a call center fails to comply with the law, it can face some very large fines. Although some exemptions apply, this law has greatly cut down the number of unwanted telemarketing calls in the United States.

In addition to enforcing the laws discussed in the preceding list, many U.S. states have registration and bonding requirements for telemarketers, as well as state-specific do-not-call lists and programs.

Both the U.S. and Canadian governments (see the next section) also have established privacy laws to protect consumers' personal information by regulating how and when companies can collect, use, and disclose personal information. These laws also regulate the length of time that these companies can retain personal information; how companies must secure it; and finally, how companies must destroy it. Violations of these laws can result in fines and criminal prosecution.

Canadian laws

Canada regulates outbound telemarketing through the Canadian Radio-Television and Telecommunications Commission (CRTC). The CRTC issues regulations called Telecom Decisions, including calling-time restrictions, disclosure requirements, and prohibitions on calls to consumers who have asked to not receive telemarketing calls. Current regulations include identification and Caller ID requirements, as well as the maintenance of a company-specific do-not-call list.

Organizations that conduct unsolicited telemarketing activity must honor a consumer do-not-call request for three years. The National Do Not Call List (DNCL) gives consumers a choice about whether to receive telemarketing calls. The National DNCL rules introduce responsibilities for Canada's telemarketers. Consumers can choose to reduce the number of telemarketing calls they receive by registering their residential, wireless, fax, or VoIP telephone numbers on the National DNCL. Violations of CRTC rules can result in the termination of telecommunications services to the call center.

The Personal Information Protection and Electronic Documents Act (PIPEDA) governs the collection, use, and disclosure of personally identifiable information by companies in Canada. All organizations engaged in commercial activity must designate a privacy officer or contact, have written policies and procedures outlining how the organization handles and protects personal information, and train employees in data-handling procedures. In addition, PIPEDA meets the requirements set forth in the European Union's Data Protection Directive (see the following section), thereby allowing Canada-based organizations to handle data about consumers in EU member states.

European Union laws

The European Union (EU), currently comprising 27 member countries, has two primary directives that affect call centers:

- **Distance Selling Regulations of 2000:** This directive protects consumers throughout Europe who buy goods and services, regardless of whether the companies selling these goods or services are located within the EU. The regulations cover sales made by mail order, Internet, telephone, and all other means of distance communication. They require suppliers to give certain information to consumers, offer the right to cancel the contract within seven working days of receiving the goods or concluding the contract for services, meet set deadlines for delivery of goods or performance of services, and offer consumer protection against fraudulent use of card payments. The regulations also prohibit *inertial selling,* which is the practice of sending unrequested goods to customers and sending them an invoice for the goods in the hope that they'll pay it.

✔ **Data Protection Directive:** The second EU directive establishes how public- and private-sector organizations can collect, use, disclose, hold, and destroy personal data, whether within or outside a member country.

Each member country's national laws must implement these consumer rights under both directives, and these national laws vary from country to country. Many EU member countries have established preference services that include do-not-call lists. Requirements regarding do-not-call laws vary from country to country.

Chapter 16

Mastering Change in Your Organization

· ·

In This Chapter

▶ Anticipating situations that call for change leadership

▶ Becoming an effective change manager

▶ Helping your staff adjust to change

· ·

*Y*ou need strong leaders to introduce change and get agents (and managers) to adapt, stay focused, and stay productive. Most people call this process *change management,* but we prefer to call it *change leadership.*

When you read the word *change,* you might think of big changes, such as layoffs, outsourcing, or the implementation of a brand-new piece of technology. But call centers have far more constant, incremental changes — changes in metrics, expectations, products, billing, new hires, system upgrades, and so on. If you get good at dealing with these small changes, you don't have to deal with lost agent productivity and a lack of trust between agents and management.

In this chapter, we discuss how to manage all the change that goes on around you, how to keep your agents productive, and how to announce and implement change in a seamless way.

Recognizing When Change Leadership Is Needed

As we mention in Chapter 1, call centers have been changing and improving for more than 40 years — ever since a call center consisted of a single operator taking ticket orders to a Frank Sinatra concert. Look at call centers now! A modern call center features many technology choices, hundreds of agents in one room, managers everywhere, and online content in place of the bulging three-ring binders of the past.

Also, company mergers and complexity have forced agents to use three to six online systems just to fill one order. To paraphrase an old saying, "The only thing that's constant is change in call centers." (In case you couldn't tell, we added the part about call centers.)

Call centers are constant-change machines, and great call center leaders develop their personal skills to refine and continually improve changes in a call center. If your team never misses a beat during turbulent times, you have achieved change mastery. As Charles Darwin said, "It is not the strongest of the species that survive, nor the most intelligent, but the one most responsive to change."

Understanding common changes in call centers

The following list goes through a few common changes that most call centers experience at some point:

- **Customer expectations:** Customers want faster service, 24-hour Web self-service, and order confirmation by e-mail.

- **Technology:** These changes can include updates to systems and networks, Web chat, interactive voice response (IVR) prompts, and new call-monitoring processes. (See Part III for more information on technology in the call center.)

- **Procedures:** Your call center may require new procedures and processes, as well as a new coaching program.

- **Marketing or products:** Your call center may have to deal with a credit-card launch, a new infomercial that increases calls, or retirement-planning season.

- **People:** Your call center gets new leaders, as well as new recruits (but you get new recruits so often, that change doesn't even feel like change anymore). Promoted employees also have to deal with new tasks, higher expectations, and confusing job titles.

- **Job security:** The call center may need to eliminate individual jobs, or it may experience a drop in revenue or a decreasing number of calls.

- **Operations:** Your call center may impose extended hours, new schedules, new performance metrics, a new quality process, or (horror!) no more free coffee.

Change never takes a break. Everyone is trying to improve the business, fix problems, and grow sales. New ideas lead to more projects and more changes. New people join and old people leave, and after you achieve successful results, management wants better results. Go figure!

Don't underestimate the impact of change. Big or small, every new thing that you want your team to do falls under this definition and requires thoughtful planning. The following sections help you figure out how to get call center agents to welcome change with open arms.

Knowing how people react to change

To implement change effectively, you need to understand the perceptions that shape people's responses to change. You can't lead change successfully if you don't have at least a basic understanding of how and why people respond to change.

Perceptions of change

Resistance to change comes about for a variety of reasons. People are simply risk-averse; they like things the way they are and may worry that change will create a worse situation. Often, agents don't trust management if past changes went poorly, making their jobs more difficult. Also, the degree of resistance directly relates to the size of the change you're making. Changing the coffee system may not evoke long-term hostile response, but a change in the bonus system can, if agents see this change as a way for management to avoid paying the agents their fair share.

Your call center agents may have these types of perceptions of change:

- ✔ **Process changes can be confusing.** Agents have to figure out these changes, and during the transition period, they may work more slowly, make mistakes, and lose confidence.

- ✔ **Technology changes lead to changes in processes.** These changes require retraining and cause system instability, which can lead to agent frustration.

- ✔ **Changes in leaders mean that trust, friendship, and mentorship disappear.** Agents don't know how a new leader will treat them.

- ✔ **Changes may mean a change in work/life balance.** Agents may have new hours, more calls, and no weekends off.

- ✔ **Agents may fear failure.** Agents may worry that they'll have to work harder to reach the level of success they currently have or that changes will leave them with fewer career options.

- ✔ **Agents could lose income if expectations are raised.** If agents have to work harder to get their regular bonuses, they may lose that income if they can't increase their productivity.

- ✔ **Agents may worry that they'll lose their jobs.** An agent's viability can be affected by new processes, technology, leaders, or unions; a drop in revenue; an increase in revenue; and so on.

Not every agent has all the concerns in the preceding list, but most agents think about some of them, because they wonder how the changes will affect them personally. A new mom, for example, might focus most on work/life balance (getting out at 5 p.m. to pick up little Melissa at day care). A team leader might be more focused on career advancement and fear of failure in a challenging new role.

People can be pretty emotional (and often irrational) about change. A strong leader needs to help them get through the emotion and become productive again.

Stages of reaction to change

Change has as much to do with context as content. You need to understand what people think about change if you want to help them accept change.

People go through four stages in reaction to change:

- ✓ **Shock or fear:** The news causes an emotional reaction that often gets in the way of hearing the facts.

- ✓ **Defensive retreat:** They aren't ready to deal with change yet and often push back or act out.

- ✓ **Acknowledgment:** They're ready to listen but haven't yet accepted the change.

- ✓ **Acceptance and adaptation:** They're ready to move forward productively (although they may still have anxiety about some aspects of the change).

Every agent remains in each stage for a different period. Also, positive change for one agent may be negative change for another. A strong salesperson may like the new bonus system, which provides lower base income with more opportunity for bonuses, but an unskilled sales agent may see the change as creating a loss of income.

Often, when managers think that their agents aren't accepting the change, those agents are merely confused about what the change means. Don't assume that an agent's need for clarity equals nonacceptance.

Seeing why things go wrong sometimes

Clients often ask us, "Why, despite my best efforts, do my agents have so much resistance to change?" Here are some common missteps that can derail a smooth transition to agent acceptance:

- You don't explain why the call center needs the change.

- You don't think that agents can handle the truth, so you try to sugar-coat it and lose credibility.

- You try to rush acceptance and don't respect the four stages of reaction that agents go through (as discussed in the preceding section).

- You send confusing or conflicting messages, or you try to explain by using data that doesn't seem relevant.

- You give up communicating with and listening to your agents, thinking that they should understand the change by now.

- You don't describe the change in terms of personal effects on agents; you focus only on company and customer needs, ignoring the needs of your agents.

- Instead of having an empathetic conversation, you answer emotional questions about personal effects with data and facts — terms that offer no comfort.

What you're thinking and what your agents are thinking may not be the same thing. It can be difficult to guess the context in which agents will take the news and even more difficult to anticipate their emotional reactions.

Improving Your Personal Change-Leadership Style

When you're dealing with a lot of changes in your call center, remember that each change has its own effects on employees, and its own data and metrics, but all changes have common themes that tell you how to make your agents accept the change without a lot of bother.

Avoiding change pitfalls

Managers at all levels may struggle to deliver change messages because they inadvertently follow the wrong behaviors. Do you recognize yourself in any of the following examples?

- **Situation:** You haven't personally bought into the company's decision.

  Wrong behavior: You create an us-versus-them mentality by telling the agents that you don't agree with the change either, but the muckety-mucks are insisting that you impose it.

- **Situation:** You avoid conflict at any cost, and implementing this change feels like conflict.

Wrong behavior: You avoid handling the introduction of the change face to face with your agents. Instead, you deliver the messages by e-mail or through other people, and you don't do individual follow-up.

✔ **Situation:** You don't know how to explain vision and context because you're not sure why the company decided to impose this change.

Wrong behavior: You wait to tell your team until after senior management has made all the decisions and planned every step. You avoid explaining why you're imposing the change and discussing the effect, and you focus instead on the easier "what and when" discussions.

✔ **Situation:** You don't have all the information that your agents want, you can't answer all their questions, and you find some of the information provided by senior management or other teams to be confusing.

Wrong behavior: You conduct your team meeting without preparing properly for it or getting all your facts clear in advance.

Following the Rule of Change Success

The Rule of Change Success can help you decide which elements need most of your attention. This rule uses a sort of formula to spell out how to achieve change success:

Discontent + Clear future state + Action plan > Degree of resistance

---

Keeping communication transparent

One of our clients recently had to implement a sales program in his organization's service-oriented call center, which provides diagnostic service or repair advice and dispatches technicians to repair faulty equipment. Many of the agents had worked for the company for years and were well entrenched in their current roles. Our client had to ensure that the team would fully support the new sales program.

His management team focused on transparency of communication, communicating with agents openly and frequently so that the agents felt respected and excited about the center's new direction. Actively engaging the agents, and giving them a clear understanding of the direct benefits for themselves and the company, was fundamental to the program's success because the agents had to implement this new program themselves.

By openly discussing the program, our client gained commitment from the majority of the center's agents. Those agents even provided recommendations on how to introduce the program, and our client made several enhancements to the program based on agent feedback.

The transparent approach produced dramatic results for our client's company — sooner than expected and at a lower cost than budgeted — because it got agents involved in making the sales program a success.

Here's a breakdown of the elements of this formula:

- ✔ **Discontent:** No one changes easily if he's very comfortable with the current state. Acceptance of change typically occurs when enough discontent breaks down organizational inertia.

- ✔ **Clear future state:** Agents can see a positive, or even exciting, outcome of the change. Explain the positive outcomes of change, as well as what isn't changing. Be sure to discuss the possible effects and how you plan to work them out with your agents.

- ✔ **Action plan:** Lay out the next steps you plan to take and the key milestones to watch for. Also explain what you *won't* be working on to reinforce what isn't changing. Even if your next step involves only creating a committee to plan the implementation, that step gives agents a sense of control and an opportunity to be involved.

  The leadership team needs to design some changes — such as staff reduction — without agent involvement.

- ✔ **Degree of resistance:** You need to gauge the level of resistance and potential opposition to the change at organizational level (you get different responses in a bureaucratic culture compared with an entrepreneurial startup) and at employee level. Some company cultures don't handle any change well, and in all companies, some people don't handle it well.

If the call center employees aren't accepting change well, you usually can look to the elements of the Rule of Change Success to understand why. If you don't understand how these elements work in your call center, even weak opposition to change could hamper your success in implementing that change.

Reducing Resistance to Change

Resistance to change is natural. (We discuss agent resistance to changes in "Knowing how people react to change," earlier in this chapter.) Follow the best practices that we talk about in the following sections to reduce the degree of resistance.

Earn — and keep — agents' trust

Organizations that have high levels of trust between employees and management can almost always get through change more easily than organizations that have little or no trust. When you talk to them, agents really listen and know that you have their best interests at heart.

You can't start earning trust at the point when you need to impose the big change; make trust a preexisting condition.

You earn the trust of your agents over a long period by building strong relationships with them and — most important — keeping your promises. This idea sounds simple (you probably remember hearing it in grade school), but a history of broken promises is a certain trust-buster.

Reducing agents' resistance to change also involves including them in the process: communicating with them early, openly, and honestly; respecting their points of view and their emotions; setting the context for why the call center needs change; and helping them understand the effect of the change.

If you're not sure whether your organization's trust level may hold back future change initiatives, you may want to find out. Consider the following:

- ✓ **Think about the last change that you implemented.** Experience may help you predict the future, so figure out how many agents expressed satisfaction and happiness with past changes. If you received little positive feedback, and adaptation took a long time, you may have to build up more trust before you make the next change.

- ✓ **Do an anonymous agent survey.** This survey can measure satisfaction with the past few changes and get honest answers to questions about those changes and their effects. Specifically, ask whether the agent's team leader was clear, honest, and trustworthy during recent changes. Ask at least one open-ended question to capture comments and reactions that you can't anticipate.

- ✓ **Bring in an expert.** Hire a third-party expert on change leadership. (Often, consulting companies provide this service.) Have the expert do a full analysis of your call center's ability to accept change and train management in methods for implementing future change.

Communicate well

In the absence of factual information, people get together and make up stories to fill in the information gap (and their stories are usually worse than reality). As a leader, you need to communicate change to your agents effectively.

Communicate accurately

If you create a communication plan that contains omissions, confusing data or charts, formulas that no one can decipher, vague references to the future, or just too much information, you make all the other best practices less effective. Spend enough time to build the communication template, test-drive it with your peers, edit as required for your agents, and communicate in phases so that agents start with the big picture and get more details later.

Communicate completely

If you want change success, you need to communicate completely with your agents. Partial explanations typically lead to confusion and sometimes mistrust.

In Figure 16-1, the pie chart includes all the pieces of complete communication. *Note:* Most managers report on the "what" and "when" of a change, but they should also include context — the "why" and the "how."

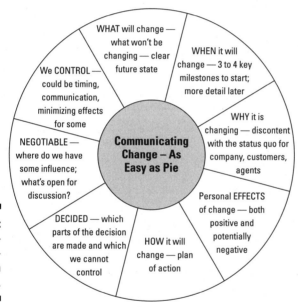

Figure 16-1: The change-communication process.

Communicate early

Figure 16-2 illustrates that if you start communicating during the planning stage as opposed to during implementation, you get several benefits:

- Agents feel that you're collaborating with them — not doing something to them.
- You control the message before the rumor mill takes control away from you.

✔ The four stages of acceptance (which we talk about in "Stages of reaction to change," earlier in this chapter) starts at this early point, and by the time the change arrives, many agents have already accepted the change.

✔ You can get smart insights from those who are affected by the change about how to manage the change better. Your team may not have control of whether the change moves forward, but using agent input always creates a better implementation plan.

Figure 16-2: Communicate early in the change process.

Decision to Change — Planning the Change — Implementing the Change

BETTER HERE ... THAN HERE

Although agents may not be included here...

... and you can choose to communicate anywhere in the process ...

... the sooner you communicate, the better your chances of getting benefits

Communicate frequently

Managers need the patience to communicate until agents accept the change to the required degree. Some agents accept the change at the first announcement; some need to hear about the change, think about it, ask a few questions, and then accept it; and some may not accept it until you have it in place and everyone else is already doing it.

The chart in Figure 16-3 shows example agents and how much time they've needed to accept change in the past. Mike (who has a generally high resistance to change) needs more information before he can accept the change. Bob, on the other hand, generally likes and accepts change quickly; he's less risk-averse than Mike is.

How much you communicate with an agent often depends on the complexity of the issue, how much information the agent needs to understand, and whether the change will create a negative effect on someone. In the High-Impact Change column in Figure 16-3, Mary needs a long acceptance cycle (longer than her normal response), almost equal to Mike (the risk-averse guy). Some part of this specific high-impact change felt risky or negative to Mary. The opposite occurred for Edith, who accepted the high-impact change more quickly than her norm.

Figure 16-3:
The number
of com-
munication
sessions
needed
to accept
change,
based
on each
agent's
past level of
resistance
to change.

	Resistance to change	Low-Impact Change	Medium-Impact Change	High-Impact Change
Bob	Low	1	2	3
Mary		1	2	5
Juan		1	3	3
Edith		1	3	2
Mike	High	2	4	6

Number of communications, coaching sessions
needed to accept this change

No matter how well you handle the situation, some people always resist change. If some agents resist months after everyone else has accepted the change, be blunt. Let them know that if they're going to remain productively on the team, it's time to accept the change; then get them to agree to do so.

Leading change doesn't involve only your agents, but also your peers and managers senior to you in the call center. They have similar emotional responses to your agents when it comes to not knowing what's happening, feeling that they haven't been consulted, or wondering what advantages they can get from the change.

Show empathy

You can't focus only on facts; emotions play the biggest role in the four stages of acceptance (discussed in "Stages of reaction to change," earlier in this chapter). Often, agents don't even need an answer, new facts, or a solution; they just want you to listen while they sort things out for themselves.

After you announce a change, plan time to follow up with people individually so that you can find out how they feel about the change and whether you can answer any questions they may have. Announce facts and context in a group, but handle emotions one person at a time.

Be careful not to confuse what your agents say with how they say it. Also, you need to be patient; some of your agents may have trouble expressing themselves, so their points may sound abrupt or negative, but they may have great ideas if you listen without becoming defensive.

Building trust through communication

Bernie Herenberg, an associate of Winston's, worked as a call center manager for a Canadian not-for-profit organization and had to merge the organization's donations-processing team with its call centers. Several cross-country branches had to be centralized with the full commitment of staff.

Herenberg did several things to tackle the issues:

✔ He visited the regional offices to meet and reassure staff members. He explained the plan for centralization, listened to agents' concerns, and promoted the benefits of the planned national contact center.

✔ He worked with the managers of each center to develop guiding principles, agree on allocation of work for extended hours, and determine what new skills agents would need to service customers from across the country.

✔ When talking with agents, he described the department mergers as an arranged marriage, adding that many cultures have a high arranged-marriage success rate and that love grows over time. The humor helped reduce resistance.

✔ He submitted an article about the project to internal publications.

✔ When each province transitioned successfully, he sent announcements to all staff members. Each small success built support and lowered resistance for the next team.

Ultimately, the centers merged successfully — on time and with a lot of staff support.

Identify and work with influential agents

An *influential agent* — one whom other agents respect and listen to — can provide support for the change you need to implement. You might recruit this person early in the change process so that she can help explain the message about the positive aspects of the change. An influential agent who opposed change in the past but agrees with the need for this particular change can influence a group of fence-sitters, because they respect her for not always agreeing with everything.

Try to get influential agents to join validation groups. Give these group members a sneak peek at the change; then ask them to help you refine the change and communicate it to the rest of the staff. You can have a truly effective team meeting when, say, 4 of 18 agents are already on your side and can help with the question-and-answer session.

Don't ignore those agents who are respectfully critical but also respected among their peers as informal leaders. When they agree to support the change, others will follow.

Involve the team

Many changes (such as systems upgrades and process fixes), which are never completely figured out when they reach your operation, require final input from your agents. You need to involve the agents in finalizing the details, fixing the errors in real time, or seeking clarification about how to implement the change.

Some new programs, such as establishing home agents (see Chapter 11), need agent involvement starting very early in the change. You can safely start with a relatively small number of agents transitioning to working at home. You're likely to find a small number of agents who want to participate while the other agents wait to see how the change turns out.

Launch a pilot program

A pilot program allows staff members to participate — not in the initial decision, but in the implementation and refinement of the decision. A pilot program lets you try out a planned change and see how it goes. If it doesn't work, you can discuss with your agents what they think you need to do differently. Giving your agents input in the process can minimize their anxiety about the change.

Chapter 17

Quality-Control Programs and Certifications

*I*n the service world — and the call center industry in particular — the meaning of *quality* has changed from the original dictionary definition of "an inherent or distinguishing characteristic of something (or someone)." *Quality* has come to mean something of superior grade, as in a quality wine. So when people talk of improving quality, it's kind of like saying seeking perfection — or, as we define it in this book, continuously improving.

In many organizations, *quality control* is a system for ensuring the maintenance of proper standards, which we interpret as a system designed to ensure continuous process improvement. We define and discuss process improvement in some detail in Chapter 15. In this chapter, you can find suggestions and resources to help ensure that process improvement happens in your center.

Certifying Your Management Team

Certification involves taking your existing, new, or potential call center management through a training program that covers call center definitions, concepts, and practices. You want to produce a management team that's familiar with call center operations and skilled in managing call center processes so that each operation achieves excellent results.

Call center management certification isn't new, but its popularity has exploded in recent years — which is a good thing, because certification can enhance the performance of your management team by providing them the knowledge, skills, and tools they need to run your call center efficiently.

The increase in demand for this type of program is largely a response to a shortage of skilled call center managers. The diversity of skills and knowledge required — from managing service level and occupancy (see Chapter 6) to labor relations and the psychology of motivation — make call center management a fairly specialized profession.

A good certification program can take smart people and develop them into competent call center operators.

In-house versus external programs

Certification programs come in two varieties: homegrown and external. Don't assume that a program's no good just because it was developed in-house; good programs can be created internally or purchased externally. If you get external help from people who've already gone through the process of creating the course, you can benefit from training based on industry standards. This training helps your staff adapt to new work methods and technology, and you can tailor it to meet your requirements, saving you a lot of time and trouble.

You can find a handy-dandy reference of certification-program suppliers in Appendix B.

A course is a course, of course, of course . . .

To develop a good program, assume that participants know very little about call centers. Start with the basics so that you can use your certification course as indoctrination for managers who are new to the call center environment (meaning smart people hired to perform call center management functions).

Going beyond the basics, you may want to create a general call center management certification program, targeted to managers and executives who need an overall understanding of how the call center operates.

Here are some topics you might include in your certification course:

- Call center definitions
- The business model, mission, and vision
- Call center business goals and metrics
- Unique call center concepts, such as managing service levels and occupancy
- Call center logistics (location, building, setup, and so on)
- Organizational structure, roles, and responsibilities
- The uses and benefits of technology in the call center
- Supervision and agent performance management, including labor relations
- Call center budgeting models
- Forecasting and scheduling
- Quality assurance
- Process management, including policies, procedures, and best practices
- Legislation that affects the call center
- Important skills for team leaders
- Priorities and use of time — a clear description of a day in the life of a front-line manager that defines roles and responsibilities, priorities, and use of time
- Behavioral skills, such as role modeling and developing direct reports

Courses that provide a general overview can take a week to complete. In each *module* (self-contained course unit), however, you can go into a great deal of depth, making the course considerably longer. Each module should cover several training goals.

A more feasible approach involves creating a separate certification course for each discipline within the call center, such as forecasting and scheduling, team leader and agent performance management, analysis and reporting, and technology management. Then you can prioritize the courses as optional, suggested, or required for specific roles within your center. Forecasting and scheduling courses would be required for the folks on your resource management team, for example.

Who should attend management certification courses?

Certification programs can help smart new managers run all or part of your call center operations. Those managers may have been transferred from other departments, promoted from within, or recruited from other companies; they may have good management credentials but little or no call center experience.

Senior managers who are responsible for call center operations can also benefit from certification programs because these programs provide clear performance standards. Executives who just got the responsibility of running the call center, for example, may use these programs to familiarize themselves with the day-to-day operations of running a call center, and executives who've worked in call centers for some time and want to make sense of the operation can benefit from getting a refresher on the technical side of the center.

Finally, certification can help call center agents, team leaders, and junior managers achieve a better overall understanding of call center operations. It can also be a great career move for these employees, setting them up for advancement after they successfully complete the course.

Instituting a Quality-Control Program

You can do a great deal on your own to improve processes (see Chapter 15) and ensure quality control within your call center. Still, you can find people out there who are certified in quality-control programs, helping you better understand your business's processes and build systems of improvement so that you can identify gaps in your processes and then implement solutions to improve those processes.

If you turn to one of these organizations, you don't have to reinvent the wheel. Such an organization can implement time-tested methods in your company quickly, allowing you to start improving your operation sooner and probably with a better-defined approach than if you'd built a quality-control program on your own. Try to get someone senior in your organization to sponsor this program so that you can get the resources you need to build and run your quality-control program.

Because of their methodology and inherent metrics, quality-control programs provide numerous benefits, including the following:

✔ They offer a standardized approach to problem-solving.

✔ They improve operational efficiencies by raising productivity and lowering costs.

✔ They often include rigorous reporting, data gathering, and disciplined documentation, helping you determine a point of reference for measuring performance improvements and allowing the business to be certified as a quality-regulated organization.

✔ They help businesses demonstrate that they comply with industry operating standards or regulations.

In the following sections, we discuss some of the quality-control programs that are most commonly used in the call center industry.

ISO 9001/2000

ISO 9001/2000 is an international standard for the creation and maintenance of a quality-assurance system within a company. This standard, developed by the International Organization for Standardization (ISO; www.iso.org), provides a template for building and documenting a quality-control system.

Key elements of ISO 9001/2000 include standards for training employees, maintenance of equipment, recordkeeping, inspection of processes, customer relations, and continuous improvement. You can ensure adherence to these standards by allowing a third-party, ISO-accredited auditor to conduct an annual audit.

ISO certification doesn't ensure that your company has high-quality products or services. It merely provides a means to ensure that your company documents and follows its own internal procedures, including those for correcting problems and improving processes. "Say what you do and do what you say" is a common ISO motto.

You can tailor ISO to the call center environment, integrating measurable outputs of success. You, as the user, have to determine what those outputs should be.

If you want to standardize and document work processes, ISO can help you reach that goal, but ISO is the beginning — not the end — of process management and control. (We talk about process management in Chapter 15.)

If you're interested in using ISO, be aware that it's not a quick process; converting your processes to the ISO standard may take a year or more. The more you have documented already, the better.

Criticisms of ISO certification

The application of ISO certification to call centers has generated some criticism. Some observers suggest that it's a manufacturing standard that isn't suited to service operations such as call centers; others argue that ISO doesn't focus enough on measurable outputs, especially quality outputs. Also, some companies simply fake their adherence to ISO just for the purpose of marketing themselves as ISO shops, and when a registrar audits their quality systems, these companies try to cover up the fact that they haven't been faithful to it.

Although all these criticisms are legitimate, they're probably not fair in their assessment of the standard. As with many business practices, if you use an ISO framework in a sincere attempt to build a structure for documenting work processes, it's a great tool that can lead to substantial process improvements in your organization. It certainly has in ours.

You need a consultant and a third-party auditor (called a *registrar)* to get ISO-certified. We offer some suggestions on where to find these resources in Appendix B.

COPC-2000

Created in 1995, Customer Operations Performance Center, Inc. (COPC) is a privately held customer service support company that defines industry standards for call center excellence. COPC certifies organizations to the call center–specific COPC-2000 standard. This standard focuses on measurable criteria in the areas of customer service, customer satisfaction, and operational efficiency, and on the application of effective processes in those areas.

A committee made up of industry professionals from high-profile organizations that use and purchase call center services maintains the COPC-2000 standard.

COPC-2000 was originally intended for use in evaluating third-party providers of call center services, but it has evolved into a standard that's used by both in-house and external/outsourced call center operations.

For more information on COPC and on COPC-2000, visit www.copc.com.

Six Sigma

Six Sigma is a quality-control program that uses data and statistical analysis to improve efficiency and control, and reduce variation, in business processes for the purpose of increasing profits, customer satisfaction, and employee morale.

Six Sigma, which literally means *six standard deviations,* refers to the reduction of errors to six standard deviations from the center of process output, which translates to about 3.4 defects per million outputs (approximately none!). Imagine your call center having fewer than four bad calls per million customer interactions.

In the call center, a defect occurs when a customer call ends without the desired outcome for the customer or the organization, probably resulting in an unsatisfied customer. Indicators of call defects include abandoned calls, repeat calls, customer complaints, low customer satisfaction scores, and errors in call-monitoring scores. Defects occur because of inadequacies in the call-handling process and your internal processes, and because of errors made by your call center agents. Identifying your levels of defects and grouping them by cause can help you start to reduce these defects and create improved customer satisfaction.

A detailed discussion of Six Sigma is beyond the scope of this book, but you can find much more information in *Six Sigma For Dummies,* by Craig Gygi, Neil DeCarlo, and Bruce Williams (Wiley Publishing, Inc.).

Finding Other Sources of Help

Over the past decade, call center management has become a discipline and industry unto itself — a very large industry. As a result, subindustries have developed solely for the purpose of providing call center support. The following sections discuss some resources that can help you meet your call center's goals.

Consulting firms

Call center consulting services have become readily available through a variety of firms, covering everything from general call center management and technology to very specific disciplines such as call handling, location selection and development, recruitment, and scheduling.

Most large consulting firms have a division of experts who can help you with your call center projects. You can also find a lot of small, independent call center consulting and support companies.

We provide a list of some places to look for call center support in Appendix B. An Internet search for *call center consulting* can also give you a good place to start.

Trade shows

The number of call center trade shows has grown along with the industry itself. These shows take place around the world, often specializing in specific trends in the industry. They're busy, fun, and often held in far-off exotic locations.

For information on call center trade shows, visit the Direct Marketing Association's Web site at www.the-dma.org, or contact your local or regional call center association.

Trade magazines

You can buy trade magazines much more cheaply than you can attend trade shows. These magazines are full of great current information on the call center industry.

Everyone who's responsible in any way for the operation of a call center — or a department within a call center — should subscribe to call center–industry and related magazines, such as those that focus on marketing or technology. A good trade magazine covers every hot issue, trend, and discipline of running call centers over the course of a one-year subscription. You can even get information from the advertisements, in which vendors strut their latest and greatest developments.

Here are some magazines that we like:

- ✔ *Call Center Magazine:* Archives at www.callcentermagazine.com
- ✔ *Customer Interaction Solutions:* www.tmcnet.com/call-center
- ✔ *Contact Management:* www.contactmanagement.ca

Part VI
The Part of Tens

The 5th Wave   By Rich Tennant

"...for technical support, press 7; for product information, press 8; if you're bored and just want to argue with someone, press 9..."

That's me...

In this part . . .

In Part VI, you can find a collection of pointers from the call center industry that can boost your company's revenue, efficiency, employee morale, and customer satisfaction. The Part of Tens — a *For Dummies* tradition — gives you a fast and easy way to pick up some helpful tips on improving agent job satisfaction, lists questions that every call center manager should answer, and provides techniques for reducing costs and increasing efficiency.

Chapter 18

Ten Ways to Improve Agents' Job Satisfaction

*I*n the business world, a generally accepted principle — which we agree with — says that companies that have happy employees tend to have happy customers. By improving your agents' job satisfaction, you can likely improve your customers' satisfaction as well.

In this chapter, we provide tips that can help you maximize your agents' satisfaction with their jobs.

Recruit People Who Value the Work

When recruiting, you need to look for two key things in a candidate: skill and motivation. (For more on recruiting, see Chapter 12.) Most employers know how to find candidates who have skill, but many employers have difficulty finding candidates with motivation.

Finding employees who value the work means that you have employees who continue to feel motivated after doing the job for some time. By choosing agents who have a positive outlook and energy, you set yourself up for success in your center, even if some of those candidates don't have all the skills that you need. By building a trusting relationship and employing good coaching skills, you can quickly develop employees' skills and keep their motivation high.

The knee-jerk reaction is to hire the most skilled person who knocks on your door, but you often end up hiring a highly skilled person who's between jobs. Don't be surprised if such a person quits after finding a job elsewhere that he considers to be better.

Even worse than losing a skilled agent is hiring an unmotivated agent, who can end up resenting your call center work for not challenging her enough. This type of employee may quit emotionally but stay on the payroll.

Clarify Expectations

Tell your agents what your company expects of them and what they can get for meeting and exceeding those expectations. (We talk more about developing and communicating expectations in Chapter 3.)

Employees often fail to do what's expected of them because no one tells them what's expected of them. Be clear in your expectations — even before a potential agent accepts the job — so you can make sure that your agents aren't disappointed (and you aren't, either). Confusion about roles and contributions frustrates everyone.

Clear expectations set the road for achievement, and your agents may feel an enhanced sense of job satisfaction when they meet those expectations.

Provide Thorough Job-Specific Training

Train your agents in the skills that they need to succeed in the call center. (See Chapter 12 for more on training.) Know the top ten reasons why your customers call, and be able to provide your newly hired agents the knowledge and skills to answer these questions or solve these problems. Typically, your new-hire training involves imparting knowledge of products and process, explaining how to use the computer systems, and training in basic customer service and sales skills.

The key to coaching and building proficiency is working on one skill at a time. After an agent can consistently demonstrate the use of a skill, move on to the next skill that needs development until that agent has mastery of all service and sales skills.

Ask, Don't Tell

Agents are more likely to change their behavior if you coach and lead them to discover the change themselves. In many centers, team leaders tell their agents what they should say or do; then they wonder why the requested changes don't stick. Effective coaching sounds like a natural conversation, and it helps agents fully understand what they need to work on. When you add value to your agent by giving him a suggestion to do or say something very specific, he'll welcome your input again and again. See Chapter 13 for a rundown of the principles of coaching.

 Coaching can work only if a high level of trust exists between agents and their team leaders. An effective coach keeps her promises, pays attention to the small things that agents find important, and remains consistent in her interactions with agents.

Remove Roadblocks to Success

Obstacles occur in almost every endeavor, and your agents will likely run into a lot of them. Common call center roadblocks include processes and tools that don't work, policies that customers complain about, and unhelpful management. Obstacles in themselves don't demotivate staff, but if management does little to help remove them, agents can find roadblocks to be very demotivating. By removing roadblocks, you show your agents that you understand their challenges and are actively working to make their situations better.

Calm Fears

Call centers can become scary places for employees because they have a very high level of accountability, and in an increasingly competitive world, the drive for results is only increasing. Poorly trained or bad team leaders compound the problem of fear because they talk or act without thinking about the effect of their behavior on agents.

Fear makes people shut down, so they don't express their feelings and often feel trapped. It dampens their enthusiasm and prevents innovation and improvement. Fear makes agents feel that they have no voice in the company or control of their jobs. A lot of good people leave call center jobs because of fear.

Your management team must step in to ensure that hard-working employees don't have to be afraid that if they make a mistake, they may lose their jobs. You can reduce fear by using the change management techniques discussed in Chapter 16.

Adapt policies to ensure that accountability goes both ways. Agents are accountable for doing their best in their positions, and management is accountable for contributing to agents' success.

You can use regular (at least quarterly) employee opinion surveys to ensure that your call center maintains a fear-free culture. Make team leaders responsible for the job satisfaction of the employees they supervise. Also, exit interviews can help determine how successful management has been in creating a supportive working environment. Check out Chapter 14 for tips on creating a motivated workforce.

Establishing an appeals process can ensure that you address agent dissatisfaction and maintain employee rights. If it's done well, this process can go a long way toward reducing agent anxiety in the workplace. Make the appeals process well-thought-out and well-designed, and train the staff in how to use it.

Don't Ask Agents to Do Anything You Wouldn't Want to Do

Set an example by doing some of the tough work that you ask your agents to do, such as answering calls from angry customers or making cold calls.

Have your team leaders do an agent's job from time to time; it can really help build a bridge between agents and the leadership team. Some of the very best team leaders sit down in an agent's seat to demonstrate a technique or a specific skill. By taking this approach, the team leader can quickly get the respect of call center agents and move the coaching from something theoretical to something practical that agents can actually achieve.

Communicate Honestly

Effective communication is critical to agent job satisfaction. If you've worked in a call center for any length of time, you can probably attest that call centers are rumor machines, which isn't surprising when you consider that so many people are brought together in one place.

By using team meetings, e-mail, portals, internal Web sites, and chat sessions, you can communicate openly and honestly — and a lot. The more information that you communicate to agents, the less active the rumor mill will become.

Ask for Feedback

Communication needs to go both ways. On a regular basis (we suggest monthly), ask employees for their feedback on whether management is creating a healthy and effective workplace. You should ask a variety of questions, but the one that's most important finds out whether employees value their jobs.

Also provide a mechanism for employees to give open-ended comments and suggestions. You may have to make the survey anonymous. Even in the best environments, some people don't feel comfortable opening up completely.

Based on the findings of your employee satisfaction survey, pick out specific positive and negative trends. Work to either improve the most critical areas, as defined by your employees, or communicate why these things are the way they are. In subsequent months, add specific questions to the feedback forms regarding key areas of dissatisfaction so that you can figure out whether your agents feel that you're improving the work environment and overall employee satisfaction. Chapter 14 provides more information about employee surveys.

Tying part of team leaders' rewards to employee satisfaction engages the entire management team in improving job satisfaction.

Be Positive

In call centers, you can track accountability easily, and in the quest for constant improvement, you may tend to focus on things that aren't right. This narrow focus, however, can lead you and your team leaders to concentrate mainly on catching people doing something wrong. Although you may adopt this management style with good intentions, it's inherently negative and can dampen enthusiasm and morale.

Constant improvement is a worthy goal. When your suggestions for improvement come in a predominantly positive environment, employees receive them much more enthusiastically. (We talk more about process improvement in Chapter 15.)

As basic as it may sound, we subscribe to the idea of a 10-to-1 positive-to-negative ratio. Give people in the office ten pieces of positive reinforcement for every suggestion for improvement, and frame suggestions for improvement in a positive manner ("Jane, you're already good at this. Imagine what can happen when you start following the troubleshooting guidelines!").

You should be able to offer encouragement easily. Catch people doing something right! If you can't easily find things to praise, you're not doing enough to create a positive environment.

We're not suggesting that you don't hold employees accountable. You just need to create accountability in a very positive environment.

Chapter 19

Ten Questions Every Call Center Manager Should Answer

*M*anaging a call center can be a rewarding and exciting job. If you want to be a successful call center manager, you need to know the answers to the important questions that we cover in this chapter.

How Does Your Call Center Fit into the Bigger Company Picture?

You can easily forget that a call center is a cog in the wheel of a larger enterprise. Everything starts with understanding how the call center fits into the big picture and answering the question "What does the business need the call center to do?"

If you run a specific business's call center, your direction comes from the senior executives to whom you report. If you run an outsourced call center, your direction comes from your client. In either case, you need clearly defined marching orders, ideally detailed in some form of service-level agreement that spells out the operating commitments between two internal teams. (We cover service levels in Chapter 6.)

With direction from the company that your call center is part of, you can define optimal service levels, the types of support that you offer to callers, the types of skills your employees need, and the kinds of tools that you need to fulfill your mission. No matter what type of operation you run, you must work through these issues with your internal clients and get the funding to create the operation that the business needs.

Why Are People Calling You?

First, by analyzing call driver reports, determine the top reasons why customers call; then drill deeper into each reason. If customers most often call to get billing information, for example, you can segment billing reasons into specific types of billing calls (the customer didn't understand the bill, the bill came late, the bill contained inaccurate charges, and so on).

Analyzing call drivers is one of your top ten management activities: It allows you to cut costs now and make operations more efficient in the future.

Understanding historical call types also helps you forecast staffing and the facilities' needs. (We talk more about forecasting in Chapter 7.) The call center scheduler uses call types to forecast future demand — which is especially important in the short term. Any given day may have a higher or lower call volume than forecast. The better you understand why volume is high or low, the better you can decide what to do about being understaffed or overstaffed.

What's Your Ideal Service-Level Objective?

You need to set a *service-level objective* — a call center term meaning your target for the percentage of calls that you answer within a specified period.

Often, call centers go with the crowd, setting the service-level objective at the industry average. Frequently, 80/20 (80 percent of calls answered within 20 seconds) becomes the default target, for no other reason than so many companies use it.

Although 80/20 is a good level of service, it may not be appropriate for your company. In an emergency-response call center, for example, 80/20 isn't good enough. Also, if a call center provides a very popular free service for which callers are willing to wait, 80/20 might be too costly.

Understanding this analysis (which we discuss in Chapter 6) arms you with knowledge of the right level of performance, as well as good reasons why your call center needs to achieve that level of performance.

What Does It Cost to Run Your Call Center for One Hour?

When you know the total cost of running your call center for an hour — and you need to consider *all* the costs, not just direct labor — you can quickly assess the benefits of a variety of business solutions, from the cost of an interactive voice response (IVR; see Chapter 9) system to outsourcing.

Understanding the components of cost per hour can really help you bring your costs down by eliminating inefficiencies. We discuss cost per hour in more detail in Chapter 6 and outsourcing in Chapter 5.

Are Your Employees Happy?

Too much change, unstable systems, poor implementations, and angry customers can all make employees unhappy. Whatever the reason, if your employees aren't happy, they aren't at their best when working with your customers. Not every day needs to be a love-in at your call center, but the work environment does need to be fair and challenging, with the occasional spark of excitement and fun.

The topic of understanding and affecting employee morale is a large one and could fill an entire book on its own — specifically, *Motivating Employees For Dummies,* by Max Messmer (Wiley Publishing, Inc.).

We want to point to one issue specifically: Employees often feel dissatisfied if they have poor relationships with their team leaders. A team leader needs to motivate and accelerate the skill level of her agents, which happens only if that team leader spends time coaching those agents. If a team leader consistently adds value to every interaction with her agents, those agents feel energized about the work and are willing to tackle new assignments and deliver high-quality service to customers.

No single activity can improve employee morale more than coaching by team leaders, but team leaders need the specific skills to coach well (see Chapter 13). Bring in the necessary expertise to help your team leaders be leaders.

What Will the Call Center Look Like in 12 to 18 Months?

Most call center forecasting and scheduling focuses on the relatively near term — from tomorrow to a few months from now — but call center managers need to have a slightly longer-term view as well. (We talk more about forecasting in Chapter 7.)

Major changes in caller demand, process, or products that your company offers require a good deal of planning, particularly if the changes require expansion, training, or new technology.

Failure to prepare results in a last-minute urgent rush to adapt, which causes stress on the call center's employees and degraded levels of customer service. The larger the change, the greater the effect of being unprepared.

Forecasting for the long term doesn't need to be difficult. Organize regular meetings with key people in the organization who might know about midterm changes that could affect the call center, such as the senior executive in charge of the call center or someone in marketing. With a broad understanding of what might be coming, you can work with your business analyst and scheduler to determine the effect of the changes. Then you can prepare your proposals or business plans for presentation to the senior people in the organization.

What Legislation Affects Your Call Center?

Call center management is becoming an exercise in risk management. Look no further than the do-not-call legislation affecting the call center industry.

You need to know about these laws and take steps to make sure that you comply with them. Better yet, hire a compliance officer, and make that person responsible for understanding the laws and making you comply, or get a compliance officer *and* a good lawyer.

Some areas of the law that you need to be concerned with include

- ✔ Privacy
- ✔ Outbound sales

✔ Labor

✔ Human rights

We talk more about call center legislation in Chapter 15.

How Does Technology Affect Your Call Center?

The developers of new technology address the demands of call centers in increasingly creative ways, as we describe in Chapter 9.

If you understand your call center process, as well as your operation's metrics and how to influence them, you can quickly identify the technologies that can improve your call center and drive results.

Call centers can often implement technology that pays for itself in one year. First, to keep capital expenses low, look for opportunities in old and proven technologies; then consider new technologies that can save you operating costs or deliver a higher level of service. You can't implement everything, but a few well-placed investments can make a big difference in efficiency or quality.

You need to consider some caveats before making tech changes:

✔ **How the technology can affect the drivers of your operation:** Your drivers include call length, calls per customer, occupancy, cost per hour, conversion rate, revenue per sale, employee satisfaction, and customer satisfaction.

✔ **Proof that the technology can get results:** Who has used this technology? What results did they get?

A lot of expensive technology that never realized its promise is sitting in call centers. Excitement about unsubstantiated claims can lead to a premature purchase.

✔ **Training for call center employees:** You can't effectively implement most technology in a vacuum. People in the call center need to understand the technology, what it does, how it works, and how they need to interact with it.

What's Your Disaster Recovery Plan?

Ask some people what a disaster recovery plan is, and they envision some type of James Bond scene in which the camera pans over a hidden lair — probably under a volcano — where the world's coolest agents take customer calls. The reality of disaster recovery planning is simpler (and, we admit, less cool).

You start a disaster recovery plan by first focusing on business continuity — planning how to keep your services available if you experience short, temporary outages (perhaps due to power failures or inclement weather) and then determining what to do during a prolonged outage and how to get back on your feet after power is restored. We discuss instituting a disaster recovery plan in Chapter 4.

For full details on this subject, see *IT Disaster Recovery Planning For Dummies,* by Peter Gregory, CISA, CISSP (Wiley).

What Are Your Three Initiatives for Improvement?

We like call centers that run effectively, and we *really* like call centers that are always evolving and improving. In the long run, the call centers that institute a culture of learning and improvement always seem to receive industry awards and rate high in customer-satisfaction surveys. Imagine that!

The managers of these centers frequently have ongoing initiatives — the things they're working on or planning that can lead to improvements in call center results. Often, team leaders and employees get excited about these initiatives; they can't wait until they can get the initiatives implemented and running. Not all initiatives work perfectly, of course, but constant innovation leads to successful initiatives that make these call centers leaders in their industry.

Chapter 20

Almost Ten Ways to Decrease Call Center Costs and Increase Efficiency

*G*enerally speaking, call centers provide a very efficient way to communicate with a large number of customers. Because call center operations frequently cost companies a lot of money, however, owners or leaders usually scrutinize those costs closely.

In this chapter, we provide some tips for improving efficiencies and decreasing overall call center costs.

Improve Call Control

In most call centers, implementing an effective call-control strategy can have an immediate effect, because reducing call length without sacrificing service is an effective way to reduce costs.

Most agents work hard to provide good service, and perhaps to sell additional products or services to customers, but many lack a structured plan that can guide a call to a successful conclusion. Some agents feel that if they control the call, they're not delivering good service; some even consider handling a call quickly to be rude, and as a result, their calls frequently wander. Training your agents in simple call-control techniques makes a significant difference in the length of each call. We talk more about training in Chapter 12.

You can help agents with call control by developing a customer-experience blueprint, as described in Chapter 15. This blueprint shows agents how to handle a call so that they can create an exceptional customer experience. The content of the blueprint doesn't deal with a specific call type, but with the specific phases that a good call should go through.

Effective coaching by team leaders (see Chapter 13) can help agents figure out how to control the call, reduce call length, and increase customer satisfaction.

Map and Improve Call Processes

Mapping your processes for handling various types of customer calls can help agents know exactly what they're supposed to do in a particular call situation. For a more complete discussion of how to map processes, see Chapter 15.

Start by identifying the eight to ten primary reasons why customers call. Then sit down with a group of agents, a team leader or two, and a trainer to map out (on paper or in software) how an agent needs to handle each type of call.

After you map the top call types, you can ask the group, "How might an agent answer this call more quickly, and how might he prevent the customer from calling back?" Simplifying and improving call processes can result in tremendous improvements in call length and other goals.

Achieve Your Service-Level Objective

A good *service-level objective* (a target that you set to measure how fast your call center answers the phone) creates a balance between the benefits and the costs associated with answering the phone quickly. See Chapter 6 for more information on assessing your service-level objectives.

Understanding the optimal service-level objective or *sweet spot* — the point where you maximize customer satisfaction while minimizing costs — can help you control costs. If you want to have your call center agents answer calls very quickly, you need a lot of agents waiting for customers at every hour of the day, which adds cost. In Chapter 6, we describe how to do a cost–benefit analysis to find your sweet spot.

After your call center achieves the optimal rate, you can still gain efficiency by delivering this level of service as consistently as possible. The less deviation from the optimal service level you have, the better. As a result, call center occupancy increases, and costs decrease.

Make Your Call Center Bigger

You can increase *occupancy* (how many minutes an agent talks to customers in a typical hour) without sacrificing customer satisfaction or service level by making your call center bigger. As you can read in Chapter 6, big call centers are more efficient than small centers. In large centers, you have a higher level of occupancy for the same level of service.

If your call center runs separate call-handling groups (customer service and collections, for example), by merging these two groups, you can take advantage of the economies of scale that big call centers have.

You can make your call center bigger so that you can benefit from improved agent occupancy by *blending,* or combining work in your inbound call-handling queue. A classic example of blending involves mixing outbound calling into an inbound sales or service queue. In this case, you use agent *idle time* — time that agents spend waiting for incoming calls — to do your outbound work. As a result, your agents are busier (more occupied) overall. If inbound volumes increase (or spike), your agents stop making outbound calls while they handle the inbound calls.

Blended work can include outbound collections calls, customer service, welcome calls, or telemarketing. You can also blend other types of work, such as answering e-mail or regular mail. Remember always to give priority to answering inbound calls!

Use Skills-Based Routing

After you analyze the types of calls you receive and the processes you need to handle each call, you can group work by required skill level. Simpler call types might go to one skill level (maybe to newer agents) and more complicated or challenging calls to another skill level. *Skills-based routing* — sending calls of specific types to agents who have the appropriate skills — can give you a lift in occupancy. We talk more about skills-based routing in Chapter 9.

Be careful not to go overboard in creating different skill levels. Skills-based routing still amounts to creating separate call-answering groups, so it's not as efficient as using one large pool of agents.

The closer you get to one skill group, the simpler organizing your inbound calls becomes and the higher your overall occupancy is, as long as your staff can handle the added complexity.

Turn Idle Time into Training Time

Even in large, efficient call centers, idle time makes up 15 percent or more of an agent's time on the phones. In an agent's standard eight-hour shift, 15 percent idle time equates to more than one hour doing nothing but waiting for calls. Instead of having agents wait, maybe you can use that time for something more valuable, such as modularized training that's ready to go whenever call volumes drop. This practice allows a team leader to take a few agents off the phones to work on very specific skills or knowledge.

A few companies have experimented with turning some of their agents' idle time into training time by using special technology. Some training applications monitor the activity of agents who work in a call-answering queue. When the application recognizes that an agent has sufficient idle time, it sends training material to that agent's desktop and headset.

Eliminate Unnecessary Calls

Your call center receives unnecessary calls for a variety of reasons, including agents who handle calls poorly on the first attempt, confusing marketing materials, and incorrect or confusing invoices. Reducing unnecessary calls gives you a basic way to make your call center more efficient. Nothing saves money like not having to answer the call at all!

Here are three quick fixes to help reduce the number of unnecessary calls in your call center:

✔ **Implement an interactive voice response (IVR) system.** As we discuss in Chapter 9, an IVR system gives customers a fast and efficient means of self-serving simple calling needs, such as accessing account balances, getting general information, and even ordering products and services. Also, an IVR system can handle calls around the clock.

Depending on the environment, an IVR system can handle 5 percent to 25 percent (or more) of your call center's call volume. You get a tremendous payback from reducing the number of agents (and the cost of their wages), making IVR one of the most cost-effective investments that you can make.

✔ **Transition customers to online self-service.** Many businesses allow customers to complete relatively complex transactions on the Web. Having a customer do the work himself can save tremendous costs (more than by using IVR) if you can persuade him to use a self-service system on the Web. Customers may find this method to be convenient because online services are available around the clock.

✔ **Analyze why customers are calling.** A slightly more complex way to reduce unnecessary calls involves tracking the reasons for the calls. Knowing why customers call can allow you to analyze the root cause and, in many cases, eliminate the need for the customer to contact your call center in the first place. Start with handling the calls you currently get really well so that customers don't have to call back. Then work on calls related to billing errors, confusing marketing materials, or missed technician visits. Sometimes, you can easily eliminate calls; at other times, you need to go through a more involved process and work with other departments.

Calculate the benefit — in terms of reduced costs to the call center and the company — of eliminating these unnecessary calls. Showing people this benefit can help you persuade them to invest time in eliminating unnecessary calls.

Find Out What a Change in Agent Utilization Costs

You can't chain your agents to their desks; they need time for breaks, meetings, training, and coaching. In most operations, agents also have a certain amount of time that's unaccounted for. This missing time happens for a variety of reasons, and your call center can probably accept it as long as it doesn't get out of hand, representing a small percentage of the total time agents are at work.

If everyone understands the costs, everyone may think about the benefit that each activity can yield. When managers plan meetings, training, and so on, for example, they do it with cost–benefit analysis in mind. (See Chapter 6 for more information about where agents' time goes.)

By thinking about how your agents use their off-phone time, you can effectively control your call center's use of those human resources. Turning non-production time into time spent talking to customers means that you need fewer agents, which lowers costs.

Relocate Your Call Center

Moving your call center to a different location can help you obtain labor at a lower cost. If your call center is located in the heart of Capital City, you have access to a lot of the best-qualified people who value the job, but they have relatively high pay requirements. You may be able to get the same quality of staff for a much lower cost in Rural City, USA; Frostbite, Canada; or Farfaraway, India.

You may not even have to close your existing call center; you can start by sending some of your calls to the remote center. Rather than replace staff in Capital City whom you lose to turnover, you might opt to hire additional staff for the rural operation. See Chapter 5 for more information on outsourcing options.

Appendix A

Key Call Center Definitions and Concepts

· ·

abandonment rate: The percentage of callers who hang up before an agent answers their call or before they make a selection in an interactive voice response (IVR) system. The opposite of *answer rate*.

accessibility: Measures that describe the ease with which customers can access your service, the general speed of call answering, and your customers' level of acceptance of this speed of answer.

after-call work (ACW): The average amount of time that agents spend working on customer accounts after the caller has hung up and during which the agents are unavailable to take another call; also known as not-ready time.

agent: The person with whom a customer speaks when she calls a call center. Different companies have different terms for this role, such as customer service representative, customer service consultant, or rep.

agent availability: The amount of time that agents wait to take calls.

agent utilization: The percentage of total agents who are logged into the phone system, busy handling customer calls. Agent utilization is the opposite of *agent availability*.

answer rate: The percentage of calls that a call center answers — defined by callers speaking to an agent or making a selection in the IVR system — compared with the total number of calls coming in. See also *interactive voice response*.

automatic call distributor (ACD): A call center telephone system that can hold customer calls in a queue for delivery to call center agents in a designated order.

automatic number identification (ANI): A system that identifies the telephone number of a calling customer, serving a function similar to Caller ID.

average handle time (AHT): The average amount of time that agents spend processing customer calls — including speaking directly with customers and doing work related to the call after the customer has hung up (such as filling out customer account information). AHT is usually expressed in seconds.

average speed of answer (ASA): The average amount of time that customers wait in a queue before being greeted by an agent.

average talk time (ATT): The average amount of time that agents spend speaking directly with customers, usually expressed in seconds.

blending: A process in which both inbound and outbound calls are delivered by the phone system to the same agent. See also *inbound* and *outbound*.

call center: A centralized office used to receive and transmit a large volume of telephone calls, both incoming product-support or information inquiries from consumers and outgoing calls for telemarketing, clientele, product services, and debt collection.

call control: The act of directing the flow of a conversation, usually by asking questions.

call length: How long it takes to process one customer interaction, usually expressed as an average. See also *average handle time*.

call strategy: The plan or approach that an agent takes in handling a customer call, including the desired outcome of the call.

call time: See *average handle time*.

call-review assessment: An evaluation of an agent's call-handling proficiency, usually scored and conducted by a member of your call center's quality-assurance team. See also *quality assurance*.

calls per agent: The number of calls handled by your call center divided by the total number of agents taking calls in a given period.

cancellations per contact: The number of customers canceling service divided by the total number of calls handled in a given period.

computer–telephony integration (CTI): Communication between the call center's telephone system and its computer system. CTI allows the merging of information and telecommunications technologies to provide added functionality to agents and customers.

contact: Any contact between a customer and an agent, such as a call, e-mail, online chat, fax, or letter.

contact center: Usually synonymous with *call center.* A contact center handles e-mail, online chat, faxes, and so on — not just telephone calls.

conversion rate: A measure of agents' sales proficiency, representing the number of sales made divided by the number of calls taken.

cost per call: The total costs associated with running the call center divided by the number of calls handled in a given period.

cost–benefit analysis: A comparison, used in decision-making, that assigns dollar values to gains and the expenses associated with acquiring these gains.

cross-selling: Selling a customer one product from a company and then persuading him to purchase other products from the same company.

Customer Operations Performance Center, Inc. (COPC): A family of best-practice and benchmark standards considered to be the most prestigious and rigorous measurement system in the call center industry.

customer relationship management (CRM): A strategy employed by corporations for maximizing the lifetime value of their relationships with their customers. CRM also frequently describes the technology used to manage customer relationships.

customer service: The act of assisting or working on behalf of a customer; also, the level of service provided to the customer.

customer service representative: See *agent.*

customer-experience blueprint: A tool or template that outlines the natural flow of a call, providing a guide for agents to make customers feel that they had an outstanding interaction with the company.

customer-satisfaction survey: A tool used to ask customers how satisfied they feel with the products or services an organization offers. You can build these surveys into your IVR system, offer them on your Web site, or conduct them through a phone call to the customer. See also *interactive voice response.*

data warehouse: A large computer database used to store your mountains of call center statistical data.

dialed number identification service (DNIS): Technology that identifies the number that the customer dialed and routes the call according to a specified plan.

disaster recovery plan: A planned procedure for restoring, and potentially rebuilding, your physical infrastructure in the event that some emergency shuts down (or greatly reduces the output of) your primary site.

drivers: Measures that affect whether you can reach your business goals; management and staff can influence them.

economies of scale: The cost advantages that a business obtains when it expands — specifically, reductions in unit cost while the size of a facility increases.

efficiency: The use of resources (such as money) with as little waste as possible.

efficiency metrics: Measures that gauge costs and efficiencies in the call center. See also *efficiency*.

envelope scheduling: Purposely scheduling more agents than needed to handle the forecasted number of inbound calls and then using agents who aren't busy taking inbound calls to do outbound calls or other work (such as online chat or e-mail). See also *blending*.

Erlang C: A mathematical formula that helps determine how many call center agents you need to meet forecasted demand.

first-call resolution (FCR): The percentage of callers who don't have to call back within a certain time frame (usually, a day or two) to have their issues resolved.

home agent: A call center agent who takes calls and does her work from her home instead of regularly coming in to the call center to work. Home agents connect to the call center's systems, customers, and call queues through a virtual private network by using either the Internet or a third-party platform.

idle time: The time that agents spend waiting for calls, meaning that they're not speaking with customers or doing after-call work. Idle time can be expressed as a percentage of total time logged in or as hours.

inbound: Incoming calls (or faxes, e-mails, or online chats) that customers generate. See also *outbound*.

information technology (IT): The development, installation, and implementation of computer systems and applications.

interactive voice response (IVR): A voice-processing application that provides automated services to incoming callers and that can gather information and interact with other computer systems and databases.

ISO 9001/2000: An international standard of the International Organization for Standardization (ISO) that provides for the creation and maintenance of a quality-assurance system within a company.

metrics: Measures of performance.

mission statement: A description of an organization's goals, values, and overall plan.

Net Promoter Score: A management tool that can gauge the loyalty of a firm's customer relationships. It serves as an alternative to traditional customer satisfaction research.

nonproduction time: Time for which the call center pays agents but during which the agents aren't on the phones, including time spent in meetings, training sessions, coffee breaks, and so on; also called off-phone time.

occupancy: A measure of your call center's on-phone productivity, representing the time that agents spend actively busy working on customer contacts compared with the total time logged on the phones. Occupancy is expressed as a percentage. See also *idle time*.

online chat: A system that allows any number of logged-in computer users to have a typed, real-time, online conversation.

outbound: The calls (or faxes, e-mails, or online chats) going out to customers that your agents generate. Telemarketing is the most common example.

outsourcing: The practice of sending work out to a third-party provider or manufacturer to achieve some business goal, such as reducing costs.

performance drivers: See *drivers*.

predictive dialer: A piece of equipment that dials telephone numbers for an outbound call center.

process management: A series of analyses, actions, and tools applied to a certain method so that you can execute that method more effectively.

process map: A chart that graphically represents a single business method from start to finish.

quality analyst: A person responsible for analyzing whether a business adheres to prescribed performance standards in various business processes.

quality assurance: A program that systematically monitors and evaluates the various aspects of a project, service, or facility to ensure that it meets standards of quality.

reporting analyst: A person who combines the information from all the systems and produces reports, charts, and graphs that illustrate performance and trends.

retention rate: The percentage of customers who initially called to cancel their service but decided not to after speaking with an agent; sometimes referred to as save rate.

revenue generation: Making money. See also *cross-selling* and *upselling*.

revenue metrics: Measures of income produced by the call center. See also *metrics*.

schedule adherence: The percentage of time that agents are actually on the phones when they're supposed to be.

scheduling: The process of assigning call center agents to weekly, monthly, or quarterly work shifts to get the right number of people working at all times.

server: A computer that provides some service for other computers connected to it via a network.

service level: How quickly call center agents answer customers' calls, e-mails, and so on. Service level is most commonly expressed as the percentage of incoming calls answered in a specified amount of time.

single point of failure: Any one element on which the success or failure of a process (or your entire call center) hinges.

Six Sigma: A quality improvement program developed by Motorola that focuses on gaining control of a process and attempting to drive defects, as defined by the customer, down to fewer than 3.4 per million.

skills-based routing: Technology that can send calls of specific types to certain agents based on those agents' skills.

stakeholder: Anyone who has a share or an interest in your call center, including clients, customers, managers, and agents.

standard deviation: In simple (and not exactly accurate) terms, the average amount that a set of numbers varies from the average of the set.

team leader: A manager whose primary responsibility is to coach, discipline, provide feedback to, and support call center agents.

telemarketing: A term typically used to describe outbound telephone sales and promotion — stereotypically used to describe the folks who call you just when you sit down to dinner. See also *outbound*.

upselling: A sales method that involves suggesting that a consumer who's making a purchase consider also purchasing an increase in service or a complementary product.

virtual call center: A group composed of agents working in several locations (often, their own homes) rather than in a single call center site who use the Internet as a network.

Voice over Internet Protocol (VoIP): A communications technology that transmits voice calls over a computer network.

voice recognition: Software that allows callers to speak commands instead of using a telephone keypad.

Appendix B

Call Center Support Services

● ●

*T*his appendix lists some places where you can find call center support.

Employee Testing and Evaluation

These companies provide call center employee testing and evaluation tools:

- ✔ **The DeGarmo Group, Inc.:** 101 N. Main St., Bloomington, IL 61701; phone 309-828-4344; Web site www.degarmogroup.com.

- ✔ **Employment Technologies Corp.:** 532 S. New York Ave., Winter Park, FL 32789; phone 888-332-0648, fax 407-788-1496; Web site www.etc-easy.com.

- ✔ **First Advantage Assessment Solutions:** 209 Burlington Rd., Suite 215, Bedford, MA 01730; phone 800-648-3166, fax 781-229-8108; Web site www.fadvassessments.com.

- ✔ **LIMRA International:** 300 Day Hill Rd., Windsor, CT 06095; phone 860-688-3358, fax 860-298-9555; Web site www.limra.com.

- ✔ **Pearson Assessment & Information:** 5601 Green Valley Dr., Bloomington, MN 55437; phone 800-328-6172; Web site www.pearsonassessments.com.

- ✔ **Presenting Solutions, Inc.:** 55 Santa Clara Ave., Oakland, CA 94610; phone 800-547-7554, fax 510-763-7599; Web site www.presol.com.

- ✔ **Thomas International:** 4310 Sherwoodtowne Blvd., Suite 400, Mississauga, ON L4Z 4C4, Canada; phone 888-597-6455, fax 905-270-2335; Web site www.thomasinternational.net.

Management Certification

These companies can provide call center management certification training:

- ✔ **Call Center Learning Solutions:** 44 N. Old Place Lane, Belgrade, MT 59714; phone 925-513-1010; Web site www.callcentertraining.com.

- ✔ **The Call Center School:** 568 Grant Highway, Lebanon, TN 37090; phone 615-812-8400, fax 866-452-2122; Web site www.thecallcenterschool.com.

- ✔ **Contact Center Employer of Choice (CCEOC):** 811 Hilton Blvd., Suite 101, Newmarket, ON L3X 2H7, Canada; phone 416-886-7007, fax 905-953-9680; Web site www.ccemployerofchoice.com.

- ✔ **Customer Operations Performance Center, Inc. (COPC):** 1717 W. Sixth St., Suite 105, Austin, TX 78703; phone 512-225-0544; Web site www.copc.com.

- ✔ **International Customer Management Institute:** 102 S. Tejon St., Suite 1200, Colorado Springs, CO 80903; phone 800-672-6177, fax 719-268-0184; Web site www.incoming.com.

- ✔ **SCInc.:** P.O. Box 945, Conifer, CO 80433; phone 877-916-1510; Web site www.scinc.com.

- ✔ **SwitchGear Consulting:** 67 Riverwood Parkway, Toronto, ON M8Y 4E4, Canada; phone 416-232-9842, fax 416-946-1303; Web site www.switchgear.ca.

  Full disclosure: Authors Afshan, Bruce, and Winston are partners in SwitchGear.

- ✔ **Transcom Worldwide S.A.:** 80 King St., Suite 300, St. Catharines, ON L2R 7G1, Canada; phone 877-637-2615, fax 905-641-1456; Web site www.transcom.com.

  Even more disclosure: Author Réal works for Transcom.

ISO Registration

This section gives you contact information for a few large organizations that provide International Organization for Standardization (ISO) registration services. (See Chapter 17 for more on ISO.) You can find many more registrars, small and large, by searching the Internet for *ISO registrar*. Some registrars also give courses in becoming certified, and most can provide you access to a worldwide network of consultants specializing in ISO certification. Here's a list to get you started in finding the perfect ISO registration service:

✔ **British Standards Institute:** 389 Chiswick High Rd., London W4 4AL, UK; phone +44-0-20-8996-9001, fax +44-0-20-8996-7001; Web site www.bsi group.com.

✔ **Intertek Systems Certification:** 70 Codman Hill Rd., Boxborough, MA 01710; phone 800-810-1195, fax 800-813-9287; Web site www.intertek-sc.com.

✔ **QMI-SAI Global:** 2 Summit Park Dr., Suite 425, Cleveland, OH 44131; phone 800-247-0802; Web site www.qmi.com.

✔ **SGS:** 1 Place des Alpes, P.O. Box 2152, 1211 Geneva 1, Switzerland; phone +41-22-739-91-11, fax +41-22-739-98-86; Web site www.sgs.com.

Call Center Consulting

You can find a lot of companies that provide call center consulting services — probably some located near you — by searching the Web. Here are a few that we're familiar with:

✔ **The Call Center School:** Provides standard educational programs on a variety of call center topics, customized education programs for call centers and industry vendors, and general call center consulting. See "Management Certification," earlier in this appendix, for contact information.

✔ **Contact Center Employer of Choice (CCEOC):** Provides testing and consulting services, and offers the Contact Center Employer of Choice Certification program. "Management Certification," earlier in this appendix, lists the company's contact information.

✔ **Customer Operations Performance Center, Inc. (COPC):** Conducts onsite operational audits of call centers, and provides assistance in outsourcing and offshoring operations. COPC markets a suite of monitoring systems to demonstrate return on investment on the preceding services. It also developed the COPC-2000, an industry-standard certification for call centers. You can find the contact information for this business in "Management Certification," earlier in this appendix.

✔ **International Customer Management Institute:** Offers training programs and educational resources for call center management. It produces the *Call Center Management Review* newsletter and released the book *Call Center Management on Fast Forward,* by Brad Cleveland (ICMI Press).

Look for this business's contact info in (you guessed it!) "Management Certification," earlier in this appendix.

- ✔ **Strategic Contact, Inc.:** Provides consulting to optimize the use of customer contact technology and operations through planning and executing projects such as call center outsourcing strategies, information technology planning, and virtual call center design. 9510 S.W. 151st Ave., Beaverton, OR 97007; phone 866-791-8560, fax 503-579-8657; Web site `www.strategiccontact.com`.

- ✔ **SwitchGear Consulting:** A sales and service consulting group that installs systemized programs to help implement change. See the "Management Certification" section, earlier in this appendix, for contact information.

- ✔ **Transcom Worldwide S.A.:** Examines contact centers — from management to call center agents — and provides consultation and operational audits, as well as developing database applications, interactive voice response (IVR) solutions, and call center training programs. The "Management Certification" section, earlier in this chapter, lists this company's contact information.

- ✔ **Vanguard Communications Corp.:** Provides consulting services in the design, development, and implementation of effective business solutions for customer contact. It focuses on applying technologies that work together to make contact centers more efficient. 45 S. Park Place, Suite 210, Morristown, NJ 07960; phone 973-605-8000, fax 973-605-8329; Web site `www.vanguard.net`.

Index

• D •

● *P* ●